the
ETHICAL
SHOPPER'S
GUIDE

TO CANADIAN SUPERMARKET PRODUCTS

the
ETHICAL
SHOPPER'S
GUIDE

TO CANADIAN SUPERMARKET PRODUCTS

By Joan Helson,
Kelly Green, David Nitkin, Amy Stein
& the Staff of EthicScan Canada

broadview press

Canadian Cataloguing in Publication Data

Main Entry Under Title
The Ethical Shopper's Guide to Canadian Supermarket Products

ISBN 1-55111-001-6

1. Consumer Education - Canada.   2. Corporations - Social aspects
- Canada - Directories.   3. Shopping - Canada.
I. Helson, Joan.

Copyright 1992, EthicScan Canada Limited.

broadview press, PO Box 1243, Peterborough, Ontario, K9H 7H5
In the U.S: broadview press, 269 Portage Rd, Lewiston, NY 14092, USA
In the U.K: Drake Marketing Services, Market House, Market Place,
Deddington, Oxford, OX15 OSF, UK

Broadview Press gratefully aknowledges the support of the Canada Council,
the Ontario Arts Council and the Government of Ontario.
Printed in Canada.

This book is printed on paper containing over 50% recycled paper including
10% post-consumer fibre.

Acknowledgements

We'd like to thank the people who helped us with the research and preparation of this *Guide,* including Michael Jantzi, David Moffat, Patricia Peña, and David Powell of EthicScan Canada; Nigel Blumenthal of Embersoft Inc.; Robin Brass of Robin Brass Studios; Leslie Dizgun and Irwin Fefergrad, our legal counsel; and the many volunteers across the country who helped verify the local availability of the brand-name products. Also, thanks to Lorrie Goldstein, David Olive and Ellen Roseman, who read and commented on an earlier version of the *Guide.*

We are indebted to the dozens of consumer advocates, company spokespersons, union agents and government officials who took time to share their knowledge with us. Finally, we offer special thanks to our editor, Penny Williams.

Contents

COMPANY PROFILES

Introduction

What do we really know about the companies who make the products we buy every day? Which companies have no plants here in Canada and import everything they sell? Which manufacture their products here, but persistently violate pollution limits in the process? And which are highly and admirably involved with the communities in which they operate?

Heavy product promotion bombards us with reminders of product and price, but has nothing to say about the company itself.

This book is all about the company itself. It won't tell you how to think or what products to buy, and it certainly won't suggest that the factors covered here should replace your concern for quality and price. What it offers is 289 pages of facts, figures and tables about the policies and practices of 83 companies whose products fight for space in your grocery cart. Use this information to assess which companies most closely reflect your own values and convictions, and cast your economic vote accordingly. It can change corporate behaviour.

How to Use the Guide

In the pages that follow, EthicScan measures the performance of Canada's leading grocery and consumer products companies under nine headings: Candour, Women's Issues, Charitable Giving and Community Involvement, Progressive Staff Policies, Labour Relations, Environmental Management, Environmental Performance, Management Practices and Consumer Relations, and Canadian Content. These nine were selected because there is strong consensus among people in the field (advocacy groups, consumer affairs professionals and business ethics academics) that these are the key issues in corporate social responsibility today.

Each of the nine is briefly described in an essay in the Key Issues section of the *Guide*. The essay also explains how we determined ratings in that category and presents an Honour Roll of top companies.

The ratings themselves are found in the Tables. The first set of tables lists companies; the second lists brand names by product type and then identifies the company — useful when you only know the brand name, or would like to review competing brands of, say, coffee. All the tables rate each company in all nine categories, using the schooldays system of "A+" to "F." (See the Key Issues essays for more information.) Take the book with you while you shop: the tables provide an at-a-glance review of the products on the shelves.

What the tables make clear is that no company is wholly good or wholly bad. One that is rated as progressive in its staff policies may lag in environmental issues, or vice versa. For the explanation of these ratings, turn to the Company Profiles section of the book.

Each company profile starts with some basic facts (including ownership, locations of plants and offices, employees and annual sales), followed by a section called *Making the Grade* that explains why the company received the marks you see in the Tables. Why was its score so high in Environmental Performance but so low in Environmental Management? Which specific policies won it a high score in Progressive Staff Policies? How many women are on its board of directors? Next comes Notable Facts — brief references to anything else significant about the company, from strikes and layoffs to animal testing or involvement with South Africa or (as a point of information only) significant events involving the company's parent. People interested in social responsibility issues tend to agree much less on these topics than they do on the nine Key Issues: some argue that any layoff, for example, is the mark of a bad company, while others feel the real issue is not the layoff itself but how it is handled. The Profile also lists all of that company's brand names available in Canada.

The last three sections of the book are designed to help you put your convictions more fully into practice. Options for Action describes ways to let companies know how you feel about their behaviour, while Sources for Action lists organizations where you can obtain additional information or learn about opportunities to become more involved yourself. The final section contains our comment and order forms: one, the Ethical Shopper's Action Report, to share information about what happened when you contacted a company about its products or behaviour; the other to comment on this *Guide* or order other EthicScan publications.

About EthicScan

Started in 1987, EthicScan Canada is a Toronto-based research and consulting company that reports on the social, environmental and labour performance of Canadian companies. We maintain a data base on the 1,500 largest companies in the country, both Canadian and transnational, and also function as a specialized information clearing house and resource centre.

Services of EthicScan include:

- *The Corporate Ethics Monitor*, a bi-monthly publication
- Corporate profiles for ethical investors
- Donor screening for not-for-profit organizations
- Ethics audits for institutions
- Codes of conduct for corporations, industry associations, and not-for-profits
- Social, labour and environmental screens for pension and mutual funds
- Seminars and training in ethical management

About the Research Process

We chose companies for the *Guide* that make products available in Canadian grocery stores and asked the same questions of them all. We used criteria appropriate to medium and large firms, adjusting our methods to suit the handful with fewer than 30 employees. A few of the companies did not wish to be profiled but have been included nonetheless.

Our research process took 17 months in total. After selecting the companies, we scanned government data bases, media reports, trade periodicals, freedom of information inquiries and business information data bases to compile as much information as possible. As well, we consulted with consumer, advocacy, labour and industry groups. We used this information to compile our surveys: a short survey of product lines and basic corporate organizational data, and a long one (80 items) about social and environmental performance. In all cases, the focus of our research was on the Canadian operations.

We sent these surveys to the companies for correction and completion and, in addition, interviewed company executives and labour union bargaining agents. We amended our surveys in light of the corrections and interviews, and returned them to the companies for a second review. Finally, we contacted executives and union agents one last time during the fact-checking process.

While we would not change information to suit a company's view of itself, we took care to reflect any divergence of opinion about the same event. A strike, for example, may be viewed quite differently by the company and an employee representative. Where information is not available, we note this fact: the company may have a good record, even though that information was not available to our researchers. The information reported here was accurate, to the best of our knowledge, as of June 1992.

Disclaimer

All brand names, trademarks and corporate names are the property of their respective owners. None of the companies reviewed here has authorized its inclusion or endorsed the judgements contained herein. The final responsibility for the contents of this book rests wholly with EthicScan Canada.

Key Issues And Honour Rolls

Grading System

A+	=	90%	-	100%
A	=	80%	-	89%
B	=	70%	-	79%
C	=	60%	-	69%
D	=	50%	-	59%
F	=	49%		or less

NOTE: In categories where more than half the companies received a failing grade (Charitable Giving and Community Involvement; Labour Relations; Environmental Management; and Management Practices and Consumer Relations), we introduced an F+ (40% - 49%)/F (39% or less) so as to maintain some distinctions among companies in the Tables. The grading system for Women's Issues was slightly different: see the essay for details.

Candour

As consumers, we spend billions of dollars every year on grocery products, yet know very little about the companies who make them. But that is changing, as a growing number of socially conscious shoppers ask these companies to discuss their corporate social behaviour. Most react warily: while they are accustomed to promoting brand-name recognition through expensive advertising campaigns, it's another thing to reveal internal policies, programs and practices.

In Canada, companies are not legally required to provide much information, whether to the public, their employees or even the government. A publicly-traded company, one that makes shares available for purchase on a stock exchange, must publish certain pieces of financial and other performance data in an annual report and other publicly available documents of record. The content of these documents varies, with some of the more progressive companies going beyond the regulated minimum to include statements on employee policies, environmental initiatives, community involvement and the like.

Privately-held corporations, those which do not offer shares on a stock exchange, must provide certain categories of information to government regulators but need not make any information directly available to the public. Almost three-quarters of the companies in our *Guide* are in this category, either as private Canadian companies or wholly-owned subsidiaries of foreign-based multinationals.

While governments and unions are valuable additional sources of information, particularly concerning labour and environmental issues, government regulations vary from jurisdiction to jurisdiction and not all companies are unionized. Those of us who want our purchases to reflect our social values, therefore, must rely heavily on corporate candour.

We devised a Candour Quotient to rate a company's willingness to disclose information, measuring questions answered as a percentage of questions asked. On the whole, companies were very responsive, with an average score of C (62%). Only a dozen of the 83 companies contacted did not respond to any of our surveys, while 37 companies answered more than 70% of our questions.

Candour Honour Roll

- Kellogg Canada Inc. (100%)
- Industries Lassonde Inc. (97%)
- Nestlé Canada Inc. (96%)
- Scotsburn Co-Operative Services Ltd. (95%)
- Melitta Canada Inc.
  Ogilvie Mills Ltd. (tied at 93%)
- Nabob Foods Limited (92%)
- Beatrice Foods Inc.
  Cargill Limited
  Kitchens of Sara Lee
  Scott Paper Limited (tied at 91%)

Women's Issues

Women constitute an ever-growing proportion of the Canadian work-force. Using the strength of their numbers, Canadian women are demanding, among other things, greater representation in management, employment and pay equity, better training and more progressive staff policies.

However, women have made little progress over the last 20 years toward attaining the salary and status of men of the same age and educational levels. A January, 1992, brief by the National Action Committee on the Status of Women states that Canadian salary levels for women are only 65% of those for men. And, according to its analysis of the progress of women in three large Canadian corporations from 1987 to 1990, most workers in the lowest salary quartile are still women and most promotions still go to men.[1]

Not surprisingly, then, scores for Women's Issues were lower on average than for any other category. Furthermore, we were only able to rate 45 of the 83 companies on this subject: three companies had too few employees (less than thirty) to get a score, while the other 35 firms did not provide us with enough information. We therefore adjusted the grading system in this category, awarding a C for 50% - 59%, D for 40% - 49%, F+ for 30% - 39% and F for the remainder. In this category, "top performer" is a very relative term: even with more generous grading, the average mark was 28% and the top three companies received 56% (C).

Some companies, in an effort to justify their lack of a formal employment equity program, commented that they do not need quotas because they hire and promote employees on the basis of merit, and everyone competes equally. Interestingly, a number of these firms had a high percentage of female workers (over 40%) but a very low percentage of women in management (less than 10%).

Two basic criteria determined a company's rating in this category: the percentage of female managers, senior managers and directors (worth 70% of the mark), and policies in place to increase these percentages. Companies were awarded a half-point for every 1% of women in these three areas, with a maximum of 25 possible points for management, 25 for senior management and 20 for the board of directors. To receive all 70 points available under the first criterion, therefore, a company would need to have women in 50% of its managerial positions and 40% of its directorships.

The remaining 30 points were divided equally among three areas of staff policy, with 10 marks for each of the following: a formal employment equity program concerning women; some provision for daycare, such as an on-site facility or a referral program; and a formal provision for extended maternity leave (beyond the legislated minimum). While daycare and parental leave are really family issues, policies in this area still primarily affect the careers, and thus the status, of women. We therefore evaluate these policies in this category.

Women's Issues Honour Roll

- Kraft General Foods Canada Inc.
  Melitta Canada Inc.
  Nestlé Canada Inc. (tied at 56%)
- Tambrands Canada Inc. (53%)
- McCormick Canada Inc. (50%)
- Kitchens of Sara Lee
  Old Dutch Food Limited (tied at 49%)
- Bristol-Myers Squibb Consumer Products Group (Canada) (48%)
- National Sea Products Limited (46%)
- DowBrands Canada Inc. (44%)

Note:

1. Judy Rebick and Phebe Poole, *Not Another Hundred Years: NAC Brief to the Parliamentary Committee Reviewing the Employment Equity Act* (Toronto: National Action Committee on the Status of Women, 1992), pp 1-5.

Charitable Giving And Community Involvement

The recession of the early 1990s has hit many Canadians hard. Food bank line-ups are longer than ever and demands on other charitable organizations have also risen dramatically. Yet while the need for donations is up, giving is down.[1]

One encouraging response to this situation is the Imagine campaign, a partnership between some leading Canadian corporations and the Canadian Centre for Philanthropy to encourage corporate donations to charity and community programs. Companies join the campaign by pledging to give a minimum of 1% of their pre-tax earnings (averaged over three years) to charitable causes. Those who do so join Imagine's list of Caring Companies and are part of the "One Percent Solution."

Whether under the Imagine banner or not, whether cash or in kind (product and services), corporate donations are one way companies can support and strengthen the communities in which they do business. Companies may support local sports teams, cultural events and community health programs, for example, donate an executive's time to help run fundraising programs or provide free office or warehouse space.

Some encourage their employees to get involved as well, by providing paid and unpaid time off for employee volunteer activities, publicizing those activities in company newsletters (and videos) and using matching gift programs to double employees' cash donations with an equal corporate grant.

Because the two areas are so closely linked, we have combined community involvement and charitable donations into one category. Under charitable giving, companies were awarded 20 marks for being one of Imagine's Caring Companies. In addition, they earned up to 20 marks if donations exceeded 1% of pre-tax earnings, receiving the full 20 if their donations equalled 2% of pre-tax earnings. The final 20 marks in this area went to those who disclosed the dollar amount of their 1990 or 1991 donations. We awarded the other 40 marks for community programs (5 marks per program) such as corporate equipment donations, time off for employee volunteer activity, cultural/arts support, sports team support, matching gift programs and publicity for employee volunteer activity in company publications.

The average score in this category was only 39% (F), reflecting both the unwillingness of some companies to disclose their activities and the generally low level of corporate donations.

Charitable Giving and Community Involvement Honour Roll

- Cargill Limited (95%)
- Kellogg Canada Inc. (90%)
- Alcan Aluminum Limited;
  Coca-Cola Beverages;
  McCain Foods Limited (tied at 80%)
- Scott Paper Limited (76%)
- Nestlé Canada Inc. (75%)

Note:

1. "Corporate Philanthropy in Canada," *Corporate Ethics Monitor*, Vol. 2, #3, May 1990.

Progressive Staff Policies

Progressive companies do more than say their employees are among their most valuable assets: they believe it and act on it, nurturing productivity with staff programs and policies aimed at creating a rewarding, secure and stimulating job atmosphere. When we talk about "progressive" staff policies in this *Guide*, we have these kinds of initiatives in mind.

Employee assistance programs (EAPs) are designed to help staff confront such problems as drug and alcohol abuse, marital and family difficulties and sexual harassment. Some employers make these counselling services available to retirees as well as employees and their dependents. A growing range of health promotion programs (HPPs) – anything from on-site fitness facilities and stop-smoking clinics to nutrition, stress and weight loss counselling – are being established to combat absenteeism, low morale and failing productivity. As well, leading-edge companies are beginning to offer "kincare" services: provision for daycare, adoption leave, help with elderly relatives ("eldercare") and retirement counselling. Finally, communication policies and vehicles also fit into this category, for employees benefit when the information flow is most complete, open, timely and reliable. We therefore looked for suggestion programs, newsletters and other publications, rewards for cost-saving ideas and a policy of open-door management, which requires managers to be freely available to and involved with their staff.

We designed the score sheet in this section to reflect the range of programs Canadian companies may have in place. Each element of a formal employee assistance program was worth 10 marks, to a maximum of 20. Similarly, each part of a formal health promotion program was worth 10 marks, to a maximum of 20. However, each communication vehicle or policy was only worth five marks, though again to a maximum of 20. We weighted these more lightly, since they are relatively more common and easier to implement (though not necessarily easier to do well). Finally, we awarded 10 marks each (to a maximum of 40) for any other progressive policies, such as retirement counselling, adoption leave, written annual performance reviews for all employees and scholarship programs for employees and/or their children.

Many companies received their best grade in this category: more than 30 were awarded a B (70% - 79%) or higher. The average score was 66% (C).

Progressive Staff Policies Honour Roll

- Bristol-Myers Squibb Consumer Products Group (Canada)
  DowBrands Canada Inc.
  H.J. Heinz Co. of Canada Ltd.
  Kraft General Foods Canada Inc.
  McCormick Canada Inc.
  Unilever Canada Limited (all tied at 100%)
- J.M. Schneider Inc.
  Nabob Foods Limited (tied at 95%)
- Ault Foods Limited;
  Nestlé Canada Inc.
  Procter & Gamble Inc.
  The Quaker Oats Company of Canada Limited
  Scott Paper Limited
  Tambrands Canada Inc. (all tied at 90%)

Labour Relations

In today's grim economic times, many companies are cutting jobs, downsizing or consolidating operations in an attempt to stay competitive. The side-effects of this relentless attention to the bottom line can include decreased productivity, less attention to health and safety issues, rising stress and falling morale. Progressive companies have tried to ease the impact of corporate reorganization on workers through such measures as formal job security programs, gain sharing incentives and improved training programs.

A formal job security program cannot guarantee a job. However, even the most basic program guarantees two things: proper advance notice of layoffs, and severance packages that meet or exceed government requirements. Progressive companies go further. They seek to delay, reduce or even eliminate the need for layoffs through the creative use of retraining, relocation, job-sharing, advance notice of technological change and early-retirement packages. When layoffs are unavoidable, they provide departing employees with outplacement counselling and job search assistance.[1]

Gain sharing programs can be another way to improve productivity, loyalty and morale. Share purchase, stock option and profit-sharing plans supplement employees' income and build their sense of ownership in the company.

Training programs are often the key to both job security and workplace safety, especially in operations subject to rapid change for technological, marketplace and other reasons. Problems like illiteracy, poor product knowledge and inadequate training for equipment and materials can result in accidents, injury and environmental mishaps. All of these cost the employer and employee, and often the host community as well.

We gave 20 marks for having a formal job security program, and 10 marks for each specific method of addressing layoff issues (to a maximum of 30). Companies earned another 20 marks for having any gain sharing program open to all employees. If they provided their 1989 and 1990 health and safety statistics, they received 20 marks (or 10 for partial disclosure); if they supplied the 1990 amount spent on training per employee, they earned a final 10 marks.

Because very few companies have a formal job security policy or any gain sharing plan, the average score in this area was only 42% (F+).

Labour Relations Honour Roll

- Ault Foods Limited
  Kellogg Canada Inc. (tied at 100%)
- Coca-Cola Beverages
  Pillsbury Canada Ltd. (tied at 90%)
- McCormick Canada Inc.
  Nabob Foods Limited (tied at 80%)
- Scott Paper Limited (78%)
- Scotsburn Co-Operative Services Ltd. (71%)
- Kraft General Foods Canada Inc.
  Nestlé Canada Inc.
  Ogilvie Mills Ltd. (tied at 70%)

Note:

1. "Layoffs, Loyalty, Life and Labour; the Ethics of Downsizing," *Corporate Ethics Monitor*, Vol 3, #1, January - February 1991.

Environmental Management

It would be a mistake to think that a company's pollution record is an effective or complete measure of its environmental responsibility. Laws may not exist; enforcement may be weak or non-existent. Companies can satisfy the law and still pollute.

We therefore assessed companies not only on their environmental performance, but also on their management practices. Proactive corporate management of environmental issues can prevent problems from occurring in the first place.

A company can structure its commitment to environmental stewardship in many ways. It can create and regularly update an environmental policy statement, establish an environmental committee of the board of directors and require regular (perhaps quarterly) reports to the board on environmental issues. It can appoint a full-time environmental affairs staffer with enough seniority to make decisions, develop programs and promote change in the corporation.[1]

It can also give specific environmental responsibilities to designated staff members at every level of the firm. This is particularly important when a company has more than one plant, and head office management cannot effectively co-ordinate and monitor environmental efforts for them all. Generally, the larger the plant or number of plants, the more employees are needed to help the company with its environmental commitments. Leading-edge companies may have two or three employees with environmental responsibilities for every 100 workers. In a similar spirit, the company may organize an environmental working committee at the staff level.

The overall average grade in this category was F+ (40%). Even companies with a strong showing in Environmental Performance did not always fare as well in Environmental Management. While many of the 83 companies have an environmental policy, few have a full-time environmental affairs officer or make quarterly reports to the board (or executive committee, where no board exists). Few of the companies with a board of directors have established an environmental committee of the board.

We gave 20 marks for having an environmental policy, since this is the first step toward having a defined commitment to the environment. We gave 10 marks for an environmental committee of the board and 15 marks for an environmental working committee or for regular environmental reports to the board. A full-time senior environmental affairs official earned up to 25 marks: full marks for a vice-president, 20 for a director (staff position, not board) and 15 for a manager. We awarded the final 30 marks for the percentage of staff with environmental responsibilities, giving 15 marks for each 1% so designated. A company where two employees out of every 100 carry environmental responsibilities, therefore, received full marks.

Environmental Management Honour Roll

- The Quaker Oats Company of Canada Limited (83%)
- Nabob Foods Limited (78%)
- Cadbury Beverages Canada Inc. (75%)
- Alcan Aluminum Limited
  Ault Foods Limited;
  Kraft General Foods Canada Inc.(tied at 70%)
- Pepsi-Cola Canada;
  Scott Paper Limited (tied at 67%)
- British Columbia Packers Limited;
  Tambrands Canada Inc. (tied at 65%)
- Canadian Home Products Ltd. (64%)

1. "A Pale Shade of Green: Progress to Date in Greening Canadian Business", *Corporate Ethics Monitor*, Vol 4, #3 May-June 1992.

Environmental Performance

Environmental regulation is a shared responsibility of the federal and provincial governments. Though there are exceptions to the pattern, our governments generally do not strongly enforce the laws that exist or make information about corporate performance in this area freely available to the public.

Companies, like individuals, can pollute both directly and indirectly. The environment is directly affected by the way they run their operations and generate, treat and dispose of waste. But it is also powerfully, if indirectly, affected by their choice of raw materials and suppliers, the amount and type of packaging they use in production and the efficiency of their operations.

Leading-edge companies are combining good environmental management with programs and initiatives that seek to raise standards and prevent problems rather than simply react to them. They commission internal or external comprehensive environmental audits of their plants and offices so they can plan and implement a coordinated environmental strategy. Their recycling programs go beyond white and coloured paper to include other office supplies, manufacturing by-products and packaging. They order environment-friendly products and services and help staff follow through on personal initiatives — for example, by supporting car or van pools.

Some other corporate efforts are more common, but still progressive: less packaging on company products, the introduction of a line of (genuinely) "green" products, recycled paper and reusable mugs instead of foam disposables.

The job of assessing companies for environmental performance was complicated by the fact that regulations vary across the country and are unevenly enforced. The data available to us included annual records of air and water discharges exceeding regulated levels, and of the number and frequency of environmental court cases involving convictions and fines.

Companies with no recorded violations or instances of exceeding emissions guidelines received 10 marks. (This is an inconclusive measure, however, for charges are rare, even in such badly polluted areas as the St. Lawrence and Niagara rivers.) Companies were given 15 marks for partial environmental audits and 30 marks for comprehensive audits of all operations. We awarded five marks each (to a maximum of 35) for programs and practices like paper, by-product and packaging recycling, the replacement of disposable cutlery and dishes with reusable ones, a car/van pool program, a green products line or the funding of local environmental groups. We also awarded five marks each (to a maximum of 25) for dollar investments made to improve environmental performance: product and packaging reformulation, for example, equipment replacement, energy efficiency measures, (green) advertising and promotion, and product research and development.

The average grade in this category was D (56%). Companies with no manufacturing operations in Canada were not graded, receiving an N/A (Not Applicable) instead.

Environmental Performance Honour Roll

- Nabob Foods Limited (100%)
- Cargill Limited;
  DowBrands Canada Inc.;
  National Sea Products Limited;
  Nestlé Canada Inc.;
  Scotsburn Co-Operative Services Ltd.;
  Unilever Canada Limited (all tied at 90%)
- The Quaker Oats Company of Canada Limited;
  Scott Paper Limited (tied at 85%)
- Cadbury Beverages Canada Inc.
  Kellogg Canada Inc. (tied at 75%)

Management Practices and Consumer Relations

The media have bombarded us lately with news of corporate wrong-doing, conflict of interest and occasions when the drive for profit has compromised safety, service and product integrity. Yet news about responsible corporate behaviour also creeps into the headlines and the company involved often benefits from the exposure. Increasingly, consumers use their purchasing power to reward companies that consistently offer them honest messages, service and products.

A code of ethics spells out the corporate definition of responsible business practices, providing behavioural guidelines for employee and employer alike. It addresses such topics as product integrity, customer service, proper advertising and fair competition. Some codes require an annual sign-off by all employees, a practice that keeps the guidelines fresh in everyone's mind. The company can spread and reinforce its ethical message in a variety of ways: in writing (perhaps an ethics column in the company newsletter), through videos and awards programs and with ethics training. Some rare companies have an ethics hotline or an ethics ombudsman, giving employees somewhere to turn when faced with dilemmas like potential conflict of interest, gift giving and problems with a superior.

In some companies, the code of ethics is provided by their foreign-based parent. The difficulty here is that laws governing such things as misleading advertising, conflict of interest and unfair competition are not the same from country to country.

We gave companies 25 marks for having a written code of ethics. If it came from a foreign-based parent, however, and was not customized for operations in Canada, only part marks were awarded since it would lack the specificity and total applicability of one developed here in Canada. We awarded an extra 10 marks if the code had been updated since 1988 and another 10 if it required an annual sign-off by all employees. Any other reinforcement or service (such as an ethics ombudsman or a column in the newsletter) earned 15 marks, and a publicly available report on corporate social practices or philanthropy earned 15 marks as well. We gave 15 marks to a company with no recorded violations of the Competition Act (which governs such things as price fixing, misleading advertising and corporate concentration). The final 10 marks were awarded for having a national, toll-free consumer telephone advisory service.

The average grade in this category was F (39%).

Management Practices and Consumer Relations Honour Roll

- Tambrands Canada Inc. (93%)
- Cargill Limited (72%)
- Canadian Home Products Ltd.
  Kellogg Canada Inc. (tied at 70%)
- Kraft General Foods Canada Inc.
  Robin Hood Multifoods Inc.
  Unilever Canada Limited (tied at 65%)

Canadian Content

Only 36% of the companies in this *Guide* are Canadian-owned. Consumers who wish to buy Canadian, therefore, will have a hard time of it if their sole criterion is ownership. We have rated companies on Canadian *content* instead. Depending on such factors as jobs, autonomy and responsiveness to Canadian priorities, a company may be foreign-owned yet still have considerable Canadian content and deliver significant benefits to this country.

Most companies listed here have production jobs in Canada, though five have no direct manufacturing jobs but support jobs elsewhere in Canada because they contract out production. Three others rely totally on imports but have marketing and sales jobs in Canada.

Some Canadian subsidiaries of foreign parents have their own boards of directors, with decision-making powers at the policy level. Others do not. A company without an active Canadian board may find it harder to tailor its strategies and practices to Canadian priorities. The degree of dependence on foreign-based policies can affect the way the company here deals with downsizings or plant openings, environmental concerns, support for local charities and, in general, its workforce and marketplace. Of course, the influence exerted is not necessarily for the worse: a progressive parent will impose progressive policies. In terms of Canadian Content, though, the issue is who makes the decision, rather than the quality of the decision.

Since a company's ownership is a given, the company cannot "improve" its standing and letter grades are therefore inappropriate. Instead, we ranked companies 0 - 4. We gave a 4 to a wholly Canadian-owned company or one majority-owned (defined for our purposes as 50% or more) in Canada. All other foreign-owned companies received from 0 to 3. The 3 went to companies that have production and make policy decisions in this country. Ones that have plants here but had to send our survey to a parent corporation elsewhere earned a 2, on the grounds that if they cannot complete such a survey on their own, they may not have the authority to make more important decisions, either. We gave a 1 to companies that have no direct production jobs but do have sales-related jobs in this country. Finally, a company that provides no Canadian jobs received a 0.

There is no Honour Roll for this category. You'll find details on each company's ownership status in its profile.

Tables By Company Name

Grading System

A+	=	90%	-	100%
A	=	80%	-	89%
B	=	70%	-	79%
C	=	60%	-	69%
D	=	50%	-	59%
F	=	49%		or less

(See Index, p. 278 for explanation of company abbreviations.)

NOTE: Some boxes are marked N/A (Not Applicable). This occurs when the company has fewer than 30 employees or, in the case of Environmental Performance, has no manufacturing operations in Canada. Question marks ("?") appear where we were not supplied with enough information with which to produce a grade. For an explanation of scores in Canadian content please see p. 32.

In categories where more than half the companies received a failing grade (Charitable Giving and Community Involvement; Labour Relations; Environmental Management; and Management Practices and Consumer Relations), we introduced an F+ (40% - 49%)/F (39% or less) so as to maintain some distinctions among companies in the Tables. The grading system for Women's Issues was slightly different: see the essay for details.

Company	Company Abbreviation	Candour	Women's issues	Charity/ community	Progressive staff policies	Labour relations	Environmental management	Environmental performance	Management/ consumer	Canadian content
C O M P A N I E S										
Alberto-Culver Canada	ABCUL	F	?	?	?	?	?	?	?	3
Alcan Aluminum	ALCAN	C	?	A	?	F	B	C	?	4
Ault Foods	AULT	B	F	C	A+	A+	B	B	F	4
BC Sugar Refinery	BCSUG	F	F	F	F	F	?	F	?	4
British Columbia Packers	BPACK	A	F	D	A	F	C	C	D	4
Beatrice Foods	BEA	A+	F	F	B	F+	F	C	F	3
Borden Catelli Consumer Products	BORDEN	F	?	F	F	F+	?	?	?	3
Bristol-Myers Squibb Consumer Products	BMCP	C	D	C	A+	F	F+	N/A	F+	1
Burns Meats	BURNS	F	?	F	?	?	?	?	?	4
Cadbury Beverages Canada	CADBEV	A	F	F+	A	F	B	B	F+	3
Campbell Soup Company	CAMBEL	C	F+	F+	C	F	D	C	F	3
Canada Starch Co.	CASCO	F	?	F	C	F	?	?	F	3
Canadian Home Products	CHP	A	F+	D	F	F	C	C	B	2
Canadian Salt Company	CANSAL	F	?	F	F	?	?	?	?	3
Canbra Foods	CANBRA	F	?	?	?	?	?	?	?	4
Cargill Limited	CARGIL	A+	F+	A+	C	F	D	A+	B	3
Cavendish Farms	CAVDIS	F	?	?	?	?	?	?	?	4
Cobi Foods	COBI	A+	F	F	F	F	F	F	F	4
Coca-Cola Beverages	COKE	A	F	A	B	A+	D	D	C	4
Colgate-Palmolive Canada	COLPAL	F	?	?	?	?	?	?	?	3
Corporate Foods	CPF	F	D	F	A	D	F	F	?	3

Company	Company Abbreviation	Candour	Women's issues	Charity/community	Progressive staff policies	Labour relations	Environmental management	Environmental perfomance	Management/consumer	Canadian content
C O M P A N I E S (C O N T ' D)										
Cott Corporation	COTT	A+	F	D	C	F	F	D	F	4
Culinar	CULNR	B	F+	D	D	F	?	F	F	4
Dare Foods	DARE	F	?	?	?	F	?	?	?	4
Dial of Canada	DIAL	N/A	N/A	?	N/A	N/A	N/A	N/A	N/A	0
Dover Industries	DOVER	F	?	?	?	?	?	?	F	4
DowBrands Canada	DOWBR	A	D	D	A+	C	D	A+	D	3
Drackett Canada	DRACK	F	?	?	?	?	?	N/A	?	1
E.D. Smith and Sons	EDSMT	F	?	F	?	?	?	?	?	4
Effem Foods	EFFEM	F	?	?	A	?	?	?	F+	3
Everfresh Canada	EVFRSH	B	D	F	F	F	F	D	F	3
Fishery Products International	FPI	F	?	?	?	F	?	?	?	4
Gainers Inc	GAINR	C	F	D	B	F	F	F	F+	4
Gaines Pet Food	GPFC	F	?	F	F	?	?	?	?	4
Gay Lea Foods Co-Operative	GAYLEA	A	F	F+	D	F	F	F	F	4
General Mills Canada	GENMIL	B	F	D	A	F	D	D	D	3
George Weston	WESTON	F	?	D	?	F	?	D	?	4
Gerber (Canada)	GERBER	F	?	?	?	?	?	N/A	?	1
Gillette Canada	GILET	F	?	F	F	?	?	N/A	?	1
Hershey Canada	HERSH	A	D	F	B	F+	F	B	F	3
H.J. Heinz Co. of Canada	HEINZ	D	F	D	A+	F+	?	D	D	3
Hostess Frito-Lay	HFLAY	F	?	F	F	?	?	?	?	3
Humpty-Dumpty Foods	HUMPTY	F	?	?	?	?	?	?	?	2
Hunt-Wesson Canada	HUNT	N/A	N/A	?	N/A	N/A	N/A	N/A	?	1
Industries Lassonde	LASND	A+	F	F	D	D	F	F	F	4

COMPANIES (CONT'D)

Company	Company Abbreviation	Candour	Women's issues	Charity/ community	Progressive staff policies	Labour relations	Environmental management	Environmental performance	Management/ consumer	Canadian content
J.M. Schneider	JMSCH	B	F	F+	A+	F	F	F	D	4
Johnson & Johnson (Canada)	J&J	A	F	D	A	F	F	D	F+	3
Kellogg Canada	KELOG	A+	F	A+	A	A+	C	B	B	3
Kimberly-Clark Canada	KIMCLA	B	F	F+	A+	D	F	F	D	3
Kitchens of Sara Lee	SARLEE	A+	D	F	F	F+	F	F	F+	3
Kraft General Foods Canada	KRAFT	B	C	F+	A+	B	B	B	C	3
Lantic Sugar	LANTIC	C	F	F	C	F	F	F	F	4
Lyons Tetley Canada	TETLEY	N/A	N/A	F	N/A	N/A	N/A	N/A	?	1
Maple Leaf Foods	MALEAF	B	?	F+	F	F	F	F	F	3
Maple Lodge Farms	MAPLOD	F	?	F	?	?	?	?	F	4
McCain Foods	MCCAIN	C	?	A	A	D	F	C	F	4
McCormick Canada	MCORMK	A	D	C	A+	A	F+	D	C	2
Mead Johnson Canada	MEAD	F	?	?	?	?	?	?	?	3
Melitta Canada	MELTA	A+	C	F+	C	F	F	N/A	D	1
Nabisco Brands Canada	NABSCO	F	?	?	D	?	?	?	?	3
Nabob Foods	NABOB	A+	F	D	A+	A	B	A+	F	3
National Sea Products	NATSEA	C	D	F	B	F	F+	A+	F	4
Nestle Canada	NESTLE	A+	C	B	A+	B	C	A+	C	3
Ocean Fisheries	OCEAN	B	F	F	A	D	D	B	F	4
Ogilvie Mills	OGMILS	A+	F	F+	A	B	F	F	F	3
Old Dutch Foods	OLDCH	C	D	F	F	D	F	C	F	3
Pepsi-Cola Canada	PEPSI	D	?	F	?	?	C	D	F	3
Pillsbury Canada	PILBRY	B	D	F	B	A+	F	F	D	3

COMPANIES (CONT'D)

Company	Company Abbreviation	Candour	Women's issues	Charity/community	Progressive staff policies	Labour relations	Environmental management	Environmental performance	Management/consumer	Canadian content
Playtex Ltd	PLATX	F	?	F	?	?	?	?	?	3
Primo Foods	PRIMO	F	?	F	?	?	F	?	?	3
Procter & Gamble	P&G	C	?	F	A+	F+	D	D	F	3
Quaker Oats Company of Canada	QUAKER	B	?	D	A+	F	A	A	F	3
Ralston Purina Canada	PURINA	A	F+	F	B	F	F+	F	C	3
Redpath Sugars	REDPAT	C	F	F	A	F	?	F	?	3
Reynolds Aluminum Company of Canada	REYNLD	A	F	F+	A	C	D	C	D	3
Robin Hood Multifoods	RHOOD	B	F	F+	A	F	F	C	C	3
S.C. Johnson & Son	SCJON	F	?	F+	?	D	?	C	?	3
Scotsburn Co-Operative Services	SBURN	A+	D	C	B	B	F+	A+	F	4
Scott Paper Limited	SCOTT	A+	F	B	A+	B	C	A	D	3
SmithKline Beecham Consumer Brands	SKB	F	?	?	?	?	?	?	?	3
Specialty Brands (Canada)	SPECBD	F	?	F	F	F	?	?	F	
Tambrands Canada	TAMBRD	B	C	F	A+	D	C	N/A	A+	2
Unilever Canada	UNILV	A+	F	F+	A+	D	F+	A+	C	1

Tables By Product Group / Brand Name

Grading System

A+	= 90%	-	100%
A	= 80%	-	89%
B	= 70%	-	79%
C	= 60%	-	69%
D	= 50%	-	59%
F	= 49%		or less

(See the Company Abbreviations Index, p. 278 for an explanation of company abbreviations.)

NOTE: Some boxes are marked N/A (Not Applicable). This occurs when the company has fewer than 30 employees or, in the case of Environmental Performance, has no manufacturing operations in Canada. Question marks ("?") appear where we were not supplied with enough information with which to produce a grade. For an explanation of scores in Canadian content please see p. 32.

In categories where more than half the companies received a failing grade (Charitable Giving and Community Involvement; Labour Relations; Environmental Management; and Management Practices and Consumer Relations), we introduced an F+ (40% - 49%)/F (39% or less) so as to maintain some distinctions among companies in the Tables. The grading system for Women's Issues was slightly different: see the essay for details.

Brand Name	Company Abbreviation	Candour	Women's issues	Charity/ community	Progressive staff policies	Labour relations	Environmental management	Environmental perfomance	Management/ consumer	Canadian content
BABY FOOD										
Alactamil	MEAD	F	?	?	?	?	?	?	?	3
Carnation Good Start	NESTLE	A+	C	B	A+	B	C	A+	C	3
Enfalac	MEAD	F	?	?	?	?	?	?	?	3
First Foods	GERBER	F	?	?	?	?	?	N/A	?	1
Gerber	GERBER	F	?	?	?	?	?	N/A	?	1
Heinz	HEINZ	D	F	D	A+	F+	?	D	?	3
Isocal	MEAD	F	?	?	?	?	?	?	?	3
Nutramigen	MEAD	F	?	?	?	?	?	?	?	3
Pablum	MEAD	F	?	?	?	?	?	?	?	3
Prosobee	MEAD	F	?	?	?	?	?	?	?	3
Sustacal	MEAD	F	?	?	?	?	?	?	?	3
BAKING MIXES										
Added Touch	MALEAF	B	?	F+	F	F	F	F	F	3
Aunt Jemima	QUAKER	B	?	D	A+	F	A	A	F	3
Betty Crocker	GENMIL	B	F	D	A	F	D	D	D	3
Bisquick	GENMIL	B	F	D	A	F	D	D	D	3
Celebration	RHOOD	B	F	F+	A	F	F	C	C	3
Cream of the West	MALEAF	B	?	F+	F	F	F	F	F	3
Duncan Hines	P&G	C	?	F	A+	F+	D	D	F	3
Monarch	MALEAF	B	?	F+	F	F	F	F	F	3
Pillsbury	PILBRY	B	D	F	B	A+	F	F	D	3
Robin Hood	RHOOD	B	F	F+	A	F	F	C	C	3
Tea-Bisk	MALEAF	B	?	F+	F	F	F	F	F	3

Brand Name	Company Abbreviation	Candour	Women's issues	Charity/ community	Progressive staff policies	Labour relations	Environmental management	Environmental perfomance	Management/ consumer	Canadian content
B A K I N G N E E D S										
Baker's Choice	REYNLD	A	F	F+	A	C	D	C	D	3
Baker's Joy	ABCUL	F	?	?	?	?	?	?	?	3
Baker's	KRAFT	B	C	F+	A+	B	B	B	C	3
Benson's	CASCO	F	?	F	C	F	?	?	F	3
Blue Ribbon	SPECBD	F	?	F	F	F	?	?	F	2
Cake Mate	MCORMK	A	D	C	A+	A	F+	D	C	2
Cadbury	CADBEV	A	F	F+	A	F	B	B	F+	3
Canada	CASCO	F	?	F	C	F	?	?	F	3
Chipits	HERSH	A	D	F	B	F+	F	B	F	3
Club House	MCORMK	A	D	C	A+	A	F+	D	C	2
Crosse & Blackwell	NESTLE	A+	C	B	A+	B	C	A+	C	3
Dromedary	SPECBD	F	?	F	F	F	?	?	F	2
Durham	CASCO	F	?	F	C	F	?	?	F	3
Egg Beaters	UNILV	A+	F	F+	A+	D	F+	A+	C	3
Fleischmann's	SPECBD	F	?	F	F	F	?	?	F	2
French's	SPECBD	F	?	F	F	F	?	?	F	2
Fry's	CADBEV	A	F	F+	A	F	B	B	F+	3
Hershey	HERSH	A	D	F	B	F+	B	B	F	3
Knox	UNILV	A+	F	F+	A+	D	F+	A+	C	3
Libby's	NESTLE	A+	C	B	A+	B	C	A+	C	3
Lite n' Fruity	EDSMT	F	?	F	?	?	?	?	?	4
Magic Baking Powder	NABSCO	F	?	?	D	?	?	?	?	3
Maple Leaf	MALEAF	B	?	F+	F	F	F	F	F	3
McNair	WESTON	F	?	D	?	F	?	D	?	3
Neilson	WESTON	F	?	D	?	F	?	D	?	4
Toll House	NESTLE	A+	C	B	A+	B	C	A+	C	3

BAKING NEEDS (CONT'D)

Brand Name	Company Abbreviation	Candour	Women's issues	Charity/community	Progressive staff policies	Labour relations	Environmental management	Environmental perfomance	Management/consumer	Canadian content
Pam	CHP	A	F+	D	F	F	C	C	B	2
QuickSet	REDPAT	C	F	F	A	F	?	F	?	3
ReaLemon	BORDEN	F	?	F	F	F+	?	?	?	3
Reese	HERSH	A	D	F	B	F+	F	B	F	3
Rose & LaFlamme	WESTON	F	?	D	?	F	?	D	?	4
Schwartz	SPECBD	F	?	F	F	F	?	?	F	2
Shake 'n Bake	KRAFT	B	C	F+	A+	B	B	B	C	3
Shirriff	KELOG	A+	F	A+	A	A+	C	B	B	3
Sun-Ripe	EDSMT	F	?	F	?	?	?	?	?	4
Tenderflake	MALEAF	B	?	F+	F	F	F	F	F	3
Toll House	NESTLE	A+	C	B	A+	B	C	A+	C	3
Traditional	WESTON	F	?	D	?	F	?	D	?	4
Wasco	WESTON	F	?	D	?	F	?	D	?	4
York	MALEAF	B	?	F+	F	F	F	F	F	3

BOTTLED WATER

Brand Name	Company Abbreviation	Candour	Women's issues	Charity/community	Progressive staff policies	Labour relations	Environmental management	Environmental perfomance	Management/consumer	Canadian content
Carignan	COTT	A+	F	D	C	F	F	D	F	4
Eau Naturelle	COTT	A+	F	D	C	F	F	D	F	4
Elite	COTT	A+	F	D	C	F	F	D	F	4
Everfresh	EVFRSH	B	D	F	F	F	F	D	F	3
Scotsburn	SBURN	A+	D	C	B	B	F+	A+	F	4

Brand Name	Company Abbreviation	Candour	Women's issues	Charity/community	Progressive staff policies	Labour relations	Environmental management	Environmental performance	Management/consumer	Canadian content
BREADS & ROLLS										
Arnold	CPF	F	D	F	A	D	F	F	?	3
Bamby	CPF	F	D	F	A	D	F	F	?	3
Bon Matin	CPF	F	D	F	A	D	F	F	?	3
Brownberry	CPF	F	D	F	A	D	F	F	?	3
Buttercup	MALEAF	B	?	F+	F	F	F	F	F	3
Butternut	CPF	F	D	F	A	D	F	F	?	3
Dietrich's	WESTON	F	?	D	?	F	?	D	?	4
Country Harvest	WESTON	F	?	D	?	F	?	D	?	4
Deli World	WESTON	F	?	D	?	F	?	D	?	4
Dempster's	CPF	F	D	F	A	D	F	F	?	3
Diana	CPF	F	D	F	A	D	F	F	?	3
Durivage	CPF	F	D	F	A	D	F	F	?	3
Ellenzweig	WESTON	F	?	D	?	F	?	D	?	4
Fibre Goodness	WESTON	F	?	D	?	F	?	D	?	4
Fun Buns	CPF	F	D	F	A	D	F	F	?	3
Gailuron	CPF	F	D	F	A	D	F	F	?	3
Grain's	CPF	F	D	F	A	D	F	F	?	3
Hollywood	CPF	F	D	F	A	D	F	F	?	3
Holsum	CPF	F	D	F	A	D	F	F	?	3
Home Pride	WESTON	F	?	D	?	F	?	D	?	4
Homestead	MALEAF	B	?	F+	F	F	F	F	F	3
Karnes	CPF	F	D	F	A	D	F	F	?	3
McGavin	MALEAF	B	?	F+	F	F	F	F	F	3

BREADS & ROLLS (CONT'D)

Brand Name	Company Abbreviation	Candour	Women's issues	Charity/ community	Progressive staff policies	Labour relations	Environmental management	Environmental perfomance	Management/ consumer	Canadian content
Olivieri	CPF	F	D	F	A	D	F	F	?	3
Pride of Montreal	CPF	F	D	F	A	D	F	F	?	3
Sara Lee	SARLEE	A+	D	F	F	F+	F	F	F+	3
Stonehouse Farms	WESTON	F	?	D	?	F	?	D	?	4
Sunmaid	CPF	F	D	F	A	D	F	F	?	3
Sunny Bee	CPF	F	D	F	A	D	F	F	?	3
Sunshine	CPF	F	D	F	A	D	F	F	?	3
Toastmaster	CPF	F	D	F	A	D	F	F	?	3
Weight Watchers	HEINZ	D	F	D	A+	F+	?	D	?	3
Weston's	WESTON	F	?	D	?	F	?	D	?	4
Wonder	WESTON	F	?	D	?	F	?	D	?	4

BUTTER

Brand Name	Company Abbreviation	Candour	Women's issues	Charity/ community	Progressive staff policies	Labour relations	Environmental management	Environmental perfomance	Management/ consumer	Canadian content
Gay Lea	GAYLEA	A	F	F+	D	F	F	F	F	4
Lactantia	AULT	B	F	C	A+	A+	B	B	F	4
Maple Leaf	MALEAF	B	?	F+	F	F	F	F	F	3
Medo-Land	BEA	A+	F	F	B	F+	F	C	F	3
Modern	BEA	A+	F	F	B	F+	F	C	F	3
Pure & Simple	AULT	B	F	C	A+	A+	B	B	F	4
Scotsburn	SBURN	A+	D	C	B	B	F+	A+	F	4
Tatamagouche	SBURN	A+	D	C	B	B	F+	A+	F	4

Brand Name	Company Abbreviation	Candour	Women's issues	Charity/ community	Progressive staff policies	Labour relations	Environmental management	Environmental perfomance	Management/ consumer	Canadian content
CANNED & FROZEN FRUITS & VEGETABLES										
Allen's	CADBEV	A	F	F+	A	F	B	B	F+	3
Avon	COBI	A+	F	F	F	F	F	F	F	4
Aylmer	NABSCO	F	?	?	D	?	?	?	?	3
Bon Appetit	MALEAF	B	?	F+	F	F	F	F	F	3
Cloverleaf	BPACK	A	F	D	A	F	C	C	D	4
Cobi	COBI	A+	F	F	F	F	F	F	F	4
Del Monte	NABSCO	F	?	?	D	?	?	?	?	3
FraserVale	PILBRY	B	D	F	B	A+	F	F	D	3
Graves	COBI	A+	F	F	F	F	F	F	F	4
Green Giant	PILBRY	B	D	F	B	A+	F	F	D	3
Hardee Farms	COBI	A+	F	F	F	F	F	F	F	4
Heinz	HEINZ	D	F	D	A+	F+	?	D	?	3
Hunt's	HUNT	N/A	N/A	?	N/A	N/A	?	N/A	?	1
Hi Lo	COBI	A+	F	F	F	F	F	F	F	4
Le Sieur	PILBRY	B	D	F	B	A+	F	F	D	3
Libby's	NESTLE	A+	C	B	A+	B	C	A+	C	3
McCain	MCCAIN	C	?	A	A	B	F	C	F	4
Mitchell's	CADBEV	A	F	F+	A	F	B	B	F+	3
Mott's Fruit Pak	CADBEV	A	F	F+	A	F	B	B	F+	3
Nature's Best	COBI	A+	F	F	F	F	F	F	F	4
Ocean Spray	CADBEV	A	F	F+	A	F	B	B	F+	3
Omstead	HEINZ	D	F	D	A+	F+	?	D	?	3
Primo	PRIMO	F	?	F	?	?	F	?	?	3
Stokely Van Camp	COBI	A+	F	F	F	F	F	F	F	4
Unico	CULNR	B	F+	D	D	F	?	F	F	4

CANNED & PROCESSED SEAFOOD

Brand Name	Company Abbreviation	Candour	Women's issues	Charity/ community	Progressive staff policies	Labour relations	Environmental management	Environmental perfomance	Management/ consumer	Canadian content
Blazin' Redfish	FPI	F	?	?	?	F	.	?	?	?	4
Blue Water	GENMIL	B	F	D	A	F	D	D	D	D	3
Brunswick	WESTON	F	?	D	?	F	?	D	?	?	4
Cloverleaf	BPACK	A	F	D	A	F	C	C	C	D	4
Connaisseur	WESTON	F	?	D	?	F	?	D	D	?	4
Heritage	WESTON	F	?	D	?	F	?	D	D	?	4
High Liner	NATSEA	C	D	F	B	F	F+	A+	A+	F	4
Holmes	WESTON	F	?	D	?	F	?	D	?	?	4
Maple Leaf	BPACK	A	F	D	A	F	C	C	C	D	4
Mirabel	FPI	F	?	?	?	F	?	?	?	?	4
North Pacific	OCEAN	B	F	F	A	D	D	B	B	F	4
Ocean's	OCEAN	B	F	F	A	D	D	B	B	F	4
Paramount	BPACK	A	F	D	A	F	C	C	C	D	4
Port Clyde	WESTON	F	?	D	?	F	?	D	D	?	4
Queen Charlotte	BPACK	A	F	D	A	F	C	C	C	D	4
Red Rose	BPACK	A	F	D	A	F	C	C	C	D	4
Royale	OCEAN	B	F	F	A	D	D	B	B	F	4
Sea Nuggets	FPI	F	?	?	?	F	?	?	?	?	4
Sea Strips	FPI	F	?	?	?	F	?	?	?	?	4
Sea Teasures	FPI	F	?	?	?	F	?	?	?	?	4
Seafood Elites	FPI	F	?	?	?	F	?	?	?	?	4
Snow's	BORDEN	F	?	F	F	F+	?	?	?	?	3
Starkist	HEINZ	D	F	D	A+	F+	?	D	D	?	3
Unico	CULNR	B	F+	D	D	F	?	F	F	F	4

Brand Name	Company Abbreviation	Candour	Women's issues	Charity/community	Progressive staff policies	Labour relations	Environmental management	Environmental performance	Management/consumer	Canadian content
C E R E A L S										
100% Bran	NABSCO	F	?	?	D	?	?	?	?	3
All-Bran	KELOG	A+	F	A+	A	A+	C	B	B	3
Alpha-Bits	KRAFT	B	C	F+	A+	B	B	B	C	3
Balance	NABSCO	F	?	?	D	?	?	?	?	3
Bran Buds	KELOG	A+	F	A+	A	A+	C	B	B	3
Cap'n Crunch	QUAKER	B	?	D	A+	F	A	A	F	3
Cheerios	GENMIL	B	F	D	A	F	D	D	D	3
Cinnamon Toast Crunch	GENMIL	B	F	D	A	F	D	D	D	3
Cocoa Puffs	GENMIL	B	F	D	A	F	D	D	D	3
Common Sense	KELOG	A+	F	A+	A	A+	C	B	B	3
Corn Flakes	KELOG	A+	F	A+	A	A+	C	B	B	3
Corn Pops	KELOG	A+	F	A+	A	A+	C	B	B	3
Corn Bran	QUAKER	B	?	D	A+	F	A	A	F	3
Count Chocula	GENMIL	B	F	D	A	F	D	D	D	3
Cracklin' Oatmeal	KELOG	A+	F	A+	A	A+	C	B	B	3
Cream of Rice	NABSCO	F	?	?	D	?	?	?	?	3
Cream of Wheat	NABSCO	F	?	?	D	?	?	?	?	3
Crispix	KELOG	A+	F	A+	A	A+	C	B	B	3
Crispy Wheats 'n Raisins	GENMIL	B	F	D	A	F	D	D	D	3
Cruncheroos	KELOG	A+	F	A+	A	A+	C	B	B	3
Frosted Flakes	KELOG	A+	F	A+	A	A+	C	B	B	3
Fruit Wheats	NABSCO	F	?	?	D	?	?	?	?	3
Fruit 'n Fibre	KRAFT	B	C	F+	A+	B	B	B	C	3
Fruit Loops	KELOG	A+	F	A+	A	A+	C	B	B	3
Fruitful Bran	KELOG	A+	F	A+	A	A+	C	B	B	3

CEREALS (CONT'D)

Brand Name	Company Abbreviation	Candour	Women's issues	Charity/community	Progressive staff policies	Labour relations	Environmental management	Environmental performance	Management/consumer	Canadian content
Fruity Marshmallow Krispies	KELOG	A+	F	A+	A	A+	C	B	B	3
Fun Pack/Variety Pack	KELOG	A+	F	A+	A	A+	C	B	B	3
Golden Grahams	GENMIL	B	F	D	A	F	D	D	D	3
Grape-Nuts	KRAFT	B	C	F+	A+	B	B	B	C	3
Harvest Crunch	QUAKER	B	?	D	A+	F	A	A	F	3
Honey Bran Crunchies	NABSCO	F	?	?	D	?	?	?	?	3
Honeycomb	KRAFT	B	C	F+	A+	B	B	B	C	3
Just Right	KELOG	A+	F	A+	A	A+	C	B	B	3
Kellogg's Raisin Bran	KELOG	A+	F	A+	A	A+	C	B	B	3
Kenmei	KELOG	A+	F	A+	A	A+	C	B	B	3
Kretschmer	QUAKER	B	?	D	A+	F	A	A	F	3
Life	QUAKER	B	?	D	A+	F	A	A	F	3
Lifestream	NABOB	A+	F	D	A+	A	B	A+	F	3
Lucky Charms	GENMIL	B	F	D	A	F	D	D	D	3
McNair	WESTON	F	?	D	?	F	?	D	?	4
Mini Wheats	KELOG	A+	F	A+	A	A+	C	B	B	3
Muslix	KELOG	A+	F	A+	A	A+	C	B	B	3
Nuts 'n Crunch	NABSCO	F	?	?	D	?	?	?	?	3
Oat Squares	QUAKER	B	?	D	A+	F	A	A	F	3
Oatmeal Raisin Crisp	GENMIL	B	F	D	A	F	D	D	D	3
Ogilvie	OGMILS	A+	F	F+	A	B	F	F	F	3
Oh's	QUAKER	B	?	D	A+	F	A	A	F	3
Old Mill	RHOOD	B	F	F+	A	F	F	C	C	3
Pac-Man	GENMIL	B	F	D	A	F	D	D	D	3
Post Raisin Bran	KRAFT	B	C	F+	A+	B	B	B	C	3

CEREALS (CONT'D)

Brand Name	Company Abbreviation	Candour	Women's issues	Charity/ community	Progressive staff policies	Labour relations	Environmental management	Environmental perfomance	Management/ consumer	Canadian content
Pro*Stars	GENMIL	B	F	D	A	F	D	D	D	3
Quaker	QUAKER	B	?	D	A+	F	A	A	F	3
Red River Cereal	MALEAF	B	?	F+	F	F	F	F	F	3
Rice Krispies	KELOG	A+	F	A+	A	A+	C	B	B	3
Robin Hood	RHOOD	B	F	F+	A	F	F	C	C	3
Shredded Wheat	NABSCO	F	?	?	D	?	?	?	?	3
Shreddies	NABSCO	F	?	?	D	?	?	?	?	3
Special K	KELOG	A+	F	A+	A	A+	C	B	B	3
Spoon Size	NABSCO	F	?	?	D	?	?	?	?	3
Strawberry Squares	KELOG	A+	F	A+	A	A+	C	B	B	3
Team	NABSCO	F	?	?	D	?	?	?	?	3
Trix	GENMIL	B	F	D	A	F	D	D	D	3

Brand Name	Company Abbreviation	Candour	Women's issues	Charity/ community	Progressive staff policies	Labour relations	Environmental management	Environmental perfomance	Management/ consumer	Canadian content
CHEESE										
Balderson	AULT	B	F	C	A+	A+	B	B	F	4
Beatrice	BEA	A+	F	F	B	F+	F	C	F	3
Black Diamond	AULT	B	F	C	A+	A+	B	B	F	4
Cape Breton Dairymen	SBURN	A+	D	C	B	B	F+	A+	F	4
Country Choice	AULT	B	F	C	A+	A+	B	B	F	4
Cracker Barrel	KRAFT	B	C	F+	A+	B	B	B	C	3
Crescent	BEA	A+	F	F	B	F+	F	C	F	3
Gay Lea	GAYLEA	A	F	F+	D	F	F	F	F	4
Kraft	KRAFT	B	C	F+	A+	B	B	B	C	3
McCain	MCCAIN	C	?	A	A	D	F	C	F	4
Nordica	GAYLEA	A	F	F+	D	F	F	F	F	4
Oxford Farms	GAYLEA	A	F	F+	D	F	F	F	F	3
Philadelphia	KRAFT	B	C	F+	A+	B	B	B	C	3
Scotsburn	SBURN	A+	D	C	B	B	F+	A+	F	4
Sealtest	AULT	B	F	C	A+	A+	B	B	F	4
Snackeroos	KRAFT	B	C	F+	A+	B	B	B	C	3
Velveeta	KRAFT	B	C	F+	A+	B	B	B	C	3
Weight Watchers	HEINZ	D	F	D	A+	F+	?	D	?	3

COCOA & OTHER DRINK MIXES

Brand Name	Company Abbreviation	Candour	Women's issues	Charity/ community	Progressive staff policies	Labour relations	Environmental management	Environmental perfomance	Management/ consumer	Canadian content
Boost	MEAD	F	?	?	?	?	?	?	?	3
Brown Cow	HERSH	A	D	F	B	F+	F	B	F	3
Cadbury	CADBEV	A	F	F+	A	F	B	B	F+	3
Carnation	NESTLE	A+	C	B	A+	B	C	A+	C	3
Chipits	HERSH	A	D	F	B	F+	F	B	F	3
Coffee-Mate	NESTLE	A+	C	B	A+	B	C	A+	C	3
Country Time	KRAFT	B	C	F+	A+	B	B	B	C	3
Fry's	CADBEV	A	F	F+	A	F	B	B	F+	3
Gatorade	QUAKER	B	?	D	A+	F	A	A	F	3
Hawaiian Punch	P&G	C	?	F	A+	F+	D	D	F	3
Hershey	HERSH	A	D	F	B	F+	F	B	F	3
Horlicks	SKB	F	?	?	?	?	?	?	?	3
Jolly Miller	MALEAF	B	?	F+	F	F	F	F	F	3
Kool-Aid	KRAFT	B	C	F+	A+	B	B	B	C	3
Lipton	UNILV	A+	F	F+	A+	D	F+	A+	C	3
Milk Mate	BORDEN	F	?	F	F	F+	?	?	?	3
Quik	NESTLE	A+	C	B	A+	B	C	A+	C	3
Strawberry Cow	HERSH	A	D	F	B	F+	F	B	F	3
Tang	KRAFT	B	C	F+	A+	B	B	B	C	3
Thirst Ade	MALEAF	B	?	F+	F	F	F	F	F	3
Weight Watchers	HEINZ	D	F	D	A+	F+	?	D	?	3

COFFEE

Brand Name	Company Abbreviation	Candour	Women's issues	Charity/ community	Progressive staff policies	Labour relations	Environmental management	Environmental perfomance	Management/ consumer	Canadian content
Amore	TETLEY	N/A	N/A	F	N/A	N/A	N/A	N/A	?	1
Cellini	CULNR	B	F+	D	D	F	?	F	F	4
Coffee-Mate	NESTLE	A+	C	B	A+	B	C	A+	C	3
Columbia	NESTLE	A+	C	B	A+	B	C	A+	C	3
Encore	NESTLE	A+	C	B	A+	B	C	A+	C	3
Folgers	P&G	C	?	F	A+	F+	D	D	F	3
General Foods International	KRAFT	B	C	F+	A+	B	B	B	C	3
Gold Roast	TETLEY	N/A	N/A	F	N/A	N/A	N/A	N/A	?	1
Hills Bros	NESTLE	A+	C	B	A+	B	C	A+	C	3
Maxwell House	KRAFT	B	C	F+	A+	B	B	B	C	3
Melitta	MELITA	A+	C	F+	C	F	F	N/A	D	1
MJB	NESTLE	A+	C	B	A+	B	C	A+	F	3
Nabob	NABOB	A+	F	D	A+	A	B	A+	F	3
Nescafé	NESTLE	A+	C	B	A+	B	C	A+	C	3
Rich Blend	NESTLE	A+	C	B	A+	B	C	A+	C	3
Summit	NABOB	A+	F	D	A+	A	B	A+	F	3
Taster's Choice	NESTLE	A+	C	B	A+	B	C	A+	C	3
Tradition	NABOB	A+	F	D	A+	A	B	A+	F	3
Viva	NESTLE	A+	C	B	A+	B	C	A+	C	3

CONDIMENTS & SAUCES

Brand Name	Company Abbreviation	Candour	Women's issues	Charity/ community	Progressive staff policies	Labour relations	Environmental management	Environmental perfomance	Management/ consumer	Canadian content
A-1	CAMBEL	C	F+	F+	C	F	D	C	F	3
Allen's	SPECBD	F	?	F	F	F	?	?	F	2
Bick's	RHOOD	B	F	F+	A	F	F	C	C	3
Bisto	CAMBEL	C	F+	F+	C	F	D	C	F	3
Bravo	BORDEN	F	?	F	F	F+	?	?	?	3
Casa Italiana	JMSCH	B	F	F+	A+	F	F	F	D	4
Catelli	BORDEN	F	?	F	F	F+	?	?	?	3
Chef Boyardee	CHP	A	F+	D	F	F	C	C	B	2
Chicken Tonight	UNILV	A+	F	F+	A+	D	F+	A+	C	3
Classico	BORDEN	F	?	F	F	F+	?	?	?	3
Crosse & Blackwell	NESTLE	A+	C	B	A+	B	C	A+	C	3
Del Monte	NABSCO	F	?	?	D	?	?	?	?	3
E.D. Smith	EDSMT	F	?	F	?	?	?	?	?	4
Franco American	CAMBEL	C	F+	F+	C	F	D	C	F	3
Gattuso (sauces)	BORDEN	F	?	F	F	F+	?	?	?	3
Gattuso (condiments)	RHOOD	B	F	F+	A	F	F	C	C	3
Gulden's	CHP	A	F+	D	F	F	C	C	B	2
Habitant	RHOOD	B	F	F+	A	F	F	C	C	3
Heinz	HEINZ	D	F	D	A+	F+	?	D	C	3
Hellmann's	CASCO	F	?	F	C	F	?	?	F	3
HP Sauce	EDSMT	F	?	F	?	?	?	?	?	4
Hunt's	HUNT	N/A	N/A	?	N/A	N/A	N/A	N/A	?	1
Knorr	CASCO	F	?	F	C	F	?	?	F	3
Kraft	KRAFT	B	C	F+	A+	B	B	B	C	3
Lawry's	UNILV	A+	F	F+	A+	D	F+	A+	C	3

CONDIMENTS & SAUCES (CONT'D)

Brand Name	Company Abbreviation	Candour	Women's issues	Charity/ community	Progressive staff policies	Labour relations	Environmental management	Environmental performance	Management/ consumer	Canadian content
Lea & Perrin	EDSMT	F	?	F	?	?	?	?	?	4
Manwich	HUNT	N/A	N/A	?	N/A	N/A	N/A	N/A	?	1
McLarens	RHOOD	B	F	F+	A	F	F	C	C	3
Meal Makers	EFFEM	F	?	?	A	?	?	?	F+	3
Meister	UNILV	A+	F	F+	A+	D	F+	A+	C	3
Mexicasa	UNILV	A+	F	F+	A+	D	F+	A+	C	3
Miracle Whip	KRAFT	B	C	F+	A+	B	B	B	C	3
Monarch	MALEAF	B	?	F+	F	F	F	F	F	3
Old El Paso	PRIMO	F	?	F	?	?	F	?	?	3
Palm	RHOOD	B	F	F+	A	F	F	C	C	3
Paterson's	CAMBEL	C	F+	F+	C	F	D	C	F	3
Prego	CAMBEL	C	F+	F+	C	F	D	C	F	3
Ragu	UNILV	A+	F	F+	A+	D	F+	A+	C	3
Rose	RHOOD	B	F	F+	A	F	F	C	C	3
Safflo	CULNR	B	F+	D	D	F	?	F	F	4
Unico	CULNR	B	F+	D	D	F	?	F	F	4
Weight Watchers	HEINZ	D	F	D	A+	F+	?	D	?	3
Winston House	SPECBD	F	?	F	F	F	?	?	F	2

Brand Name	Company Abbreviation	Candour	Women's issues	Charity/community	Progressive staff policies	Labour relations	Environmental management	Environmental performance	Management/consumer	Canadian content
CONFECTIONERY										
Aero	NESTLE	A+	C	B	A+	B	C	A+	C	3
After Eight	NESTLE	A+	C	B	A+	B	C	A+	C	3
All Nuts	HERSH	A	D	F	B	F+	F	B	F	3
Almondillos	HERSH	A	D	F	B	F+	F	B	F	3
Beech-Nut	HERSH	A	D	F	B	F+	F	B	F	3
Big Turk	NESTLE	A+	C	B	A+	B	C	A+	C	3
Black Magic	NESTLE	A+	C	B	A+	B	C	A+	C	3
Bounty	EFFEM	F	?	?	A	?	?	?	F+	3
Breath Savers	HERSH	A	D	F	B	F+	F	B	F	3
Bridge Mixture	HERSH	A	D	F	B	F+	F	B	F	3
Burnt Almond	WESTON	F	?	D	?	F	?	D	?	4
Cadbury's	WESTON	F	?	D	?	F	?	D	?	4
Cailler	NESTLE	A+	C	B	A+	B	C	A+	C	3
Capri	NESTLE	A+	C	B	A+	B	C	A+	C	3
Caramilk	WESTON	F	?	D	?	F	?	D	?	4
Caravan	HERSH	A	D	F	B	F+	F	B	F	3
Cerises	WESTON	F	?	D	?	F	?	D	?	4
Cherry Blossom	HERSH	A	D	F	B	F+	F	B	F	3
Coconut	WESTON	F	?	D	?	F	?	D	?	4
Coffee Crisp	NESTLE	A+	C	B	A+	B	C	A+	C	3
Cream Eggs	WESTON	F	?	D	?	F	?	D	?	4
Crispy Crunch	WESTON	F	?	D	?	F	?	D	?	4
Crunchie	WESTON	F	?	D	?	F	?	D	?	4
Dairy Milk	WESTON	F	?	D	?	F	?	D	?	4
Dairy Box	NESTLE	A+	C	B	A+	B	C	A+	C	3
Dare	DARE	F	?	?	?	F	?	?	?	4

CONFECTIONERY (CONT'D)

Brand Name	Company Abbreviation	Candour	Women's issues	Charity/community	Progressive staff policies	Labour relations	Environmental management	Environmental performance	Management/consumer	Canadian content
Eat-More	HERSH	A	D	F	B	F+	F	B	F	3
Elegante	NESTLE	A+	C	B	A+	B	C	A+	C	3
Fiesta	NESTLE	A+	C	B	A+	B	C	A+	C	3
Fruit and Nut	WESTON	F	?	D	?	F	?	D	?	4
Glosettes	HERSH	A	D	F	B	F+	F	B	F	3
Gold	WESTON	F	?	D	?	F	?	D	?	4
Goodies	HERSH	A	D	F	B	F+	F	B	F	3
Grifo	NESTLE	A+	C	B	A+	B	C	A+	C	3
Hazelnut	WESTON	F	?	D	?	F	?	D	?	4
Hershey	HERSH	A	D	F	B	F+	F	B	F	3
Jelly Tots	NESTLE	A+	C	B	A+	B	C	A+	C	3
Jersey Milk	WESTON	F	?	D	?	F	?	D	?	4
Kit Kat	NESTLE	A+	C	B	A+	B	C	A+	C	3
Kraft	KRAFT	B	C	F+	A+	B	B	B	C	3
Laura Secord	NESTLE	A+	C	B	A+	B	C	A+	C	3
Life Savers	HERSH	A	D	F	B	F+	F	B	F	3
Lowney	HERSH	A	D	F	B	F+	F	B	F	3
M&M's	EFFEM	F	?	?	A	?	?	?	F+	3
Mackintosh	NESTLE	A+	C	B	A+	B	C	A+	C	3
Malted Milk	WESTON	F	?	D	?	F	?	D	?	4
Maltesers	EFFEM	F	?	?	A	?	?	?	F+	3
Maple Buds	NESTLE	A+	C	B	A+	B	C	A+	C	3
Mars	EFFEM	F	?	?	A	?	?	?	F+	3
McCormicks'	CULNR	B	F+	D	D	F	?	F	F	4
Milka	KRAFT	B	C	F+	A+	B	B	B	C	3
Mint Patties	NESTLE	A+	C	B	A+	B	C	A+	C	3

CONFECTIONERY (CONT'D)

Brand Name	Company Abbreviation	Candour	Women's issues	Charity/ community	Progressive staff policies	Labour relations	Environmental management	Environmental performance	Management/ consumer	Canadian content
Mint Royale	NESTLE	A+	C	B	A+	B	C	A+	C	3
Minuet Cherries	NESTLE	A+	C	B	A+	B	C	A+	C	3
Mirage	NESTLE	A+	C	B	A+	B	C	A+	C	3
Moirs	HERSH	A	D	F	B	F+	F	B	F	3
Mr. Big	WESTON	F	?	D	?	F	?	D	?	4
Neilson	WESTON	F	?	D	?	F	?	D	?	4
Nestlé	NESTLE	A+	C	B	A+	B	C	A+	C	3
Nibs	HERSH	A	D	F	B	F+	F	B	F	3
Nut Milk	HERSH	A	D	F	B	F+	F	B	F	3
Nutchos	NESTLE	A+	C	B	A+	B	C	A+	C	3
Oh Henry!	HERSH	A	D	F	B	F+	F	B	F	3
Ovation	HERSH	A	D	F	B	F+	F	B	F	3
Paulins	CULNR	B	F+	D	D	F	?	D	F	4
Pep	WESTON	F	?	D	?	F	?	D	?	4
Perugina	NESTLE	A+	C	B	A+	B	C	A+	C	3
Pot of Gold	HERSH	A	D	F	B	F+	F	B	F	3
Quality Street	NESTLE	A+	C	B	A+	B	C	A+	C	3
Raisinets	NESTLE	A+	C	B	A+	B	C	A+	C	3
Reese Peanut Butter Cups	HERSH	A	D	F	B	F+	F	B	F	3
Reese's Pieces	HERSH	A	D	F	B	F+	F	B	F	3
Rolo	NESTLE	A+	C	B	A+	B	C	A+	C	3
Rosebuds	WESTON	F	?	D	?	F	?	D	?	4
Rossana	NESTLE	A+	C	B	A+	B	C	A+	C	3
Rum and Butter	WESTON	F	?	D	?	F	?	D	?	4
Selection	HERSH	A	D	F	B	F+	F	B	F	3

CONFECTIONERY (CONT'D)

Brand Name	Company Abbreviation	Candour	Women's issues	Charity/ community	Progressive staff policies	Labour relations	Environmental management	Environmental perfomance	Management/ consumer	Canadian content
Skittles	EFFEM	F	?	?	A	?	?	?	F+	3
Skor	HERSH	A	D	F	B	F+	F	B	F	3
Smarties	NESTLE	A+	C	B	A+	B	C	A+	C	3
Snack Bar	WESTON	F	?	D	?	F	?	D	?	4
Snickers	EFFEM	F	?	?	A	?	?	?	F+	3
Special Dark	HERSH	A	D	F	B	F+	F	B	F	3
Special Crisp	HERSH	A	D	F	B	F+	F	B	F	3
Starburst	EFFEM	F	?	?	A	?	?	?	F+	3
Super 8	NESTLE	A+	C	B	A+	B	C	A+	C	3
Sweet Marie	WESTON	F	?	D	?	F	?	D	?	4
Temptation	HERSH	A	D	F	B	F+	F	B	F	3
Three Musketeers	EFFEM	F	?	?	A	?	?	?	F+	3
Toblerone	KRAFT	B	C	F+	A+	B	B	B	C	3
Tradition	HERSH	A	D	F	B	F+	F	B	F	3
Turtles	NESTLE	A+	C	B	A+	B	C	A+	C	3
Twix	EFFEM	F	?	?	A	?	?	?	F+	3
Twizlets	HERSH	A	D	F	B	F+	F	B	F	3
Twizzlers	HERSH	A	D	F	B	F+	F	B	F	3
Viau	CULNR	B	F+	D	D	F	?	F	F	4
Virginia	WESTON	F	?	D	?	F	?	D	?	4
Wunderbar	WESTON	F	?	D	?	F	?	D	?	4
Y&S	HERSH	A	D	F	B	F+	F	B	F	3
Yorkie	NESTLE	A+	C	B	A+	B	C	A+	C	3

COOKIES

Brand Name	Company Abbreviation	Candour	Women's issues	Charity/ community	Progressive staff policies	Labour relations	Environmental management	Environmental performance	Management/ consumer	Canadian content
Barnum's Animals	NABSCO	F	?	?	D	?	?	?	?	3
Bear Paws	CULNR	B	F+	D	D	F	?	F	F	4
Chips Ahoy!	NABSCO	F	?	?	D	?	?	F	?	3
Christie	NABSCO	F	?	?	D	?	?	?	?	3
Coffee Breaks	NABSCO	F	?	?	D	?	?	?	?	3
Colonial	BEA	A+	F	F	B	F+	F	C	F	3
Dads	NABSCO	F	?	?	D	?	?	?	?	3
Dare	DARE	F	?	?	?	F	?	?	?	4
Fig Newtons	NABSCO	F	?	?	D	?	?	?	?	3
Fudgee-O	NABSCO	F	?	?	D	?	?	?	?	3
Lido's	CULNR	B	F+	D	D	F	?	F	F	4
Maxi Fruits	CULNR	B	F+	D	D	F	?	F	F	4
McCormicks'	CULNR	B	F+	D	D	F	?	F	F	4
Meteo	CULNR	B	F+	D	D	F	?	F	F	4
Mr. Christie's	NABSCO	F	?	?	D	?	?	?	?	3
Normandie	CULNR	B	F+	D	D	F	?	F	F	4
Oreo	NABSCO	F	?	?	D	?	?	?	?	3
Pantry	NABSCO	F	?	?	D	?	?	?	?	3
Peek Freans	NABSCO	F	?	?	D	?	?	?	?	3
Pirate	NABSCO	F	?	?	D	?	?	?	?	3
Primo	PRIMO	F	?	F	?	?	F	?	?	3
Quaker	QUAKER	B	?	D	A+	F	A	A	F	3
Sultana's	NABSCO	F	?	?	D	?	?	?	?	3
Sunmaid	DARE	F	?	?	?	F	?	?	?	4
Teddy Grahams	NABSCO	F	?	?	D	?	?	?	?	3
Viau's	CULNR	B	F+	D	D	F	?	F	F	4

Brand Name	Company Abbreviation	Candour	Women's issues	Charity/ community	Progressive staff policies	Labour relations	Environmental management	Environmental perfomance	Management/ consumer	Canadian content
C O O K I E S (C O N T ' D)										
Wagon Wheels	CULNR	B	F+	D	D	F	?	F	F	4
Whippet	CULNR	B	F+	D	D	F	?	F	F	4
Windsor	BEA	A+	F	F	B	F+	F	C	F	3
C R A C K E R S										
Breton	DARE	F	?	?	?	F	?	?	?	4
Christie	NABSCO	F	?	?	D	?	?	?	?	3
Colonial	BEA	A+	F	F	B	F+	F	C	F	3
Dare	DARE	F	?	?	?	F	?	?	?	4
Grissol	CULNR	B	F+	D	D	F	?	F	F	4
Honey Maid	NABSCO	F	?	?	D	?	?	?	?	3
Lifestream	NABOB	A+	F	D	A+	A	B	A+	F	3
McCormicks'	CULNR	B	F+	D	D	F	?	F	F	4
McKay	NESTLE	A+	C	B	A+	B	C	A+	C	3
Old London	CASCO	F	?	F	C	F	?	?	F	3
Paulins	CULNR	B	F+	D	D	F	?	F	F	4
Premium Plus	NABSCO	F	?	?	D	?	?	?	?	3
Ritz	NABSCO	F	?	?	D	?	?	?	?	
Rusks	CULNR	B	F+	D	D	F	?	F	F	4
Snacking Crackers	NABSCO	F	?	?	D	?	?	?	?	3
Triscuit	NABSCO	F	?	?	D	?	?	?	?	3
Wheatsworth	NABSCO	F	?	?	D	?	?	?	?	3
Windsor	BEA	A+	F	F	B	F+	F	C	F	3

Brand Name	Company Abbreviation	Candour	Women's issues	Charity/ community	Progressive staff policies	Labour relations	Environmental management	Environmental perfomance	Management/ consumer	Canadian content
DEODORANTS										
Ban	BMCP	C	D	C	A+	F	F+	N/A	F+	1
Brut	UNILV	A+	F	F+	A+	D	F+	A+	C	3
Dry Idea	GILET	F	?	F	F	?	?	N/A	?	1
Impulse	UNILV	A+	F	F+	A+	D	F+	A+	C	3
Irish Spring	COLPAL	F	?	?	?	?	?	?	?	3
Johnson's	J&J	A	F	D	A	F	F	D	F+	3
Old Spice	P&G	C	?	F	A+	F+	D	D	F	3
Pears	UNILV	A+	F	F+	A+	D	F+	A+	C	3
Right Guard	GILET	F	?	F	F	?	?	N/A	?	1
Secret	P&G	C	?	F	A+	F+	D	D	F	3
Shower to Shower	J&J	A	F	D	A	F	F	D	F+	3
Soft & Dri	GILET	F	?	F	F	?	?	N/A	?	1

Brand Name	Company Abbreviation	Candour	Women's issues	Charity/community	Progressive staff policies	Labour relations	Environmental management	Environmental perfomance	Management/consumer	Canadian content
DESSERTS										
All Natural	AULT	B	F	C	A+	A+	B	B	F	4
Beatrice	BEA	A+	F	F	B	F+	F	C	F	3
Bluenose	SBURN	A+	D	C	B	B	F+	A+	F	4
Chipwich	AULT	B	F	C	A+	A+	B	B	F	4
Christie	NABSCO	F	?	?	D	?	?	?	?	3
Cool Whip	KRAFT	B	C	F+	A+	B	B	B	C	3
Crosse & Blackwell	NESTLE	A+	C	B	A+	B	C	A+	C	3
Dallaire	AULT	B	F	C	A+	A+	B	B	F	4
Delys	AULT	B	F	C	A+	A+	B	B	F	4
Drake's	CULNR	B	F+	D	D	F	?	F	F	4
Drumstick	AULT	B	F	C	A+	A+	B	B	F	4
Famous	AULT	B	F	C	A+	A+	B	B	F	4
Fruit Fantasy	AULT	B	F	C	A+	A+	B	B	F	4
Good Humor	BEA	A+	F	F	B	F+	F	C	F	3
Häagen Dazs	AULT	B	F	C	A+	A+	B	B	F	4
J. Higby's	AULT	B	F	C	A+	A+	B	B	F	4
Jell-O	KRAFT	B	C	F+	A+	B	B	B	C	3
Laura Secord	NESTLE	A+	C	B	A+	B	C	A+	C	3
Light 'n' Lively	AULT	B	F	C	A+	A+	B	B	F	4
Magic Moments	KRAFT	B	C	F+	A+	B	B	B	C	3
McCain	MCCAIN	C	?	A	A	D	F	C	F	4
Meadowgold	AULT	B	F	C	A+	A+	B	B	F	4
Movenpick	AULT	B	F	C	A+	A+	B	B	F	4
Mrs. Smith's	KELOG	A+	F	A+	A	A+	C	B	B	3
Nestlé	NESTLE	A+	C	B	A+	B	C	A+	C	3

Brand Name	Company Abbreviation	Candour	Women's issues	Charity/ community	Progressive staff policies	Labour relations	Environmental management	Environmental performance	Management/ consumer	Canadian content
D E S S E R T S (C O N T ' D)										
Nutriwhip	MALEAF	B	?	F+	F	F	F	F	F	3
Oh Henry! Ice Cream Bar	HERSH	A	D	F	B	F+	F	B	F	3
Parlour	AULT	B	F	C	A+	A+	B	B	F	4
Pepperidge Farms	CAMBEL	C	F+	F+	C	F	D	C	F	3
Perfect Endings	CULNR	B	F+	D	D	F	?	F	F	4
Reddi Wip	BEA	A+	F	F	B	F+	F	C	F	3
Reese Ice Cream Bar	HERSH	A	D	F	B	F+	F	B	F	3
Robinson	DOVER	F	?	?	?	?	?	?	F	4
Sara Lee	SARLEE	A+	D	F	F	F+	F	F	F+	3
Scotsburn	SBURN	A+	D	C	B	B	F+	A+	F	4
Sealtest	AULT	B	F	C	A+	A+	B	B	F	4
Staffords	EDSMT	F	?	F	?	?	?	?	?	4
Sydney Sandwich	SBURN	A+	D	C	B	B	F+	A+	F	4
Weight Watchers	HEINZ	D	F	D	A+	F+	?	D	?	3
D I A P E R S										
Curity	GERBER	F	?	?	?	?	?	N/A	?	1
Huggies	KIMCLA	B	F	F+	A+	D	F	F	D	3
Luvs	P&G	C	?	F	A+	F+	D	D	F	3
Pampers	P&G	C	?	F	A+	F+	D	D	F	3
Pull-Ups	KIMCLA	B	F	F+	A+	D	F	F	D	3

63

Brand Name	Company Abbreviation	Candour	Women's issues	Charity/ community	Progressive staff policies	Labour relations	Environmental management	Environmental perfomance	Management/ consumer	Canadian content
DISH DETERGENTS										
all	UNILV	A+	F	F+	A+	D	F+	A+	C	3
Cascade	P&G	C	?	F	A+	F+	D	D	F	3
Dove	UNILV	A+	F	F+	A+	D	F+	A+	C	3
Excel	UNILV	A+	F	F+	A+	D	F+	A+	C	3
Ivory	P&G	C	?	F	A+	F+	D	D	F	3
Joy	P&G	C	?	F	A+	F+	D	D	F	3
Mir	UNILV	A+	F	F+	A+	D	F+	A+	C	3
Palmolive	COLPAL	F	?	?	?	?	?	?	?	3
Sunlight	UNILV	A+	F	F+	A+	D	F+	A+	C	3
FEMININE HYGIENE										
Always	P&G	C	?	F	A+	F+	D	D	F	3
Anyday	KIMCLA	B	F	F+	A+	D	F	F	D	3
Carefree	J&J	A	F	D	A	F	F	D	F+	3
Compak	TAMBRD	B	C	F	A+	D	C	N/A	A+	1
FDS	ABCUL	F	?	?	?	?	?	?	?	3
K-Y	J&J	A	F	D	A	F	F	D	F+	3
Kotex	KIMCLA	B	F	F+	A+	D	F	F	D	3
Lightdays	KIMCLA	B	F	F+	A+	D	F	F	D	3
Massengil	SKB	F	?	?	?	?	?	?	?	3
Maxithins	TAMBRD	B	C	F	A+	D	C	N/A	A+	1
New Freedom	KIMCLA	B	F	F+	A+	D	F	F	D	3
o.b.	J&J	A	F	D	A	F	F	D	F+	3
Playtex	PLATX	F	?	F	?	?	?	?	?	3
Stayfree	J&J	A	F	D	A	F	F	D	F+	3
Sure and Natural Prima	J&J	A	F	D	A	F	F	D	F+	3
Tampax	TAMBRD	B	C	F	A+	D	C	N/A	A+	1

Brand Name	Company Abbreviation	Candour	Women's issues	Charity/community	Progressive staff policies	Labour relations	Environmental management	Environmental performance	Management/consumer	Canadian content
FLOUR										
Cream of the West	MALEAF	B	?	F+	F	F	F	F	F	3
Dover	DOVER	F	?	?	?	?	?	?	F	4
Five Roses	OGMILS	A+	F	F+	A	B	F	F	F	3
Hi-Fibre	DOVER	F	?	?	?	?	?	?	F	4
Monarch	MALEAF	B	?	F+	F	F	F	F	F	3
Purity	MALEAF	B	?	F+	F	F	F	F	F	3
Robin Hood	RHOOD	B	F	F+	A	F	F	C	C	3
Swan's Down	DOVER	F	?	?	?	?	?	?	F	4
FOOD WRAPS										
Alcan	ALCAN	C	?	A	?	F	B	C	?	4
Baggies	DOWBR	A	D	D	A+	C	D	A+	D	3
Baker's Choice	REYNLD	A	F	F+	A	C	D	C	D	3
Brown-In-Bag	REYNLD	A	F	F+	A	C	D	C	D	3
Cut-Rite	SCOTT	A+	F	B	A+	B	C	A	D	3
Diamond	REYNLD	A	F	F+	A	C	D	C	D	3
Handi Wrap	DOWBR	A	D	D	A+	C	D	A+	D	3
Presto	REYNLD	A	F	F+	A	C	D	C	D	3
Reynolds	REYNLD	A	F	F+	A	C	D	C	D	3
Saran Wrap	DOWBR	A	D	D	A+	C	D	A+	D	3
Stretch 'N Seal	DOWBR	A	D	D	A+	C	D	A+	D	3
Ziploc	DOWBR	A	D	D	A+	C	D	A+	D	3

Brand Name	Company Abbreviation	Candour	Women's issues	Charity/ community	Progressive staff policies	Labour relations	Environmental management	Environmental perfomance	Management/ consumer	Canadian content
FRESH & FROZEN MEAT/POULTRY										
Citadel	MALEAF	B	?	F+	F	F	F	F	F	3
Maple Lodge Farms	MAPLOD	F	?	F	?	?	?	?	F	4
Maple Leaf	MALEAF	B	?	F+	F	F	F	F	F	3
Prime	MALEAF	B	?	F+	F	F	F	F	F	3
Schneider	JMSCH	B	F	F+	A+	F	F	F	D	4
Sherwood Farms	MALEAF	B	?	F+	F	F	F	F	F	3
Stillmeadow	MALEAF	B	?	F+	F	F	F	F	F	3
Tend-R-Fresh	MALEAF	B	?	F+	F	F	F	F	F	3
Tendercut	CARGIL	A+	F+	A+	C	F	D	A+	B	3
FRESH & FROZEN SEAFOOD										
BC Packers	BPACK	A	F	D	A	F	C	C	D	4
Blue Water	GENMIL	B	F	D	A	F	D	D	D	3
Catch O' the Day	FPI	F	?	?	?	F	?	?	?	4
High Liner	NATSEA	C	D	F	B	F	F+	A+	F	4
Light Tonight	NATSEA	C	D	F	B	F	F+	A+	F	4
Mirabel	FPI	F	?	?	?	F	?	?	?	4
Newfoundland Imperial Cod	FPI	F	?	?	?	F	?	?	?	4
North Pacific	OCEAN	B	F	F	A	D	D	B	F	4
SeaFresh	NATSEA	C	D	F	B	F	F+	A+	F	4
Treasure Isle	NATSEA	C	D	F	B	F	F+	A+	F	4

FROZEN PREPARED FOODS

Brand Name	Company Abbreviation	Candour	Women's issues	Charity/ community	Progressive staff policies	Labour relations	Environmental management	Environmental performance	Management/ consumer	Canadian content
Aunt Jemima	QUAKER	B	?	D	A+	F	A	A	F	3
Carnation	NESTLE	A+	C	B	A+	B	C	A+	C	3
Caterpac	MCCAIN	C	?	A	A	D	F	C	F	4
Cavendish Farms	CAVDIS	F	?	?	?	?	?	?	?	4
Eggo	KELOG	A+	F	A+	A	A+	C	B	B	3
Handi Meals	JMSCH	B	F	F+	A+	F	F	F	D	4
Healthy Choice	HUNT	N/A	N/A	?	N/A	N/A	N/A	N/A	?	1
Jeno's	PILBRY	B	D	F	B	A+	F	F	D	3
Le Menu	CAMBEL	C	F+	F+	C	F	D	C	F	3
McCain	MCCAIN	C	?	A	A	D	F	C	F	4
Micro Marvels	MALEAF	B	?	F+	F	F	F	F	F	3
Nutri-Grain	KELOG	A+	F	A+	A	A+	C	B	B	3
Old El Paso	PRIMO	F	?	F	?	?	F	?	?	3
Omstead	HEINZ	D	F	D	A+	F+	?	D	?	3
Pepperidge Farms	CAMBEL	C	F+	F+	C	F	D	C	F	3
Pillsbury	PILBRY	B	D	F	B	A+	F	F	D	3
Pizza Pops	PILBRY	B	D	F	B	A+	F	F	D	3
Schneider	JMSCH	B	F	F+	A+	F	F	F	D	4
Lean Cuisine	NESTLE	A+	C	B	A+	B	C	A+	C	3
Stouffer's	NESTLE	A+	C	B	A+	B	C	A+	C	3
Superiore	CHP	A	F+	D	F	F	C	C	B	2
Swanson	CAMBEL	C	F+	F+	C	F	D	C	F	3
Totino's	PILBRY	B	D	F	B	A+	F	F	D	3
Valley Farms	MCCAIN	C	?	A	A	D	F	C	F	4
Weight Watchers	HEINZ	D	F	D	A+	F+	?	D	?	3
York	MALEAF	B	?	F+	F	F	F	F	F	3

Brand Name	Company Abbreviation	Candour	Women's issues	Charity/community	Progressive staff policies	Labour relations	Environmental management	Environmental performance	Management/consumer	Canadian content
FROZEN & REFRIGERATED DOUGHS & PASTRY										
Gainsborough	CPF	F	D	F	A	D	F	F	?	3
Pepperidge Farms	CAMBEL	C	F+	F+	C	F	D	C	F	3
Pillsbury	PILBRY	B	D	F	B	A+	F	F	D	3
Tenderflake	MALEAF	B	?	F+	F	F	F	F	F	3
HAIR CARE										
Agree	SCJON	F	?	F+	?	D	?	C	?	3
Alberto	ABCUL	F	?	?	?	?	?	?	?	3
Aqua Net	UNILV	A+	F	F+	A+	D	F+	A+	C	3
Body on Tap	BMCP	C	D	C	A+	F	F+	N/A	F+	1
Bold Hold	ABCUL	F	?	?	?	?	?	?	?	3
Breck	DIAL	N/A	N/A	?	N/A	N/A	N/A	N/A	N/A	0
Brylcreem	SKB	F	?	?	?	?	?	?	?	3
Clairol	BMCP	C	D	C	A+	F	F+	N/A	F+	1
Clubman's	SCJON	F	?	F+	?	D	?	C	?	3
Condition	BMCP	C	D	C	A+	F	F+	N/A	F+	1
Consort	ABCUL	F	?	?	?	?	?	?	?	3
Dry Look	GILET	F	?	F	F	?	?	N/A	?	1
Final Net	BMCP	C	D	C	A+	F	F+	N/A	F+	–
French Formula	SCJON	F	?	F+	?	D	?	C	?	3
HALO	COLPAL	F	?	?	?	?	?	?	?	3
Halsa	SCJON	F	?	F+	?	D	?	C	?	3
Head and Shoulders	P&G	C	?	F	A+	F+	D	D	F	3
Ivory	P&G	C	?	F	A+	F+	D	D	F	3
Jhirmack	PLATX	F	?	F	?	?	?	?	?	3
Johnson's	J&J	A	F	D	A	F	F	D	F+	3

HAIR CARE (CONT'D)

Brand Name	Company Abbreviation	Candour	Women's issues	Charity/community	Progressive staff policies	Labour relations	Environmental management	Environmental perfomance	Management/consumer	Canadian content
Lustrasilk	GILET	F	?	F	F	?	?	N/A	?	1
Pantene	P&G	C	?	.F	A+	F+	D	D	F	3
Pears	UNILV	A+	F	F+	A+	D	F+	A+	C	3
Pert	P&G	C	?	F	A+	F+	D	D	F	3
Silkience	GILET	F	?	F	F	?	?	N/A	?	1
Tame	GILET	F	?	F	F	?	?	N/A	?	1
TCB	ABCUL	F	?	?	?	?	?	?	?	3
Timotei	UNILV	A+	F	F+	A+	D	F+	A+	C	3
Toni	GILET	F	?	F	F	?	?	N/A	?	1
TRESemme	ABCUL	F	?	?	?	?	?	?	?	3
Vitalis	BMCP	C	D	C	A+	F	F+	N/A	F+	1
Vidal Sassoon	P&G	C	?	F	A+	F+	D	D	F	3
VO5	ABCUL	F	?	?	?	?	?	?	?	3

HOUSEHOLD CLEANERS

Brand Name	Company Abbreviation	Candour	Women's issues	Charity/community	Progressive staff policies	Labour relations	Environmental management	Environmental performance	Management/consumer	Canadian content
Ajax	COLPAL	F	?	?	?	?	?	?	?	3
Amex	COLPAL	F	?	?	?	?	?	?	?	3
Behold	DRACK	F	?	?	?	?	?	N/A	?	1
Bon Ami	SCJON	F	?	F+	?	D	?	C	?	3
Borax	DIAL	N/A	N/A	?	N/A	N/A	N/A	N/A	N/A	0
Bravo	SCJON	F	?	F+	?	D	?	C	?	3
Brillo	DIAL	N/A	N/A	?	N/A	N/A	N/A	N/A	N/A	0
Comet	P&G	C	?	F	A+	F+	D	D	F	3
Dow	DOWBR	A	D	D	A+	C	D	A+	D	3
Drano	DRACK	F	?	?	?	?	?	N/A	?	1
Endust	DRACK	F	?	?	?	?	?	N/A	?	1
Fantastik	DOWBR	A	D	D	A+	C	D	A+	D	3
Favor	SCJON	F	?	F+	?	D	?	C	?	3
Fine Wood Buffing Wax	SCJON	F	?	F+	?	D	?	C	?	3
Freedom	SCJON	F	?	F+	?	D	?	C	?	3
Future	SCJON	F	?	F+	?	D	?	C	?	3
Glade	SCJON	F	?	F+	?	D	?	C	?	3
Glass Plus	DOWBR	A	D	D	A+	C	D	A+	D	3
Glory	SCJON	F	?	F+	?	D	?	C	?	3
Javex	COLPAL	F	?	?	?	?	?	?	?	3
Johnson	SCJON	F	?	F+	?	D	?	C	?	3
Klear	SCJON	F	?	F+	?	D	?	C	?	3
Lestoil	P&G	C	?	F	A+	F+	D	D	F	3
Mop Magic	SCJON	F	?	F+	?	D	?	C	?	3
Mr. Clean	P&G	C	?	F	A+	F+	D	D	F	3
Mr. Muscle	DRACK	F	?	?	?	?	?	N/A	?	1

HOUSEHOLD CLEANERS (CONT'D)

Brand Name	Company Abbreviation	Candour	Women's issues	Charity/ community	Progressive staff policies	Labour relations	Environmental management	Environmental perfomance	Management/ consumer	Canadian content
Murphy Oil Soap	COLPAL	F	?	?	?	?	?	?	?	3
Pledge	SCJON	F	?	F+	?	D	?	C	?	3
Renuzit	DRACK	F	?	?	?	?	?	N/A	?	1
Scrub 'n Shine	COLPAL	F	?	?	?	?	?	?	?	3
Spic 'n Span	P&G	C	?	F	A+	F+	D	D	F	3
Toilet Duck	SCJON	F	?	F+	?	D	?	C	?	3
Twinkle	DRACK	F	?	?	?	?	?	N/A	?	1
Vanish	DRACK	F	?	?	?	?	?	N/A	?	1
Vim	UNILV	A+	F	F+	A+	D	F+	A+	C	3
Wax-Strip	SCJON	F	?	F+	?	D	?	C	?	3
Windex	DRACK	F	?	?	?	?	?	N/A	?	1

INCONTINENCE PRODUCTS

Brand Name	Company Abbreviation	Candour	Women's issues	Charity/ community	Progressive staff policies	Labour relations	Environmental management	Environmental perfomance	Management/ consumer	Canadian content
Assure	J&J	A	F	D	A	F	F	D	F+	3
Attends	P&G	C	?	F	A+	F+	D	D	F	3
Depends	KIMCLA	B	F	F+	A+	D	F	F	D	3
Profile	KIMCLA	B	F	F+	A+	D	F	F	D	3
Serenity	J&J	A	F	D	A	F	F	D	F+	3

71

JAMS & JELLIES

Brand Name	Company Abbreviation	Candour	Women's issues	Charity/community	Progressive staff policies	Labour relations	Environmental management	Environmental performance	Management/consumer	Canadian content
Canadiana	CULNR	B	F+	D	D	F	?	F	F	4
Double Fruit	CULNR	B	F+	D	D	F	?	F	F	4
E.D. Smith	EDSMT	F	?	F	?	?	?	?	?	4
Grenache	CULNR	B	F+	D	D	F	?	F	F	4
Guest	CULNR	B	F+	D	D	F	?	F	F	4
Habitant	EDSMT	F	?	F	?	?	?	?	?	4
Kraft Pure	KRAFT	B	C	F+	A+	B	B	B	C	3
Laura Secord	NESTLE	A+	C	B	A+	B	C	A+	C	3
Old Homestead	CULNR	B	F+	D	D	F	?	F	F	4
Tradition	CULNR	B	F+	D	D	F	?	F	F	4
Vachon	CULNR	B	F+	D	D	F	?	F	F	4
Welch's	CADBEV	A	F	F+	A	F	B	B	F+	3

JUICES & FRUIT DRINKS

Brand Name	Company Abbreviation	Candour	Women's issues	Charity/community	Progressive staff policies	Labour relations	Environmental management	Environmental performance	Management/consumer	Canadian content
Beatrice	BEA	A+	F	F	B	F+	F	C	F	3
Caesar's Choice	CAMBEL	C	F+	F+	C	F	D	C	F	3
Campbell's	CAMBEL	C	F+	F+	C	F	D	C	F	3
Citrus Hill	P&G	C	?	F	A+	F+	D	D	F	3
Cool Down	EVFRSH	B	D	F	F	F	F	D	F	3
Country Time	KRAFT	B	C	F+	A+	B	B	B	C	3
Del Monte	NABSCO	F	?	?	D	?	?	?	?	3
Everfresh	EVFRSH	B	D	F	F	F	F	D	F	3
Five Alive	COKE	A	F	A	B	A+	D	D	C	4
Fruite	LASND	A+	F	F	D	D	F	F	F	4
Garden Cocktail	CADBEV	A	F	F+	A	F	B	B	F+	3
Gatorade	QUAKER	B	?	D	A+	F	A	A	F	3
Graves	COBI	A+	F	F	F	F	F	F	F	4
Hawaiian Punch	P&G	C	?	F	A+	F+	D	D	F	3
Heinz	HEINZ	D	F	D	A+	F+	?	D	?	3
Honeydew	COBI	A+	F	F	F	F	F	F	F	4
Kent	MCCAIN	C	?	A	A	D	F	C	F	4
Libby's	NESTLE	A+	C	B	A+	B	C	A+	C	3
McCain	MCCAIN	C	?	A	A	D	F	C	F	4
Mont-Rouge	LASND	A+	F	F	D	D	F	C	F	4
Mott's	CADBEV	A	F	F+	A	F	B	B	F+	3
Mr. Citrus	EVFRSH	B	D	F	F	F	F	D	F	3
Oasis	LASND	A+	F	F	D	D	F	F	F	3
Oasis Del Sol	LASND	A+	F	F	D	D	F	F	F	4
Ocean Spray	CADBEV	A	F	F+	A	F	B	B	F+	3
Picnic	MCCAIN	C	?	A	A	D	F	C	F	4

JUICES & FRUIT DRINKS (CONT'D)

Brand Name	Company Abbreviation	Candour	Women's issues	Charity/community	Progressive staff policies	Labour relations	Environmental management	Environmental perfomance	Management/consumer	Canadian content
Pure Sun	COKE	A	F	A	B	A+	D	D	C	4
ReaLemon	BORDEN	F	?	F	F	F+	?	?	?	3
Ribena	SKB	F	?	?	?	?	?	?	?	3
Rougemont	LASND	A+	F	F	D	D	F	F	F	4
Scotsburn	SBURN	A+	D	C	B	B	F+	A+	F	4
Sunny Delight	P&G	C	?	F	A+	F+	D	D	F	3
V-8	CAMBEL	C	F+	F+	C	F	D	C	F	3
Vegetable Cocktail	HEINZ	D	F	D	A+	F+	?	D	?	3
Welch's	CADBEV	A	F	F+	A	F	B	B	F+	3
Wright's	NABSCO	F	?	?	D	?	?	?	?	3

LAUNDRY SUPPLIES

Brand Name	Company Abbreviation	Candour	Women's issues	Charity/ community	Progressive staff policies	Labour relations	Environmental management	Environmental perfomance	Management/ consumer	Canadian content
ABC	COLPAL	F	?	?	?	?	?	?	?	3
all	UNILV	A+	F	F+	A+	D	F+	A+	C	3
Amaze	UNILV	A+	F	F+	A+	D	F+	A+	C	3
Arctic Power	COLPAL	F	?	?	?	?	?	?	?	3
Bio-Ad	COLPAL	F	?	?	?	?	?	?	?	3
Bold	P&G	C	?	F	A+	F+	D	D	F	3
Borateem	DIAL	N/A	N/A	?	N/A	N/A	N/A	N/A	N/A	0
Borax	DIAL	N/A	N/A	?	N/A	N/A	N/A	N/A	N/A	0
Bounce	P&G	C	?	F	A+	F+	D	D	F	3
Chanteclerc	COLPAL	F	?	?	?	?	?	?	?	3
Cheer	P&G	C	?	F	A+	F+	D	D	F	3
Dash	P&G	C	?	F	A+	F+	D	D	F	3
Downy	P&G	C	?	F	A+	F+	D	D	F	3
Dreft	P&G	C	?	F	A+	F+	D	D	F	3
Fleecy	COLPAL	F	?	?	?	?	?	?	?	3
Glide	COLPAL	F	?	?	?	?	?	?	?	3
Ivory Snow	P&G	C	?	F	A+	F+	D	D	F	3
Javex	COLPAL	F	?	?	?	?	?	?	?	3
Kleen Guard	ABCUL	F	?	?	?	?	?	?	?	3
Mix O Bleaches	COLPAL	F	?	?	?	?	?	?	?	3
Nu-Fluff	COLPAL	F	?	?	?	?	?	?	?	3
Oxydol	P&G	C	?	F	A+	F+	D	D	F	3
Perfex	COLPAL	F	?	?	?	?	?	?	?	3
Shout	SCJON	F	?	F+	?	D	?	C	?	3
Snuggle	UNILV	A+	F	F+	A+	D	F+	A+	C	3
Spray'N Wash	DOWBR	A	D	D	A+	C	D	A+	D	3

Brand Name	Company Abbreviation	Candour	Women's issues	Charity/ community	Progressive staff policies	Labour relations	Environmental management	Environmental perfomance	Management/ consumer	Canadian content
LAUNDRY SUPPLIES (CONT'T)										
Spray 'N Starch	DOWBR	A	D	D	A+	C	D	A+	D	3
Stainaway	COLPAL	F	?	?	?	?	?	?	?	3
Static Guard	ABCUL	F	?	?	?	?	?	?	?	3
Sunbrite	COLPAL	F	?	?	?	?	?	?	?	3
Sunlight	UNILV	A+	F	F+	A+	D	F+	A+	C	3
Surf	UNILV	A+	F	F+	A+	D	F+	A+	C	3
Tide	P&G	C	?	F	A+	F+	D	D	F	3
Wisk	UNILV	A+	F	F+	A+	D	F+	A+	C	3

Brand Name	Company Abbreviation	Candour	Women's issues	Charity/ community	Progressive staff policies	Labour relations	Environmental management	Environmental perfomance	Management/ consumer	Canadian content
M A R G E R I N E , S H O R T E N I N G & O I L S										
Becel	UNILV	A+	F	F+	A+	D	F+	A+	C	3
Blue Bonnet	UNILV	A+	F	F+	A+	D	F+	A+	C	3
Burns	MALEAF	B	?	F+	F	F	F	F	F	3
Canola Harvest	CANBRA	F	?	?	?	?	?	?	?	4
Country Crock	UNILV	A+	F	F+	A+	D	F+	A+	C	3
Crisco	P&G	C	?	F	A+	F+	D	D	F	3
Domestic	MALEAF	B	?	F+	F	F	F	F	F	3
EverSweet	UNILV	A+	F	F+	A+	D	F+	A+	C	3
Fleischmann's	UNILV	A+	F	F+	A+	D	F+	A+	C	3
Fluffo	P&G	C	?	F	A+	F+	D	D	F	3
Gallo	CULNR	B	F+	D	D	F	?	F	F	4
Golden Girl	UNILV	A+	F	F+	A+	D	F+	A+	C	3
Good Luck	UNILV	A+	F	F+	A+	D	F+	A+	C	3
I Can't Believe It's Not										
Butter	UNILV	A+	F	F+	A+	D	F+	A+	C	3
Imperial	UNILV	A+	F	F+	A+	D	F+	A+	C	3
Lactantia	AULT	B	F	C	A+	A+	B	B	F	4
Krona	UNILV	A+	F	F+	A+	D	F+	A+	C	3
Mazola	CASCO	F	?	F	C	F	?	?	F	3
Mom's	UNILV	A+	F	F+	A+	D	F+	A+	C	3
Monarch	UNILV	A+	F	F+	A+	D	F+	A+	C	3
Parkay	KRAFT	B	C	F+	A+	B	B	B	C	3
Planters	HERSH	A	D	F	B	F+	F	B	F	3
Primo	PRIMO	F	?	F	?	?	F	?	?	3
Purelight	CASCO	F	?	F	C	F	?	?	F	3
Saflo	CULNR	B	F+	D	D	F	?	F	F	4

MARGERINE, SHORTENING & OILS (CONT'D)

Brand Name	Company Abbreviation	Candour	Women's issues	Charity/ community	Progressive staff policies	Labour relations	Environmental management	Environmental perfomance	Management/ consumer	Canadian content
Sno'Flake	MALEAF	B	?	F+	F	F	F	F	F	3
St. Lawrence	CASCO	F	?	F	C	F	?	?	F	3
Tenderflake	MALEAF	B	?	F+	F	F	F	F	F	3
Unico	CULNR	B	F+	D	D	F	?	F	F	4
West	CANBRA	F	?	?	?	?	?	?	?	4

MILK & CREAM

Brand Name	Company Abbreviation	Candour	Women's issues	Charity/ community	Progressive staff policies	Labour relations	Environmental management	Environmental perfomance	Management/ consumer	Canadian content
Beatrice	BEA	A+	F	F	B	F+	F	C	F	3
Cape Breton Dairymen	SBURN	A+	D	C	B	B	F+	A+	F	4
Carnation	NESTLE	A+	C	B	A+	B	C	A+	C	3
Coffee-Mate	NESTLE	A+	C	B	A+	B	C	A+	C	3
Copper Cliff	AULT	B	F	C	A+	A+	B	B	F	4
Dallaire	AULT	B	F	C	A+	A+	B	B	F	4
Eagle Brand	BORDEN	F	?	F	F	F+	?	?	?	3
Fussell's	NESTLE	A+	C	B	A+	B	C	A+	C	3
Gay Lea	GAYLEA	A	F	F+	D	F	F	F	F	4
Heritage Farms	BEA	A+	F	F	B	F+	F	C	F	3
Nestlé	NESTLE	A+	C	B	A+	B	C	A+	C	3
Nordica	GAYLEA	A	F	F+	D	F	F	F	F	4
Royal Oak	AULT	B	F	C	A+	A+	B	B	F	4
Schneider	JMSCH	B	F	F+	A+	F	F	B	F	4
Scotsburn	SBURN	A+	D	C	B	B	F+	A+	D	4
Sealtest	AULT	B	F	C	A+	A+	B	B	F	4

Brand Name	Company Abbreviation	Candour	Women's issues	Charity/ community	Progressive staff policies	Labour relations	Environmental management	Environmental perfomance	Management/ consumer	Canadian content
MISCELLANEOUS HOUSEHOLD SUPPLIES										
Carousel	DOVER	F	?	?	?	?	?	?	F	4
Crystal	CANSAL	F	?	F	F	?	?	?	?	3
Melitta	MELTA	A+	C	F+	C	F	F	N/A	D	1
Playtex	PLATX	F	?	F	?	?	?	?	?	3
Raid House and Garden	SCJON	F	?	F+	?	D	?	C	?	3
Safe-T-Salt	CANSAL	F	?	F	F	?	?	?	?	3
MISCELLANEOUS PERSONAL CARE										
Q-Tips	UNILV	A+	F	F+	A+	D	F+	A+	C	3
Cutex	UNILV	A+	F	F+	A+	D	F+	A+	C	3
Off	SCJON	F	?	F+	?	D	?	C	?	3
Deep Woods	SCJON	F	?	F+	?	D	?	C	?	3
Skintastic	SCJON	F	?	F+	?	D	?	C	?	3
Sundown	J&J	A	F	D	A	F	F	D	F+	3

ORAL HYGIENE

Brand Name	Company Abbreviation	Candour	Women's issues	Charity/ community	Progressive staff policies	Labour relations	Environmental management	Environmental perfomance	Management/ consumer	Canadian content
Aim	UNILV	A+	F	F+	A+	D	F+	A+	C	3
Aquafresh	SKB	F	?	?	?	?	?	?	?	3
Close-Up	UNILV	A+	F	F+	A+	D	F+	A+	C	3
Colgate	COLPAL	F	?	?	?	?	?	?	?	3
Crest	P&G	C	?	F	A+	F+	D	D	F	3
Dentotape	J&J	A	F	D	A	F	F	D	F+	3
Fasteeth	P&G	C	?	F	A+	F+	D	D	F	3
Fixodent	P&G	C	?	F	A+	F+	D	D	F+	3
Johnson & Johnson	J&J	A	F	D	A	F	F	D	F+	3
Macleans	SKB	F	?	?	?	?	?	?	?	3
Orafix	SKB	F	?	?	?	?	?	?	?	3
Oral-B	GILET	F	?	F	F	?	?	N/A	?	1
Pepsodent	UNILV	A+	F	F+	A+	D	F+	A+	C	3
Prevent	J&J	A	F	D	A	F	F	D	F+	3
Reach	J&J	A	F	D	A	F	F	D	F+	3
Scope	P&G	C	?	F	A+	F+	D	D	F	3
Stim-U-Dent	J&J	A	F	D	A	F	F	D	F+	3

OTHER BABY NEEDS

Brand Name	Company Abbreviation	Candour	Women's issues	Charity/ community	Progressive staff policies	Labour relations	Environmental management	Environmental perfomance	Management/ consumer	Canadian content
Baby Fresh	SCOTT	A+	F	B	A+	B	C	A	D	3
Baby's Own	SKB	F	?	?	?	?	?	?	?	3
Cherubs	PLATX	F	?	F	?	?	?	?	?	3
Gerber	GERBER	F	?	?	?	?	?	N/A	?	1
Johnson's	J&J	A	F	D	A	F	F	D	F+	3
Nuk	GERBER	F	?	?	?	?	?	N/A	?	1
Playtex	PLATX	F	?	F	?	?	?	?	?	3

PAPER PRODUCTS

Brand Name	Company Abbreviation	Candour	Women's issues	Charity/ community	Progressive staff policies	Labour relations	Environmental management	Environmental perfomance	Management/ consumer	Canadian content
Baby Fresh	SCOTT	A+	F	B	A+	B	C	A	D	3
Cashmere	SCOTT	A+	F	B	A+	B	C	A	D	3
Cottonelle	SCOTT	A+	F	B	A+	B	C	A	D	3
Delsey	KIMCLA	B	F	F+	A+	D	F	F	D	3
Dove	P&G	C	?	F	A+	F+	D	D	F	3
Facelle	P&G	C	?	F	A+	F+	D	D	F	3
Facettes	P&G	C	?	F	A+	F+	D	D	F	3
Festival	P&G	C	?	F	A+	F+	D	D	F	3
Florelle	P&G	C	?	F	A+	F+	D	D	F	3
Hi-Dri	KIMCLA	B	F	F+	A+	D	F	F	D	3
Kleenex	KIMCLA	B	F	F+	A+	D	F	F	D	3
Melitta	MELTA	A+	C	F+	C	F	F	N/A	D	1
Pronto	P&G	C	?	F	A+	F+	D	D	F	3
Purex	SCOTT	A+	F	B	A+	B	C	A	D	3
Royale	P&G	C	?	F	A+	F+	D	D	F	3
Scotowels	SCOTT	A+	F	B	A+	B	C	A	D	3
Scott	SCOTT	A+	F	B	A+	B	C	A	D	3
Scotties	SCOTT	A+	F	B	A+	B	C	A	D	3
Viva	SCOTT	A+	F	B	A+	B	C	A	D	3
White Swan	SCOTT	A+	F	B	A+	B	C	A	D	3

Brand Name	Company Abbreviation	Candour	Women's issues	Charity/ community	Progressive staff policies	Labour relations	Environmental management	Environmental perfomance	Management/ consumer	Canadian content
PASTA										
Buitoni Fresco	NESTLE	A+	C	B	A+	B	C	A+	C	3
Catelli	BORDEN	F	?	F	F	F+	?	?	?	3
Creamette	BORDEN	F	?	F	F	F+	?	?	?	3
Gattuso	BORDEN	F	?	F	F	F+	?	?	?	3
Golden Wheat	BORDEN	F	?	F	F	F+	?	?	?	3
Lancia	BORDEN	F	?	F	F	F+	?	?	?	3
Nelia	BORDEN	F	?	F	F	F+	?	?	?	3
Primo	PRIMO	F	?	F	?	?	F	?	?	3
Romi	BORDEN	F	?	F	F	F+	?	?	?	3
Splendor	BORDEN	F	?	F	F	F+	?	?	?	3
Unico	CULNR	B	F+	D	D	F	?	F	F	4
PEANUT BUTTER & OTHER SPREADS										
Cheese Pot	KRAFT	B	C	F+	A+	B	B	B	C	3
Cheese Eeze	JMSCH	B	F	F+	A+	F	F	F	D	4
Cheese Whiz	KRAFT	B	C	F+	A+	B	B	B	C	3
Country Crock	UNILV	A+	F	F+	A+	D	F+	A+	C	3
Kraft	KRAFT	B	C	F+.	A+	B	B	B	C	3
Monarch	UNILV	A+	F	F+	A+	D	F+	A+	C	3
Skippy	CASCO	F	?	F	C	F	?	?	F	3
Squirrel	CASCO	F	?	F	C	F	?	?	F	3

PET FOODS & SUPPLIES

Brand Name	Company Abbreviation	Candour	Women's issues	Charity/ community	Progressive staff policies	Labour relations	Environmental management	Environmental perfomance	Management/ consumer	Canadian content
9-Lives	HEINZ	D	F	D	A+	F+	?	D	?	3
Butcher's Blend	PURINA	A	F+	F	B	F	F+	F	C	3
Cat's Choice	GPFC	F	?	F	F	?	?	?	?	4
Champion	NESTLE	A+	C	B	A+	B	C	A+	C	3
Chew-Eez	NESTLE	A+	C	B	A+	B	C	A+	C	3
Chicken Cuts	QUAKER	B	?	D	A+	F	A	A	F	3
Cycle	QUAKER	B	?	D	A+	F	A	A	F	3
Dr Ballard	NESTLE	A+	C	B	A+	B	C	A+	C	3
Fancy Feast	NESTLE	A+	C	B	A+	B	C	A+	C	3
Friskies	NESTLE	A+	C	B	A+	B	C	A+	C	3
Gaines	GPFC	F	?	F	F	?	?	?	?	4
Gainesburgers	GPFC	F	?	F	F	?	?	?	?	4
Grrravy	PURINA	A	F+	F	B	F	F+	F	C	3
Grand Gourmet	NESTLE	A+	C	B	A+	B	C	A+	C	3
Happy Cat	PURINA	A	F+	F	B	F	F+	F	C	3
Hill's	COLPAL	F	?	?	?	?	?	?	?	3
Kal Kan	EFFEM	F	?	?	A	?	?	?	F+	3
Ken-L-Ration	QUAKER	B	?	D	A+	F	A	A	F	3
Kibbles 'N Bits 'N Bits 'N Bits	QUAKER	B	?	D	A+	F	A	A	F	3
Kibbles and Chews	PURINA	A	F+	F	B	F	F+	F	C	3
Master	GPFC	F	?	F	F	?	?	?	?	4
Me and My Cat	GPFC	F	?	F	F	?	?	?	?	4
Meow Mix	PURINA	A	F+	F	B	F	F+	F	C	3
Milk Bone	NABSCO	F	?	?	D	?	?	?	?	3
Miss Mew	NESTLE	A+	C	B	A+	B	C	A+	C	3

PET FOODS & SUPPLIES (CONT'D)

Brand Name	Company Abbreviation	Candour	Women's Issues	Charity/ community	Progressive staff policies	Labour relations	Environmental management	Environmental performance	Management/ consumer	Canadian content
Nuggets and Nibbles	GPFC	F	?	F	F	?	?	?	?	4
O.N.E.	PURINA	A	F+	F	B	F	F+	F	C	3
Pamper	QUAKER	B	?	D	A+	F	A	A	F	3
Pedigree	EFFEM	F	?	?	A	?	?	?	F+	3
Pep	QUAKER	B	?	D	A+	F	A	A	F	3
Pounce	QUAKER	B	?	D	A+	F	A	A	F	3
Pro Plan	PURINA	A	F+	F	B	F	F+	F	C	3
Purina	PURINA	A	F+	F	B	F	F+	F	C	3
Puss 'n Boots	QUAKER	B	?	D	A+	F	A	A	F	3
Rover	QUAKER	B	?	D	A+	F	A	A	F	3
Science Diet	COLPAL	F	?	?	?	?	?	?	?	3
Sheba	EFFEM	F	?	?	A	?	?	?	F+	3
Snausages	QUAKER	B	?	D	A+	F	A	A	F	3
Society	QUAKER	B	?	D	A+	F	A	A	F	3
T-Bone	QUAKER	B	?	D	A+	F	A	A	F	3
Tender Vittles	PURINA	A	F+	F	B	F	F+	F	C	3
Tender Chunks	QUAKER	B	?	D	A+	F	A	A	F	3
Top Choice	GPFC	F	?	F	F	?	?	?	?	4
Total Diet	QUAKER	B	?	D	A+	F	A	A	F	3
Treats	QUAKER	B	?	D	A+	F	A	A	F	3
Wagtime	NESTLE	A+	C	B	A+	B	C	A+	C	3
Whiskas	EFFEM	F	?	?	A	?	?	?	F+	3

Brand Name	Company Abbreviation	Candour	Women's issues	Charity/community	Progressive staff policies	Labour relations	Environmental management	Environmental performance	Management/consumer	Canadian content
PREPARED FOODS										
Alphagetti	HEINZ	D	F	D	A+	F+	?	D	?	3
Betty Crocker	GENMIL	B	F	D	A	F	D	D	D	3
Breakfast Tyme	JMSCH	B	F	F+	A+	F	F	F	D	4
Catelli	BORDEN	F	?	F	F	F+	?	?	?	3
Chef Boyardee	CHP	A	F+	D	F	F	C	C	B	2
Enviro-getti	HEINZ	D	F	D	A+	F+	?	D	?	3
Exquisine	EFFEM	F	?	?	A	?	?	?	F+	3
Franco American	CAMBEL	C	F+	F+	C	F	D	C	F	3
Hamburger Helper	GENMIL	B	F	D	A	F	D	D	D	3
Kraft	KRAFT	B	C	F+	A+	B	B	B	C	3
Libby's	NESTLE	A+	C	B	A+	B	C	A+	C	3
Lipton	UNILV	A+	F	F+	A+	D	F+	A+	C	3
Lunchables	KRAFT	B	C	F+	A+	B	B	B	C	3
Lunch Tyme	JMSCH	B	F	F+	A+	F	F	F	D	4
Magic Pantry	GAINR	C	F	D	B	F	F	F	F+	4
Mexicasa	UNILV	A+	F	F+	A+	D	F+	A+	C	3
Microchef	UNILV	A+	F	F+	A+	D	F+	A+	C	3
Old El Paso	PRIMO	F	?	F	?	?	F	?	?	3
Pillsbury	PILBRY	B	D	F	B	A+	F	F	D	3
Pop-Tarts	KELOG	A+	F	A+	A	A+	C	B	B	3
Puritan	UNILV	A+	F	F+	A+	D	F+	A+	C	3
Quadelco	CAMBEL	C	F+	F+	C	F	D	C	F	3
Scario's	HEINZ	D	F	D	A+	F+	?	D	?	3
Shirriff	KELOG	A+	F	A+	A	A+	C	B	B	3
Stove Top	KRAFT	B	C	F+	A+	B	B	B	C	3
Stuff'n Such	EFFEM	F	?	?	A	?	?	?	F+	3

PREPARED FOODS (CONT'D)

Brand Name	Company Abbreviation	Candour	Women's issues	Charity/community	Progressive staff policies	Labour relations	Environmental management	Environmental performance	Management/consumer	Canadian content
Tuna Helper	GENMIL	B	F	D	A	F	D	D	D	3
U.F.O.'s	HEINZ	D	F	D	A+	F+	?	D	?	3

PREPARED MEAT/POULTRY

Brand Name	Company Abbreviation	Candour	Women's issues	Charity/community	Progressive staff policies	Labour relations	Environmental management	Environmental performance	Management/consumer	Canadian content
Baseball	UNILV	A+	F	F+	A+	D	F+	A+	C	3
Bavarians	UNILV	A+	F	F+	A+	D	F+	A+	C	3
Bitner	PRIMO	F	?	F	?	?	F	?	?	3
Burns	BURNS	F	?	F	F	?	?	?	?	4
Burns Flakes of Ham	MALEAF	B	?	F+	F	F	F	F	F	3
Burns Flakes of Meat	MALEAF	B	?	F+	F	F	F	F	F	3
Captain's Chicken	NATSEA	C	D	F	B	F	F+	A+	F	4
Chipolettes	UNILV	A+	F	F+	A+	D	F+	A+	C	3
Coorsh	PRIMO	F	?	F	?	?	F	?	?	3
Deli-Fresh	UNILV	A+	F	F+	A+	D	F+	A+	C	3
Deli-Lean	UNILV	A+	F	F+	A+	D	F+	A+	C	3
Deli-Stik	UNILV	A+	F	F+	A+	D	F+	A+	C	3
Hygrade	UNILV	A+	F	F+	A+	D	F+	A+	C	3
Kam	MALEAF	B	?	F+	F	F	F	F	F	3
Klik	MALEAF	B	?	F+	F	F	F	F	F	3
Kretchmar	GAINR	C	F	D	B	F	F	F	F+	4
La Belle Fermiere	UNILV	A+	F	F+	A+	D	F+	A+	C	3
Libby's	NESTLE	A+	C	B	A+	B	C	A+	C	3
Lifestyle	JMSCH	B	F	F+	A+	F	F	F	D	4
Maple Lodge Farms	MAPLOD	F	?	F	?	?	?	?	F	4
Maple Leaf	MALEAF	B	?	F+	F	F	F	F	F	3
McGarry's	UNILV	A+	F	F+	A+	D	F+	A+	C	3
Mini-Sizzlers	JMSCH	B	F	F+	A+	F	F	F	D	4

PREPARED MEAT/POULTRY (CONT'D)

Brand Name	Company Abbreviation	Candour	Women's issues	Charity/community	Progressive staff policies	Labour relations	Environmental management	Environmental perfomance	Management/consumer	Canadian content
Oktoberfest	JMSCH	B	F	F+	A+	F	F	F	D	4
Overlander	UNILV	A+	F	F+	A+	D	F+	A+	C	3
Pizza Sticks	UNILV	A+	F	F+	A+	D	F+	A+	C	3
Puritan	UNILV	A+	F	F+	A+	D	F+	A+	C	3
Red-Hots	JMSCH	B	F	F+	A+	F	F	F	D	4
Regal	UNILV	A+	F	F+	A+	D	F+	A+	C	3
Schneider	JMSCH	B	F	F+	A+	F	F	F	D	4
Schneider's Old Fashioned	JMSCH	B	F	F+	A+	F	F	F	D	4
Sensible	GAINR	C	F	D	B	F	F	F	F+	4
Shopsy's	UNILV	A+	F	F+	A+	D	F+	A+	C	3
Spork	MALEAF	B	?	F+	F	F	F	F	F	3
Superior	GAINR	C	F	D	B	F	F	F	F+	4
Swift	GAINR	C	F	D	B	F	F	F	F+	4
Underwood	PRIMO	F	?	F	?	?	F	?	?	3
Vienna Sausages	MALEAF	B	?	F+	F	F	F	F	F	3

87

Brand Name	Company Abbreviation	Candour	Women's issues	Charity/ community	Progressive staff policies	Labour relations	Environmental management	Environmental perfomance	Management/ consumer	Canadian content
RICE & BEANS										
Heinz	HEINZ	D	F	D	A+	F+	?	D	?	3
Libby's	NESTLE	A+	C	B	A+	B	C	A+	C	3
Minute Rice	KRAFT	B	C	F+	A+	B	B	B	C	3
Old El Paso	PRIMO	F	?	F	?	?	F	?	?	3
Primo	PRIMO	F	?	F	?	?	F	?	?	3
Ranch Style	CHP	A	F+	D	F	F	C	C	B	2
Rice a Roni	QUAKER	B	?	D	A+	F	A	A	F	3
Savoury Classics	QUAKER	B	?	D	A+	F	A	A	F	3
Uncle Ben's	EFFEM	F	?	?	A	?	?	?	F+	3
Unico	CULNR	B	F+	D	D	F	?	F	F	4
SALAD DRESSINGS										
Club House	MCORMK	A	D	C	A+	A	F+	D	C	2
Crosse & Blackwell	NESTLE	A+	C	B	A+	B	C	A+	C	3
Gardenfare	MCORMK	A	D	C	A+	A	F+	D	C	2
Kraft Free	KRAFT	B	C	F+	A+	B	B	B	C	3
Kraft	KRAFT	B	C	F+	A+	B	B	B	C	3
Weight Watchers	HEINZ	D	F	D	A+	F+	?	D	?	3

Brand Name	Company Abbreviation	Candour	Women's issues	Charity/ community	Progressive staff policies	Labour relations	Environmental management	Environmental perfomance	Management/ consumer	Canadian content
SALT, SEASONINGS & SPICES										
Ac'cent	PRIMO	F	?	F	?	?	F	?	?	3
Blue Ribbon	SPECBD	F	?	F	F	F	?	?	F	2
Club House	MCORMK	A	D	C	A+	A	F+	D	C	2
French's	SPECBD	F	?	F	F	F	?	?	F	2
Half Salt	CANSAL	F	?	F	F	?	?	?	?	3
Lawry's	UNILV	A+	F	F+	A+	D	F+	A+	C	3
McCormick	MCORMK	A	D	C	A+	A	F+	D	C	2
Molly McButter	ABCUL	F	?	?	?	?	?	?	?	3
Monarch	MALEAF	B	?	F+	F	F	F	F	F	3
Mrs. Dash	ABCUL	F	?	?	?	?	?	?	?	3
Old El Paso	PRIMO	F	?	F	?	?	F	?	?	3
Papa Dash	ABCUL	F	?	?	?	?	?	?	?	3
Schwartz	SPECBD	F	?	F	F	F	?	?	F	2
Spice Cargo	MCORMK	A	D	C	A+	A	F+	D	C	2
Spice Classics	MCORMK	A	D	C	A+	A	F+	D	C	2
Spice Island	SPECBD	F	?	F	F	F	?	?	F	2
Stange	MCORMK	A	D	C	A+	A	F+	D	C	2
Windsor	CANSAL	F	?	F	F	?	?	?	?	3

Brand Name	Company Abbreviation	Candour	Women's issues	Charity/ community	Progressive staff policies	Labour relations	Environmental management	Environmental perfomance	Management/ consumer	Canadian content
SHAVING NEEDS										
Aqua Velva	SKB	F	?	?	?	?	?	?	?	3
Atra	GILET	F	?	F	F	?	?	N/A	?	1
Brut	UNILV	A+	F	F+	A+	D	F+	A+	C	3
Edge	SCJON	F	?	F+	?	D	?	C	?	3
Foamy	GILET	F	?	F	F	?	?	N/A	?	1
Good News	GILET	F	?	F	F	?	?	N/A	?	1
Lectric Shave	SKB	F	?	?	?	?	?	?	?	3
Palmolive	COLPAL	F	?	?	?	?	?	?	?	3
Sensor	GILET	F	?	F	F	?	?	N/A	?	1
Soft Sense	SCJON	F	?	F+	?	D	?	C	?	3
Trac II	GILET	F	?	F	F	?	?	N/A	?	1

Brand Name	Company Abbreviation	Candour	Women's issues	Charity/ community	Progressive staff policies	Labour relations	Environmental management	Environmental perfomance	Management/ consumer	Canadian content
SKIN CARE										
Aapri	GILET	F	?	F	F	?	?	N/A	?	1
Aveeno	SCJON	F	?	F+	?	D	?	C	?	3
Bain de Soleil	P&G	C	?	F	A+	F+	D	D	F	3
Brut	UNILV	A+	F	F+	A+	D	F+	A+	C	3
Camay	P&G	C	?	F	A+	F+	D	D	F	3
Caress	UNILV	A+	F	F+	A+	D	F+	A+	C	3
Cashmere Bouquet	COLPAL	F	?	?	?	?	?	?	?	3
Clearasil	P&G	C	?	F	A+	F+	D	D	F	3
Coast	P&G	C	?	F	A+	F+	D	D	F	3
Dial	DIAL	N/A	N/A	?	N/A	N/A	N/A	N/A	N/A	0
Dove	UNILV	A+	F	F+	A+	D	F+	A+	C	3
Essense Magique	UNILV	A+	F	F+	A+	D	F+	A+	C	3
Irish Spring	COLPAL	F	?	?	?	?	?	?	?	3
Ivory	P&G	C	?	F	A+	F+	D	D	F	3
Johnson's	J&J	A	F	D	A	F	F	D	F+	3
Lever 2000	UNILV	A+	F	F+	A+	D	F+	A+	C	3
Lifebuoy	UNILV	A+	F	F+	A+	D	F+	A+	C	3
Lustrasilk	GILET	F	?	F	F	?	?	N/A	?	1
Lux	UNILV	A+	F	F+	A+	D	F+	A+	C	3
Noxema	P&G	C	?	F	A+	F+	D	D	F	3
Oil of Olay	P&G	C	?	F	A+	F+	D	D	F	3
Palmolive	COLPAL	F	?	?	?	?	?	?	?	3
Pond's	UNILV	A+	F	F+	A+	D	F+	A+	C	3
Pure & Natural	DIAL	N/A	N/A	?	N/A	N/A	N/A	N/A	N/A	0
Safeguard	P&G	C	?	F	A+	F+	D	D	F	3
Sea Breeze	BMCP	C	D	C	A+	F	F+	N/A	F+	1

SKIN CARE (CONT'D)

Brand Name	Company Abbreviation	Candour	Women's issues	Charity/ community	Progressive staff policies	Labour relations	Environmental management	Environmental performance	Management/ consumer	Canadian content
Shower to Shower	J&J	A	F	D	A	F	F	D	F+	3
Soft Sense	SCJON	F	?	F+	?	D	?	C	?	3
Soft Soap	COLPAL	F	?	?	?	?	?	.	?	3
Tone	DIAL	N/A	N/A	?	N/A	N/A	N/A	N/A	N/A	0
Vaseline	UNILV	A+	F	F+	A+	D	F+	A+	C	3
Wet Soap	UNILV	A+	F	F+	A+	D	F+	A+	C	3
Wondra	P&G	C	?	F	A+	F+	D	D	F	3
Zest	P&G	C	?	F	A+	F+	D	D	F	3

SNACKS

Brand Name	Company Abbreviation	Candour	Women's issues	Charity/ community	Progressive staff policies	Labour relations	Environmental management	Environmental performance	Management/ consumer	Canadian content
1/2 Moon	CULNR	B	F+	D	D	F	?	F	F	4
Beary Pals	GENMIL	B	F	D	A	F	D	D	D	3
Beaver	HERSH	A	D	F	B	F+	F	B	F	3
Betty Crocker	GENMIL	B	F	D	A	F	D	D	D	3
Bits & Bites	NABSCO	F	?	?	D	?	?	?	?	3
Bugles	GENMIL	B	F	D	A	F	D	D	D	3
Caramel	CULNR	B	F+	D	D	F	?	F	F	4
Chee-tos	HFLAY	F	?	F	F	?	?	?	?	3
Chocolate Coated Dips	QUAKER	B	?	D	A+	F	A	A	F	3
Christie	NABSCO	F	?	?	D	?	?	?	?	3
Cracker Jack	BORDEN	F	?	F	F	F+	?	?	?	3
Crunch Tators	HFLAY	F	?	F	F	?	?	?	?	3
Dinosaur Pals	GENMIL	B	F	D	A	F	D	D	D	3
Doritos	HFLAY	F	?	F	F	?	?	?	?	3
Drake's	CULNR	B	F+	D	D	F	?	F	F	4
Extra Crunchy	HFLAY	F	?	F	F	?	?	?	?	3
Flaky	CULNR	B	F+	D	D	F	?	F	F	4

Brand Name	Company Abbreviation	Candour	Women's issues	Charity/ community	Progressive staff policies	Labour relations	Environmental management	Environmental perfomance	Management/ consumer	Canadian content
Crunch & Munch	CHP	A	F+	D	F	F	C	C	B	2
Frito-Lay	HFLAY	F	?	F	F	?	?	?	?	3
Fritos	HFLAY	F	?	F	F	?	?	?	?	3
Fruit Roll-Ups	GENMIL	B	F	D	A	F	D	D	D	3
Garfield	GENMIL	B	F	D	A	F	D	D	D	3
Gibney's	HFLAY	F	?	F	F	?	?	?	?	3
Granny's	CULNR	B	F+	D	D	F	?	F	F	4
Hostess (chips)	HFLAY	F	?	F	F	?	?	?	?	3
Hostess (cakes)	WESTON	F	?	D	?	F	?	D	?	4
Humpty Dumpty	HUMPTY	F	?	?	?	?	?	?	?	2
Jiffy Pop	CHP	A	F+	D	F	F	C	C	B	2
Jos. Louis	CULNR	B	F+	D	D	F	?	F	F	4
Kettle Chips	NABOB	A+	F	D	A+	A	B	A+	F	3
May West	CULNR	B	F+	D	D	F	?	F	F	4
McCormicks'	CULNR	B	F+	D	D	F	?	F	F	4
Mexicasa	UNILV	A+	F	F+	A+	D	F+	A+	C	3
Mister Sallty	NABSCO	F	?	?	D	?	?	?	?	3
Nature Valley	GENMIL	B	F	D	A	F	D	D	D	3
Old Dutch	OLDCH	C	D	F	F	D	F	C	F	3
Orville Redenbacher's	HUNT	N/A	N/A	?	N/A	N/A	N/A	N/A	?	1
Planters	HERSH	A	D	F	B	F+	F	B	F	3
Pop-Secret	GENMIL	B	F	D	A	F	D	D	D	3
Pringles	P&G	C	?	F	A+	F+	D	D	D	3
Quaker	QUAKER	B	?	D	A+	F	A	A	F	3
Rold Gold	HFLAY	F	?	F	F	?	?	?	?	3
Ruffles	HFLAY	F	?	F	F	?	?	?	?	3

SNACKS (CONT'D)

Brand Name	Company Abbreviation	Candour	Women's issues	Charity/ community	Progressive staff policies	Labour relations	Environmental management	Environmental performance	Management/ consumer	Canadian content
Shark Bites	GENMIL	B	F	D	A	F	D	D	D	3
Smartfood	HFLAY	F	?	F	F	?	?	?	?	3
Snackeroos	KRAFT	B	C	F+	A+	B	B	B	C	3
Stuart	CULNR	B	F+	D	D	F	?	F	F	4
Sunchips	HFLAY	F	?	F	F	?	?	?	?	3
Sunkist Fun Fruit	UNILV	A+	F	F+	A+	D	F+	A+	C	3
Swiss Rolls	CULNR	B	F+	D	D	F	?	F	F	4
Thunder Jets	GENMIL	B	F	D	A	F	D	D	D	3
Tostitos	HFLAY	F	?	F	F	?	?	?	?	3
Twigs	NABSCO	F	?	?	D	?	?	?	?	3
Uneeda	NABSCO	F	?	?	D	?	?	?	?	3
Vachon	CULNR	B	F+	D	D	F	?	F	F	4

SOFT DRINKS

Brand Name	Company Abbreviation	Candour	Women's issues	Charity/ community	Progressive staff policies	Labour relations	Environmental management	Environmental performance	Management/ consumer	Canadian content
7UP	PEPSI	D	?	F	?	?	C	D	F	3
A&W	UNILV	A+	F	F+	A+	D	F+	A+	C	3
Allan Denis	COTT	A+	F	D	C	F	F	D	F	4
C-Plus	CADBEV	A	F	F+	A	F	B	B	F+	3
Canada Dry	CADBEV	A	F	F+	A	F	B	B	F+	3
Coca-Cola Classic	COKE	A	F	A	B	A+	D	D	C	4
Coke	COKE	A	F	A	B	A+	D	D	C	4
Cott	COTT	A+	F	D	C	F	F	D	F	4
Crush	CADBEV	A	F	F+	A	F	B	B	F+	3
Diet 7UP	PEPSI	D	?	F	?	?	C	D	F	3
diet Coke	COKE	A	F	A	B	A+	D	D	C	4
diet Sprite	COKE	A	F	A	B	A+	D	D	C	4
diet Minute Maid	COKE	A	F	A	B	A+	D	D	C	4

SOFT DRINKS (CONT'D)

Brand Name	Company Abbreviation	Candour	Women's issues	Charity/ community	Progressive staff policies	Labour relations	Environmental management	Environmental performance	Environmental Management/ consumer	Canadian content
Diet Mountain Dew	PEPSI	D	?	F	?	?	C	D	F	3
Diet Pepsi	PEPSI	D	?	F	?	?	C	D	F	3
Diet Rite	COTT	A+	F	D	C	F	F	D	F	4
Fanta	COKE	A	F	A	B	A+	D	D	C	4
Fresca	COKE	A	F	A	B	A+	D	D	C	4
Hires	CADBEV	A	F	F+	A	F	B	B	F+	3
KIK	COTT	A+	F	D	C	F	F	D	F	4
Minute Maid	COKE	A	F	A	B	A+	D	D	C	4
Mountain Dew	PEPSI	D	?	F	?	?	C	D	F	3
Pepsi	PEPSI	D	?	F	?	?	C	D	F	3
RC Cola	COTT	A+	F	D	C	F	F	D	F	4
Schweppes	CADBEV	A	F	F+	A	F	B	B	F+	3
Sprite	COKE	A	F	A	B	A+	D	D	C	4
Tab	COKE	A	F	A	B	A+	D	D	C	4

SOUPS

Brand Name	Company Abbreviation	Candour	Women's issues	Charity/ community	Progressive staff policies	Labour relations	Environmental management	Environmental perfomance	Management/ consumer	Canadian content
Aylmer	NABSCO	F	?	?	D	?	?	?	?	3
Bovril	CASCO	F	?	F	C	F	D	?	F	3
Campbell's	CAMBEL	C	F+	F+	C	F	C	C	F	3
Cloverleaf	BPACK	A	F	D	A	F	C	C	D	4
du Chef	CASCO	F	?	F	C	F	?	?	F	3
Gattuso	CAMBEL	C	F+	F+	C	F	D	C	F	3
Habitant	CAMBEL	C	F+	F+	C	F	D	C	F	3
Healthy Request	CAMBEL	C	F+	F+	C	F	D	C	F	3
Hearty Noodles	CAMBEL	C	F+	F+	C	F	D	C	F	3
Heinz	HEINZ	D	F	D	A+	F+	?	D	?	3
Knorr	CASCO	F	?	F	C	F	?	?	F	3
Libby's	NESTLE	A+	C	B	A+	B	C	A+	C	3
Lipton	UNILV	A+	F	F+	A+	D	F+	A+	C	3
Loney's	CULNR	B	F+	D	D	F	?	F	F	4
Maggi	NESTLE	A+	C	B	A+	B	C	A+	C	3
Milani	ABCUL	F	?	?	?	?	?	?	?	3
Oxo	UNILV	A+	F	F+	A+	D	F+	A+	C	3
Primo	PRIMO	F	?	F	?	?	F	?	?	3
Progresso	PRIMO	F	?	F	?	?	F	?	?	3
Snow's	BORDEN	F	?	F	F	F+	?	?	?	3
Unico	CULNR	B	F+	D	D	F	?	F	F	4

SUGARS, SWEETENERS & SYRUPS

Brand Name	Company Abbreviation	Candour	Women's issues	Charity/ community	Progressive staff policies	Labour relations	Environmental management	Environmental perfomance	Management/ consumer	Canadian content
Aunt Jemima	QUAKER	B	?	D	A+	F	A	A	F	3
BeeHive	CASCO	F	?	F	C	F	?	?	F	3
Brown Cow	HERSH	A	D	F	B	F+	F	B	F	3
Hershey	HERSH	A	D	F	B	F+	F	B	F	3
Lantic	LANTIC	C	F	F	C	F	F	F	F	4
Old Tyme	CASCO	F	?	F	C	F	?	?	F	3
Old Colony	CASCO	F	?	F	C	F	?	?	F	3
Quik	NESTLE	A+	C	B	A+	B	C	A+	C	3
Redpath	REDPAT	C	F	F	A	F	?	F	?	3
Rogers	BCSUG	F	F	F	F	F	?	F	?	4
Shady Maple	HEINZ	D	F	D	A+	F+	?	D	?	3
Splenda	REDPAT	C	F	F	A	F	?	F	?	3
Strawberry Cow	HERSH	A	D	F	B	F+	F	B	F	3
SugarTwin	ABCUL	F	?	?	?	?	?	?	?	3
Sugar in the Raw	PRIMO	F	?	F	?	?	F	?	?	3
Sweet 'n Low	PRIMO	F	?	F	?	?	F	?	?	3
Top Scotch	HERSH	A	D	F	B	F+	F	B	F	3

Brand Name	Company Abbreviation	Candour	Women's issues	Charity/ community	Progressive staff policies	Labour relations	Environmental management	Environmental performance	Management/ consumer	Canadian content
TEA										
Goodhost	NESTLE	A+	C	B	A+	B	C	A+	C	3
Lipton	UNILV	A+	F	F+	A+	D	F+	A+	C	3
Lyons	TETLEY	N/A	N/A	F	N/A	N/A	N/A	N/A	?	1
Nabob Deluxe	NABOB	A+	F	D	A+	A	B	A+	F	3
Nestea	NESTLE	A+	C	B	A+	B	C	A+	C	3
PGTips	UNILV	A+	F	F+	A+	D	F+	A+	C	3
Red Rose	UNILV	A+	F	F+	A+	D	F+	A+	C	3
Salada	UNILV	A+	F	F+	A+	D	F+	A+	C	3
Tetley	TETLEY	N/A	N/A	F	N/A	N/A	N/A	N/A	?	1
YOGURT										
Alpenfresh	AULT	B	F	C	A+	A+	B	B	F	4
Beatrice	BEA	A+	F	F	B	F+	F	C	F	3
Crescent	BEA	A+	F	F	B	F+	F	C	F	3
Danone	WESTON	F	?	D	?	F	?	D	?	4
Gay Lea	GAYLEA	A	F	F+	D	F	F	F	F	4
Light 'n Lively	AULT	B	F	C	A+	A+	B	B	F	4
Muppets	AULT	B	F	C	A+	A+	B	B	F	4
Sealtest	AULT	B	F	C	A+	A+	B	B	F	4

Company Profiles

Notes concerning headline data:

1. Under the heading, "Operations," an asterisk denotes the location of a plant.

2. Unless otherwise indicated, data concerning number of employees, annual sales and advertising expenditures are for Canada only.

3. Unless otherwise indicated, figures are in Canadian dollars.

4. The word in bold in the upper right hand margin is the company abbreviation. This abbreviation is also used in the tables. An index of company abbreviations may be found on p. 278

5. The information presented here was accurate, to the best of our knowledge, as of June 1992.

6. Information on business in South Africa was taken from the following two publications:

Alison Cooper, *U.S. Business in South Africa 1990:* Investor Responsibility Research Centre Inc., Washington, D.C., 1990.

Alison Cooper, *International Business in South Africa 1990*: Investor Responsibility Research Centre Inc., Washington, D.C., 1990.

Alberto-Culver Canada Inc.

506 Kipling Ave., Toronto, ON M8Z 5E2

Founded in Canada: 1957, Toronto, ON
Ownership: Alberto-Culver Company (US), 100%
Operations: ON*
Employees: 130 (est.)
Annual sales: $74 million

Alberto-Culver Canada markets a wide range of personal care and grocery products. Although its products are heavily supported by intensive advertising and promotional campaigns, very little is known about how this wholly-owned subsidiary does business. Its Chicago-based parent, the Alberto-Culver Company, reports spending $146 million (US) on advertising in 1991, the equivalent of about 16% of its total net sales in the same year, and the company's sales and marketing achievements are consistently the major focus of its annual report. The Canadian operations of Alberto-Culver consist of one non-unionized plant in Toronto. Sales are handled by brokers and representatives, working out of their own homes or distribution offices.

Making the Grade

We know even less about the Canadian company than we do about its parent. Its low Candour rating in the Tables reflects the fact that it did not respond to any of our surveys or participate in the research process in any way, to the extent of refusing even to verify which brands are marketed in Canada. Alberto-Culver is not on Imagine's Caring Companies list. It has no record of environmental court cases, fines or other related problems in Canada.

Notable Facts

The 1991 annual report released by the publicly-traded US parent company did not provide any information about the company's social or environmental performance in the US or elsewhere, although it did mention that the Canadian company managed to achieve profit growth "in a deeply recessionary economy."

BRAND NAMES
Alberto
Baker's Joy
Bold Hold
Consort
FDS
Kleen Guard
Milani
Molly McButter
Mrs. Dash
Papa Dash
Static Guard
Sugar Twin
TCB
TRESemme
VO5

Alcan Aluminum Limited

1188 Sherbrooke St. W., Montreal, PQ H3A 3G2   **ALCAN**

Founded in Canada: 1902

Ownership: widely held (46,000 shareholders)

Operations: BC*, ON*, PQ*

Employees: 15,000

Annual sales: $7.7 billion (worldwide)

The world's largest aluminum company, Canada-based Alcan Aluminum has operations in 20 countries, with 700 manufacturing plants and 53,000 employees worldwide. The company is a leading producer of flat and rolled aluminum, as well as a manufacturer of a variety of aluminum products. Alcan Aluminum's wholly-owned subsidiary, Alcan Enterprises, produces aluminum foil.

Making The Grade

CANDOUR: Although Alcan was contacted later than others in the *Guide*, the company provided considerable assistance in the limited amount of time available to it.

WOMEN'S ISSUES: The company has one woman on its 14-member board of directors. It has a formal employment equity program.

CHARITABLE GIVING AND COMMUNITY INVOLVEMENT: Alcan earned a position on the Honour Roll for this category. It is part of the Imagine campaign and in 1990 contributed $5.8 million to charity. It supports the Variety Club, L'Opera de Montréal, Les Grandes Ballets Canadiens and the United Way. It also offers gifts in kind (such as aluminum windows for a shelter for battered women), lends company facilities to charitable groups, gives paid and unpaid time off to employees for volunteer activities, has an endowment program for post-secondary institutions, supports sports teams and sponsors the Montreal International Festival.

PROGRESSIVE STAFF POLICIES: The company said only that it provides a variety of programs in its different locations, including some fitness facilities, and that it has a scholarship fund for the children of employees.

LABOUR RELATIONS: Alcan addresses job security issues with retraining and some relocation of machine operators when it makes plant production changes, although it has no formal job security program.

BRAND NAME
Alcan

ENVIRONMENTAL MANAGEMENT: On the Honour Roll in this category, the company has a written environmental policy, an environmental committee of the board, and staff committee. In addition, it has a vice-president of environment and occupational health and safety, and makes quarterly environmental reports to the board.

ENVIRONMENTAL PERFORMANCE: Alcan has undertaken a comprehensive environmental audit, and the company devotes funds to environmental research and development and to equipment replacement. It supports a variety of recycling programs for aluminum products, sponsors conferences and research into environmental problems, and funds local environmental groups. As well, the company recycles paper, packaging and manufacturing by-products.

The company has been the subject of a number of environmental court cases and has been fined a total of $175,100 since 1989 for violations in British Columbia, Ontario, and Quebec. As well, the company has been on government lists for non-compliance with effluent regulations in Kitimat and Smithers, BC, and has been cited as one of the 50 worst polluters of the St. Lawrence River. In 1987, Alcan reached an agreement with the provincial and federal governments to proceed with a $1 billion expansion of its Kemano hydro-electric site without conducting a full environmental review. The Kemano station was built in 1952 to power the company's Kitimat, BC, smelter. In 1991, a coalition of British Columbia organizations won an injunction from the Federal Court of Canada, putting the project on hold until a full environmental review was completed. The Federal Court of Appeal reversed that decision in May, 1992. The coalition stated that it would appeal that ruling to the Supreme Court of Canada. The company's US subsidiary, Alcan Aluminum Corporation, faces a number of environmental suits.

MANAGEMENT PRACTICES AND CONSUMER RELATIONS: Alcan has a statement of purpose, policies and objectives, but does not have a written code of ethics.

Notable Facts

Alcan has had more than eight strikes over the past ten years. The 1987 closure of its aluminum foil processing plant in Bracebridge, Ont., plant took place eight weeks after a strike that had halted production for four months. The firm says the two events were unrelated.

Alcan formally divested itself of its South African interests in 1986. While the company continues to provide a South African firm with technical assistance on aluminum fabrication for commercial purposes, this arrangement is scheduled to end December, 1992. It buys manganese under contract from a South African supplier.

Ault Foods Limited

405 The West Mall, Etobicoke, ON M9C 5J1

Founded in Canada: 1891, Cass Bridge, ON
Ownership: John Labatt Limited (Canada), 100%
Operations: AB, ON*, PQ*
Employees: 3,000

Ault Foods is part of the John Labatt Limited group of companies, which includes Labatt Breweries of Canada, the Toronto Blue Jays baseball team and a majority interest in broadcaster TSN. Ault began as a cheesemaker in Cass Bridge, Ont., in 1891 and became part of John Labatt Limited in 1968. A substantial presence in the dairy foods market in Ontario and Quebec, the company has gained market share by purchasing the rights to trade names such as Sealtest, Neilson (ice cream: see p.168) and Black Diamond. Ault exports to 35 countries.

Making the Grade

WOMEN'S ISSUES: Although Ault has a formal employment equity program and equity committee, only 15% of its managers are women (compared to 30% of the workforce as a whole). There are no women on its 11-man board of directors and the company has no provisions for daycare or extended maternity leave.

CHARITABLE GIVING AND COMMUNITY INVOLVEMENT: Ault donated $350,000, largely in cash, to charitable organizations in 1990. While the company is pledged to the Imagine campaign through its parent company, it did not reveal the total amount of its giving as a percentage of pre-tax earnings. It contributed to a number of community programs last year, including university matching gift programs and health and cultural activities and it is one of the founding sponsors of Kids Help Phone, a telephone counselling service for young people.

PROGRESSIVE STAFF POLICIES: Ault is on the Honour Roll in this category. It offers a broad range of staff programs and policies, including substance abuse and personal counselling, a stop-smoking program and a fitness club subsidy. It also provides an annual written performance review for all employees and scholarship programs for employees and their children.

BRAND NAMES

All Natural
Alpenfresh
Balderson
Black Diamond
Chipwich
Copper Cliff
Country Choice
Dallaire
Delys
Drumstick
Famous
Fruit Fantasy
Häagen Dazs
J. Higby's
Lactantia
Light 'n' Lively
Meadowgold
Movenpick
Muppets
Parlour
Pure & Simple
Royal Oak
Sealtest

LABOUR RELATIONS: The company is on this Honour Roll as well. Its strong job security program includes retraining, relocation, early retirement, financial compensation and advance notice of technological change in the case of layoffs or downsizing. A bonus plan is provided for salaried employees and a share-purchase plan for all employees. Ault gave us health and safety statistics.

ENVIRONMENTAL MANAGEMENT: On the Honour Roll in this category as well, the company made a strong showing under both environmental headings. It has a written environmental policy, an environmental committee of the board (in conjunction with its parent), an environmental working committee, and makes reports to the board six times a year. It is among the few companies in this *Guide* to report a full-time environmental affairs official, the director of environmental affairs, and each plant has its own environmental co-ordinator.

ENVIRONMENTAL PERFORMANCE: Ault conducts what it defines as a "detailed evaluation of all operations," and recycles oil, batteries, tires, coolants and refrigerants, paperboard and fine paper. Instead of dumping food by-products like whey into the sewers, it gives them to local farmers for use as fodder. Ault was fined $4,000 in 1989 for a violation of the Ontario Water Resources Act.

MANAGEMENT PRACTICES AND CONSUMER RELATIONS: The company has a written code of ethics and a toll-free number for retail trade customers (rather than consumers). Ault did not comment on whether or not it has been involved in any Competition Act litigation.

Notable Facts

Ault has purchased a number of operations over the past few years, increasing its corporate concentration in the ice cream and cheese markets. In some cases, the operations were closed after acquiring the brand name and production transferred to existing facilities. As well, several plants have been closed by Ault in an effort to centralize and upgrade operations. The list of layoffs over the past five years is lengthy, but Ault has used retraining, relocation, financial compensation and other aspects of its formal job security program to help ease the impact. About 75% of the company's workforce is unionized. The company has a pay equity program in addition to its formal employment equity program.

Ault has licensed Scotsburn Co-operative Services Ltd. (see p. 251) to produce products for Atlantic Canada under these Ault-controlled brand names: Sealtest, Parlour, Häagen Dazs and J. Higby's.

BC Sugar Refinery, Limited BCSUG

Box 2150, Vancouver, BC V6B 3V2

Founded in Canada: 1890, Vancouver, BC
Ownership: widely held (none over 10%)
Operations: BC*, AB*, MB*
Employees: 518
Annual sales: $161 million (worldwide)

This Vancouver-based company, founded over 100 years ago by B.T. Rogers, refines cane sugar in Vancouver and produces white sugar from sugar beets in Alberta and Manitoba. Brian Rogers, grandson of the founder, works for the company. Until last year, each province marketed the firm's sugar under its own brand (Manitoba, Alberta or BC Sugar) but the company has now adopted the Rogers name for all its products. As of October, 1992, BC Sugar will have acquired 100% of Lantic Sugar Limited (see p. 197), giving the company an eastern Canadian presence as well as connections with Lantic's New York subsidiary.

Making the Grade

CANDOUR: BC Sugar completed the product survey, did not respond to the social performance survey and provided some information during a fact-checking interview. We also interviewed a spokesperson for the Retail Wholesale Union, which represents the 230 workers at BC Sugar's Vancouver plant.

WOMEN'S ISSUES: There is one woman on the company's eight-member board of directors and none in senior management. The percentage of women in management was not supplied, but women comprise 25% of all staff.

CHARITABLE GIVING AND COMMUNITY INVOLVEMENT: Although not pledged to the Imagine campaign, the company's support for the arts and education includes donations to the Vancouver Symphony, Science World, the Vancouver Art Gallery, the University of British Columbia and the University of Victoria. The company has a sugar museum next to its Vancouver refinery, which attracts over 6,000 visitors annually.

PROGRESSIVE STAFF POLICIES: The union representative calls the company "a pretty enlightened corporation." The company has an employee newsletter, *Sugar Scoop*, and a policy of open-door management. It participates, though not financially, in a union-run employee assistance program. When one office worker's son devel-

> **BRAND NAMES**
> Rogers
> (see also Lantic
>   Sugar Limited,
>   p. 197)

oped leukemia, the company began looking for ways to support the struggle against this disease: it encourages bone marrow testing and provides paid time off to any employee who becomes a donor.

LABOUR RELATIONS: A "family atmosphere" pervades the Vancouver plant, says the union spokesperson. The company does not have a formal job security policy and normally handles layoffs through attrition. It offers a share purchase plan to all permanent employees and matches the first $300 invested.

ENVIRONMENTAL MANAGEMENT/PERFORMANCE: BC Sugar does not have a written environmental policy. However, it recycles cardboard, office paper and packaging materials and re-refines spills so that few raw materials are wasted.

MANAGEMENT PRACTICES AND CONSUMER RELATIONS: The company does not have a written code of ethics.

Notable Facts

BC Sugar expanded into chemicals in 1984 by buying US-based companies that made phenols from the distillation of toluene (coal tar). One subsidiary, Kalama Chemical Inc., is involved in an estimated $3-million (US) state-ordered cleanup at its Garfield, NJ, facility; in 1990 it spent $2.7 million (US) to clean up its Kalama, Washington, facility. The company's Chatterton Petrochemical Corp. plant is now shut down and its Kalama operations are for sale.

While recently acquired Lantic Sugar has been involved in a couple of strikes, none of BC Sugar's British Columbia, Manitoba or Alberta sugar refineries have been involved in any strikes since 1987. The Taber, Alta., refinery was shut down for one year (1985-86) when the company could not reach an agreement with sugar beet farmers, who responded by not planting a crop that year. Growers claimed that the offered purchase price was less than the cost of raising the crop.

Beatrice Foods Inc.

295 The West Mall, Suite 600, Toronto, ON M9C 4Z4

Founded in Canada: 1969, Kingston, ON
Ownership: Merrill Lynch Capital Partners (US), 72%
Operations: AB*, SK*, MB*, ON*, PQ*
Employees: 3,000
Annual sales: $746 million

Beatrice, one of the largest producers of fluid milk in Canada, manufactures a range of dairy products and baked goods. The company has 22 production facilities in 19 communities and exports Canadian-made products to the United States and Great Britain. Originally US-based, the company was split in 1987, with Onex Corporation acquiring the Canadian assets and ConAgra (owners of Hunt-Wesson, see p. 181) the US food operations. Onex, owners of Purolator Courier and Sky Chef, sold Beatrice to Merrill Lynch Capital Partners in 1991.

Making the Grade

CANDOUR: Beatrice was very responsive to our surveys, earning a place on the Honour Roll for this category.

WOMEN'S ISSUES: This was the company's lowest score. Only 17% of its workforce is female and only 7% of management and 5% of senior management positions are occupied by women. No women sit on the company's nine-man board. Beatrice has no employment equity program or staff programs specifically designed to promote the advancement of women.

CHARITABLE GIVING AND COMMUNITY INVOLVEMENT: While not one of Imagine's Caring Companies, the company's 1991 charitable donations ($200,000) approach the campaign's 1% target. Beatrice supports arts, health, environmental and sports organizations in the communities in which it operates.

BRAND NAMES
Beatrice
Colonial
Crescent
Good Humor
Heritage Farms
Medo-Land
Modern
Reddi Wip
Windsor

PROGRESSIVE STAFF POLICIES: It received high marks in this area, offering an employee assistance program, adoption leave benefits, employee suggestion program, open-door management and rewards for cost-saving ideas.

LABOUR RELATIONS: Although it has no formal job security program, Beatrice seeks to soften the impact of downsizing with retraining, relocation and advance notice of technological change. It offers a stock option plan to key employees. The company does not keep centralized health and safety or training data.

ENVIRONMENTAL MANAGEMENT: Beatrice has a written environmental policy and 23 employees with environmental responsibilities.

ENVIRONMENTAL PERFORMANCE: It conducts a comprehensive audit of all its operations, recycles paper and manufacturing by-products, and has replaced dated equipment, improved energy efficiency and reformatted its packaging. Beatrice was fined $15,000 for a 1988 violation of the Ontario Water Resources Act for polluting waterways at its Aylmer, Ontario, location.

MANAGEMENT PRACTICES AND CONSUMER RELATIONS: Beatrice has no written code of ethics, ethics advisory service, social practices report or toll-free number for consumers. On the other hand, it has no Competition Act violations on record.

Notable Facts

The company is 67% unionized. Employment totals have increased by about 1,000 since 1986, owing in part to the acquisition of Eplett and Palm Dairies in 1989 and 1990 respectively. Nonetheless, a series of layoffs occurred in 1991 when the company closed Ontario plants in Oshawa, North Bay, Thunder Bay and Sault Ste Marie, causing 219 people to lose their jobs. The company blames the Sault Ste Marie closing on cross-border shopping. It has hired more staff at its Brampton, Ont., plant, some from among staff laid off elsewhere.

Borden Catelli Consumer Products

250 Consumers Rd., Suite 900, Willowdale, ON M2J 4V6

Founded in Canada: in the 1890s
Ownership: Borden Inc. (US), 100%
Operations: BC, AB*, MB, ON*, PQ*, NS
Employees: 900

Borden Catelli is one of several divisions of Borden Inc., which also owns Sunworthy Wallcoverings and Humpty Dumpty Foods Limited (see p. 180), and operates a food wrap and two adhesive plants in this country. Borden Inc. is ranked first in the world in pasta, vinyl food wraps, and wallcoverings.

Making the Grade

CANDOUR: Borden Catelli Consumer Products completed the product survey, but referred us to its parent in Columbus, Ohio, for the rest of our research. While Borden expressed interest in the project, it did not respond to any of our surveys. Borden Catelli provided some additional data late in the process. We also talked to spokespersons for the Retail, Wholesale and Department Store (RWDS) union, which represented workers at the now defunct Ingersoll, Ont., facility, but received conflicting accounts from them of programs and practices.

WOMEN'S ISSUES: The company has introduced an employment equity plan but has no daycare program or extended maternity leave.

CHARITABLE GIVING AND COMMUNITY INVOLVEMENT:
Borden Catelli says it has a "significant budget" for donations of cash and product to charity. While not pledged to the Imagine campaign, the company does support the United Way, Salvation Army and Canadian Heart Foundation, and employees are involved in a number of volunteer activities.

LABOUR RELATIONS: The company has an employee share purchase plan for all employees. No formal job security policy is in place, but Borden Catelli did give severance pay to laid-off workers at its Winnipeg facility and used its office space to help them find other employment. Employees participate in the parent company's retirement savings plan, with the company matching eligible contributions.

BRAND NAMES
Bravo
Catelli
Classico
Cracker Jack
Creamette
Eagle Brand
Gattuso (pasta and sauces only)
Golden Wheat
Lancia
Milk Mate
Nelia
ReaLemon
Romi
Snow's
Splendor

Notable Facts

Borden Catelli produces Gattuso pasta and sauces, but Robin Hood Multifoods Inc. (p. 247) and Campbell Soup Company Ltd. (see p. 119) respectively produce the condiments and soups under this brand name.

Following a series of acquisitions in the 1980s, the parent company has spent the last three years consolidating its operations. This has meant plant closures and layoffs in Weston, Ont. (1990, 32 jobs lost), Winnipeg (1991, 69 jobs lost) and Ingersoll, Ont. (1992, 79 jobs lost). In addition, certain production lines from Borden Catelli's Lethbridge, Alta., plant were transferred to the US. The parent, Borden Inc., has one subsidiary operation and a holding company in South Africa.

Bristol-Myers Squibb Consumer Products Group (Canada)

BMCP

999 DeMaisonneuve West, 12th floor, Montreal, PQ H3A 3L4

Founded in Canada: 1936, Montreal, PQ

Ownership: Bristol-Myers Squibb Co. (US), 100%

Operations: BC, ON, PQ

Employees: 176

Toll-free number: 800-363-3930 or 800-223-5800

Bristol-Myers Squibb Consumer Products Group, formerly called Clairol Canada, is one of three operations of parent company Bristol-Myers Squibb (see also Drackett Canada, p. 153, and Mead Johnson Canada, p. 209). It markets hair care, hair colouring, shampoo and deodorant products through a unionized distribution centre in Boucherville, Que., and three offices, one each in Montreal, Toronto and Vancouver.

Making the Grade

CANDOUR: The company completed our initial products survey but did not participate further. Later in the process, American officials at the parent company answered many of our questions.

WOMEN'S ISSUES: The Group is on the Honour Roll in this category. Women represent 59% of its staff, 41% of its management and 36% of its senior management, though none of the four directors is a woman. The company provides daycare referral.

CHARITABLE GIVING AND COMMUNITY INVOLVEMENT: The company gave $58,300 to charity in 1990. While it is not on Imagine's list, Bristol-Myers Squibb Co. is pledged to the Imagine campaign.

PROGRESSIVE STAFF POLICIES: The Group ties for first place on the Honour Roll in this category. Staff can take advantage of tuition reimbursement and a counselling program that addresses a range of personal, substance abuse and financial problems. The company offers aerobics classes, and will soon offer nutrition seminars, stop-smoking clinics and other activities as well. The company has a formal hiring program for persons with disabilities and informal ones for women, minorities and Native peoples. It also has a scholarship fund for employees' children, provides unpaid time off for employee volunteer activities and publicizes their efforts in the company newsletter. All employees and retirees also receive newsletters summarizing quarterly state-of-the-business meetings.

BRAND NAMES

Ban

Body on Tap

Clairol

Condition

Final Net

Sea Breeze

Vitalis

ENVIRONMENTAL MANAGEMENT: The parent company, which provides environmental policy for all operations worldwide, has a vice-president of environmental affairs and occupational health and safety. A representative of the Canadian company sits on the parent's environmental committee.

ENVIRONMENTAL PERFORMANCE: The company recycles paper and packaging, and had no environmental charges brought against it while it had manufacturing operations in Canada. The parent company has produced several comprehensive environmental responsibility reports.

MANAGEMENT PRACTICES AND CONSUMER RELATIONS: For many years the parent company has had a worldwide document called the *Pledge and Statement of Business Conduct*, which is now under internal review. The Canadian company has an ethics ombudsman. A former employee says it is an excellent company to work for because it treats workers with respect.

Notable Facts

The company agreed to an employee buyout in 1991, which allowed managers to purchase Clairol's Knowlton, PQ, plant and save 90 jobs. The remaining 218 employees retired or were transferred or laid off. Production in Canada was moved to the US, although the Knowlton plant continues to produce some of the same products under contract.

The company says that no animal testing is conducted by or for Bristol-Myers Squibb in Canada. The parent company continues to do animal testing on new compounds, although none has been carried out on finished consumer product formulas for more than three years. The parent states that it has been involved for some time in developing non-animal tests, and notes that 99% of all its animal tests are for pharmaceutical and health care products. It has given over $1 million (US) in grants to help develop non-animal tests and sponsors a company-wide symposium on non-animal testing alternatives.

The US parent company has subsidiary operations in South Africa.

British Columbia Packers Limited

PO Box 5000, Vancouver, BC V6B 4A8

Founded in Canada: 1928, Vancouver, BC
Ownership: George Weston Limited (Canada), 100%
Operations: BC*, AB, ON, PQ
Employees: 2,000 in Canada; 4,000 worldwide
Annual sales: $180 million ($384 million worldwide)
Advertising expenditures: $1.1 million

This company is one of the world's leading canners of salmon. Acquired by George Weston Limited (see p. 168) in 1962, the company has processing, packaging and freezing plants in British Columbia, the US and the Philippines. In 1990, it purchased a government-owned tuna company in the Solomon Islands, which it says gives it a reliable supply of tuna caught by methods that do not kill dolphins. BC Packers (as it is usually called) buys fish from approximately 3,000 independent fishermen and operates three salmon farms. Under the Cloverleaf brand name, the company is Canada's market leader in canned salmon and tuna, although 62% of total sales are made to 30 foreign markets, including Japan, the European Community and the US.

Making the Grade

CANDOUR: BC Packers was the only one of the George Weston subsidiaries to respond to EthicScan's social performance survey. It was very forthcoming and received a high rating.

WOMEN'S ISSUES: While 50% of the workforce is female, only 8% of management and 6% of senior management positions are held by women. BC Packers' 10-member board of directors is all male. The company has no formal employment equity program, daycare provision or extended maternity leave.

CHARITABLE GIVING AND COMMUNITY INVOLVEMENT: BC Packers is pledged to Imagine's One Percent Solution and makes donations independent of its parent (also on the Imagine list). In 1990 the company gave $15,000 to $20,000 (cash and in kind). Staff are involved in such community programs as local salmon festivals, sports teams and school events, but on an individual rather than corporate basis.

PROGRESSIVE STAFF POLICIES: The company provides retirement counselling, and annual written performance reviews to all employees and offers counselling for drug and alcohol abuse to its 1,450 plant workers, 300 office

BRAND NAMES
BC Packers
Cloverleaf
Maple Leaf
Paramount
Queen Charlotte
Red Rose

staff and 250 directly employed Canadian fishermen. It also has employee suggestion programs, rewards for cost-saving ideas, and a newsletter, *Hook, Line and Thinker*.

LABOUR RELATIONS: The company has no formal job security policy or any specific methods of addressing layoffs or downsizing. Health and safety information was provided in part.

ENVIRONMENTAL MANAGEMENT: BC Packers earned a place on this Honour Roll. George Weston Limited provides the company's written environmental policy. Reports to the board are made as needed. There are three employees with environmental functions, the most senior being a full-time manager of environmental affairs.

ENVIRONMENTAL PERFORMANCE: Staff have conducted a comprehensive environmental audit of all operations. The company's activities include paper recycling, the replacement of disposable cutlery and dishes with reusable ones, product research and development, equipment replacement and reformulation of packaging. The firm has not had any fines for environmental violations, but in 1990-91 its largest fish processing plant (in Steveston, BC) was three times placed on a watch list for exceeding provincial effluent discharge limits. It planned to deal with the situation by relocating the outfall pipe to reduce the environmental impact on Cannery Channel. As of June, 1992, the company had not been placed on a 1992 watch list. Some environmentalists have voiced concern over the use of antibiotics in the company's northern BC fish farming operations.

MANAGEMENT PRACTICES AND CONSUMER RELATIONS: The company introduced its own written code of ethics, distinct from that of the parent company, in 1989. It does not require an annual employee sign-off on the code or provide any other ethics reinforcement (such as an advisory service, ombudsman or training). BC Packers has not been charged with any Competition Act violations.

Notable Facts

Eighty percent of the company's workforce is unionized through the United Fishermen and Allied Workers union. BC Packers was one of several companies involved in a major strike in British Columbia's fishing industry in 1989. One hundred workers were laid off in 1990 when the Victoria fish processing facility was closed. In addition, 15 office staff were laid off late in 1991. The parent company (see p. 168) has no operations in South Africa.

Burns Meats

Suite 4230 West Tower, Petro Canada Building, 150-6th Avenue SW, Calgary, AB T2P 3Y7

Founded in Canada: 1890, Calgary, AB
Ownership: A.J.E. Child (Canada), 65%
Operations: AB*, MB*, ON
Employees: 2,000
Annual sales: $700 million (Burns Foods)

Burns Meats, Canada's third largest meat packer, was founded under the name P. Burns and Company. A privately held company, it has plants in Lethbridge, Alta., and Winnipeg (and is the only remaining large meat packing firm in Manitoba). In the last ten years, Burns has closed plants in Brandon, Man., Calgary, Edmonton, Toronto and Kitchener, Ont.

Burns Meats is a division of Burns Foods (1985) Limited, which has 30 branches and plants across Canada. Burns Foods also owns Scott National, which produces frozen foods for the food service industry.

Making the Grade

CANDOUR: Burns chose not to complete most of our survey and received a low rating. The majority owner and a company employee both provided some information in interviews late in the process.

CHARITABLE GIVING AND COMMUNITY INVOLVEMENT: Most of what we know about the company is in this category. Burns is pledged to the Imagine campaign and provides significant support for the Royal Winnipeg Ballet. The company was involved in the founding of the Calgary Stampede and backs many community events, including the Stampede, the Canadian National Exhibition, the Brandon Exhibition and Winnipeg's Folkarama celebration. Burns participates in charity events, cultural programs and social activities, and encourages its employees to get involved as well.

PROGRESSIVE STAFF POLICIES: We know only that the company says it is open to ideas from employees, and that "bull pens" in its Winnipeg facilities encourage the discussion of ideas to improve operations.

ENVIRONMENTAL MANAGEMENT/PERFORMANCE: Burns provided few details about its environmental initiatives. The company has an environmental guidelines statement and environmental pledge plaques in individual plants.

BRAND NAMES
Burns

MANAGEMENT PRACTICES AND CONSUMER RELATIONS: In 1989 Burns, along with two other companies, pleaded guilty to conspiring to fix the price of slaughter hogs, in contravention of the Competition Act and was fined $125,000. A Burns spokesperson said that the company pleaded guilty to avoid legal costs.

Notable Facts

In 1987, Burns was one of 10 companies which fought to keep federal government meat inspection reports private. Its lawyers told the court that "slanted news reporting might create a distorted impression that plants are not sanitary."

Burns has had what one union representative calls "an up-and-down relationship" with the United Food and Commercial Workers union for about 50 years. There was a series of strikes in 1984 over wages and wage reduction.

In 1988, 550 former employees of the firm's Calgary plant were granted an out-of-court settlement of less than $100,000 for a $9.6-million claim for severance pay benefits for loss of jobs in 1984. The company reportedly closed the plant one week after the union refused wage rollbacks and workers voted to strike. In 1989 and 1990, the company asked workers in the Brandon, Man., plant to accept pay cuts so that the operation could remain competitive. The plant was subsequently closed, with the loss of 82 jobs.

Cadbury Beverages Canada Inc.

2700 Matheson Blvd. E., East Tower, Suite 500, Mississauga ON L4W 4X1

Founded in Canada: 1919
Ownership: Cadbury Schweppes Plc (UK), 100%
Operations: BC, AB, ON*, PQ, NS
Number of employees: 400

The company is a wholly-owned subsidiary of UK-based Cadbury Schweppes Plc, a beverage and confectionery company with operations in 110 countries. The confectionery division is now represented by Neilson Cadbury, a division of George Weston Limited (see p. 168). Cadbury Beverages Canada manufactures carbonated beverages, fruit drinks, sauces and spreads. All of its brands except the apple sauces are marketed nationally and have a significant share of their respective markets. Certain Cadbury beverages are also produced under licence in Canada by both Coca-Cola Beverages (see p. 135) and Pepsi-Cola Canada Ltd. (see p. 228). Recent company acquisitions include Crush International (1989) and Canada Dry (1986), as well as particular brands, such as both Allen's and Mitchell's apple sauces (1990) and E.D. Smith's Garden Cocktail (1989).

Making the Grade

CANDOUR: The company responded to two of the three EthicScan surveys and was forthcoming overall.

WOMEN'S ISSUES: The representation of women in management (15%) and senior management (18%) is higher at Cadbury than at any other member of the bottling industry in this *Guide*. One of the five members of the board of directors is female. The company did not provide a figure for the percentage of women in the workforce.

CHARITABLE GIVING AND COMMUNITY INVOLVEMENT: Cadbury Beverages is not on Imagine's list, but it does report $200,000 in donations in 1990. Its community activities include a matching gift program, sports team support, and a policy of publicizing employee volunteer activities in its newsletter.

PROGRESSIVE STAFF POLICIES: While the company does not have a formal employee assistance program, its score in this category was still high because of the significant number of other programs, such as a fitness club subsidy, quit-smoking program, retirement counselling and annual written performance reviews. It has a policy of open-

BRAND NAMES
Allen's
Cadbury
Canada Dry
C-Plus
Crush
Fry's
Garden Cocktail
Hires
Mitchell's
Mott's
Mott's Fruit Pak
Ocean Spray
Schweppes
Welch's

door management, provides a newsletter, suggestion programs and employee savings plan, and offers to pay tuition for job-related courses. The company has no employment equity program, but notes that it "has an operating practice within the company of promoting on the basis of merit as opposed to any program based on race, sex, age, etc."

ENVIRONMENTAL MANAGEMENT: Cadbury Beverages is on the Honour Roll for this category. It has a written environmental policy, an environmental committee of the board and makes reports to the board as needed. While there is no full-time environment officer, eight employees have some environmental responsibilities connected with their positions, the most senior being a vice-president. The managing director of Cadbury Beverages is a past chairperson of Ontario Multi-Materials Recycling Inc. (OMMRI), one of the organizations that helped develop Ontario's Blue Box recycling program.

ENVIRONMENTAL PERFORMANCE: On this honour roll as well, Cadbury conducts environmental audits of some of its operations. Its in-house environmental practices include employee education programs, an environmental suggestion program, a car/van pool service and efforts to replace disposable cutlery and dishes with reusable ones. Cadbury also recycles paper, aluminum and glass, invests in environmentally-related product research and development and packaging reformulation, and makes contributions to industry organizations.

MANAGEMENT PRACTICES AND CONSUMER RELATIONS: The company has a *Policy Statement on Business Conduct*, which does not require annual employee sign-off. It has not been fined for any Competition Act violations, although the Ministry of Consumer and Corporate Affairs did investigate Neilson's takeover of Cadbury's confectionery division. Market concentration and anticipated closure of Cadbury's Whitby, Ont., plant were key issues.

Notable Facts

The company is 40% unionized and has had no plant openings or closures in the past five years. The hot chocolate division has seasonal layoffs affecting 15-20 employees every spring. While the Canadian company has no export sales or interests in South Africa, its UK parent has five active and 19 dormant subsidiaries in that country. Cadbury Beverages cans Nestea iced tea product for Nestlé Canada (see p. 219).

Campbell Soup Company Ltd.

60 Birmingham Street, Toronto, ON, M8V 2B8

Founded in Canada: 1930, Toronto, ON
Ownership: Campbell Soup Company (US), 100%
Operations: BC, AB, MB, ON*, PQ, NS
Employees: 2,138
Annual sales: $494 million
Advertising expenditures: $5 million

Campbell Soup, whose goal is to be the "number one food company in North America," has plants in St. Mary's, Listowel, Toronto and Chatham, all in Ontario. It has market-leading brands in beverages (V-8), condiments and sauces (A-1, Franco-American and Bisto), frozen dinners (Swanson), frozen desserts (Pepperidge Farm) and, of course, soups, with its distinctive red and white label cans. The company has test kitchens and laboratories in Toronto and an agricultural research station in Chatham, where it conducted $200,000-worth of product research and development in 1990. Until mid-1991, the company was publicly-traded and produced a Canadian annual report. The parent company has since taken Campbell private.

Making the Grade

CANDOUR: Campbell participated in the research process, answering more than half of the questions posed.

WOMEN'S ISSUES: Although more than 55% of Campbell's workforce is female, only 11% of its managers and 13% of senior managers (4 out of 30) are women. The 21-member board of directors has four women in its ranks. Extended maternity leave is granted on an individual basis only and there are no daycare provisions. However, it does offer flextime and time-sharing options.

CHARITABLE GIVING AND COMMUNITY INVOLVEMENT: The company is not on Imagine's list and did not provide recent information about its charitable giving. However, a March 1990 survey conducted for the *Corporate Ethics Monitor* found that the company's 1989 donations totalled $259,000, which amounted to slightly more than the Imagine goal of 1% of pre-tax earnings. A sizable portion of the contribution came from employees at the Toronto plant and office. In 1990, Campbell co-sponsored a literacy promotion program, in addition to its other education contributions, such as university matching gift and education grants.

BRAND NAMES
A-1
Bisto
Caesar's Choice
Campbell's
Franco American
Gattuso (soups)
Habitant (soups)
Healthy Request
Hearty Noodles
Le Menu
Paterson's
Pepperidge Farms
Prego
Quadelco
Swanson
V-8 Juice

PROGRESSIVE STAFF POLICIES: The emphasis is on communications programs, with a company newsletter, suggestion programs, rewards for cost-saving ideas, annual written performance reviews and employee/management motivational seminars. President's Awards and President's Citations are given primarily to teams who demonstrate outstanding contributions to the company's goals.

LABOUR RELATIONS: The company offers no formal job security program or methods for addressing layoffs. It has full-time safety representatives at all its plants.

ENVIRONMENTAL MANAGEMENT: Campbell has a written environmental strategy, which focuses on environmentally-sound packaging and production processes and links the goals of quality, continuous improvement and the environment. At the corporate level, an environmental task force has developed policy, created committees at all plants, and commissioned energy and environmental audits at all plants.

ENVIRONMENTAL PERFORMANCE: The company reports that it has reduced the amount of packaging in its Le Menu frozen dinners and has lightened its steel cans by 24 percent. In 1989-90 it was fined a total of $15,500 under the Ontario Water Resources Act for excessive wastewater emissions at the St. Mary's plant. The plant had been named by the Ontario Ministry of the Environment as one of those that most frequently exceeded wastewater discharge limits during 1988. A company spokesperson said that waste disposal is now under control at this site. Since at least 1983, Campbell has stored significant quantities of PCBs at its Toronto plant.

MANAGEMENT PRACTICES AND CONSUMER RELATIONS: Campbell has a written code of ethics. No other information was disclosed in this category.

Notable Facts

Since 1987, the global restructuring of the parent company has been accompanied by nine layoffs in Canada, affecting 300 workers. In 1989, Campbell acquired the soups and sauces division of Habitant from Catelli (see p. 109), while Robin Hood Multifoods (p. 247) acquired the condiments division. In a similar arrangement, Campbell produces Gattuso soups while Robin Hood Multifoods makes Gattuso condiments and Borden Catelli makes Gattuso pasta and sauces.

Canda Starch Co Inc.

401 The West Mall, Etobicoke, ON M9C 5H9

Founded in Canada: 1858, Cardinal, ON
Ownership: CPC International Inc. (US), 100%
Operations: ON*, PQ
Employees: 1,100
Annual sales: $67.3 million

Canada Starch markets products to consumers through a division called Best Foods Canada Inc. It is a strong presence in the table syrup, cooking oil, corn starch and bouillon markets. As the maker of both Squirrel and Skippy brands, the company has a sizeable share of the peanut butter market. Since 1986, Canada Starch has acquired several operations, including Bovril Canada, du Chef and Old London Melba Toast, which have increased the size of its workforce by almost 200. As well, it has acquired trademarks from St. Lawrence Starch Company and now makes and markets Beehive corn syrup, St. Lawrence oil and Durham starch.

Making the Grade

CANDOUR: The company received a low rating. It did not initially respond to the surveys, though it did provide some information late in the process.

WOMEN'S ISSUES: No information was provided on the percentage of women in management and senior management or on the board of directors. The company has no daycare or extended maternity leave provisions or formal programs concerning the hiring and promotion of women.

CHARITABLE GIVING AND COMMUNITY INVOLVEMENT: Canada Starch is not on the Imagine list and did not disclose charitable donation figures. It supports sports teams and health causes.

PROGRESSIVE STAFF POLICIES: These include an on-site fitness facility, retirement counselling, adoption leave benefits, company newsletter, open-door management and scholarship funds for employees and their children.

LABOUR RELATIONS: Though there is no formal job security program, the company uses early retirement and advance notice of technological change to deal with the impact of layoffs.

BRAND NAMES
Beehive
Benson's
Bovril
Canada
du Chef
Durham
Hellman's
Knorr
Mazola
Old Colony
Old London
Old Tyme
Skippy
Squirrel
St. Lawrence

ENVIRONMENTAL MANAGEMENT: The company has no written environmental policy, although Best Foods issues a values statement to all employees that includes comments on the environment. No other environmental information was supplied.

ENVIRONMENTAL PERFORMANCE: Canada Starch's Cardinal, Ont., plant, which makes syrup and other products, was under an Ontario government control order for several years until modernization brought wastewater emissions within approved limits in 1990. The company received the Regional Industry Energy Award for energy conservation at its London, Ont., plant in 1988.

MANAGEMENT PRACTICES AND CONSUMER RELATIONS: While there is no Canadian code of ethics, all CPC International managers worldwide receive a company manual that deals with such issues as a business ethics policy. Canadian managers sign off annually on a conflict of interest statement. The company did not comment on whether it has had Competition Act violations.

Notable Facts

Twenty percent of staff are unionized. The company's Lennoxville, Que., syrup plant was closed in 1987, and its operations shifted to the Cardinal, Ont., plant.

The parent company, CPC International, has trademark agreements with a South African company, but, as of October 1989, the company says it derives no royalties from these arrangements.

Canadian Home Products Ltd., Canadian Home Foods Division

685 Third Avenue, New York, NY 10017-4085

Founded in Canada: 1943, Niagara Falls, ON

Ownership: American Home Products Corporation (US), 100%

Operations: AB, ON*, PQ

Employees: 217

Toll-free number: 800-461-4556

Canadian Home Products is a wholly-owned subsidiary of American Home Products, a huge multinational corporation that manufactures over-the-counter medication, grocery products, contraceptives, pharmaceuticals and infant formula. A number of products marketed by the Canadian foods division hold more than a 25% market share, including Chef Boyardee, PAM and Franklin Crunch & Munch. Our questionnaire concerned only the Canadian Home Foods Division of the company, not its pharmaceutical operations.

Making the Grade

CANDOUR: The decision to respond to our questionnaire was made from American Home Product's head office in New York, although the surveys were completed in conjunction with the Canadian operations. All surveys regarding American Home Products or any of its subsidiaries, regardless of country of origin, are handled through New York in order to maintain consistency. American Home Products co-operated fully with our enquiry, yet was frequently unable to supply details about specific practices in Canada. Many of the Canadian operations are consolidated with the parent's and many of the programs are plant-specific rather than determined by a Canadian head office. Therefore, while one Canadian Home Products plant may have a particular program or policy, others may not.

WOMEN'S ISSUES: Women occupy just 12% of management and 20% of senior management positions at the company, and the Canadian board of directors has no women among its eight members. There is no formal employment equity program or provision for daycare, and extended maternity leave is provided on a case-by-case basis.

CHARITABLE GIVING AND COMMUNITY INVOLVEMENT: Canadian Home Products is not on Imagine's list and did not provide us with information about donations as a percentage of pre-tax earnings. However, in 1990, it gave $10,600, mostly in product donations, to various organi-

BRAND NAMES
Chef Boyardee
Crunch and Munch
Gulden's
Jiffy Pop
Pam
Ranch Style
Superiore

zations. The company has a matching gift program and allows unpaid time off for employee volunteer activity.

PROGRESSIVE STAFF POLICIES: The US office had a difficult time determining exactly which programs are available at which plants. An employee assistance program is available on request and some employees are eligible for a fitness club subsidy. Canadian Home Foods also has a suggestion program, adoption leave and annual written employee performance reviews.

LABOUR RELATIONS: The company has no formal job security program and no method of addressing job security. No gain sharing programs are offered in the Canadian operations. The US parent provided health and safety figures, but not training data.

ENVIRONMENTAL MANAGEMENT: Canadian Home Products has a place on this Honour Roll. It has an environmental policy, provided by the parent company, and makes regular reports to the parent's board of directors. While the company has three employees with environmental duties, none has full-time environmental responsibilities. On the other hand, American Home Products, which makes most of the policy decisions for the Canadian company, recently appointed a vice-president of environmental affairs. Neither the Canadian company nor its parent has an environmental committee, although the parent has a corporate issues committee that addresses environmental concerns.

ENVIRONMENTAL PERFORMANCE: Environmental audits of all operations are conducted annually. Canadian Home Products has very few environmental programs, but it has replaced equipment and improved energy efficiency at its plants. The company has no record of environmental violations or related fines in Canada.

MANAGEMENT PRACTICES AND CONSUMER RELATIONS: Canadian Home Products made this Honour Roll. It has a written code of ethics, revised annually, and requires a yearly sign-off on the code. The company has not been charged with any Competition Act violations, and it offers a toll-free advisory service.

Notable Facts

Canadian Home Products has had no strikes since 1981-82 and employment figures have been stable for the past five years. Seventy-eight percent of its employees are unionized.

In conjunction with the Canadian Infant Formula Association, Canadian Home Products has agreed to market its infant formula only to health professionals, so as not to discourage women from breast feeding or intrude on the doctor-patient relationship. The American parent changed its policy concerning the marketing of this product because of consumer pressure and has been removed from the United Church of Christ boycott list, but remains on others. According to the US-based Interfaith Center on Corporate Responsibility, American Home Products (AHP) has developed a clear policy and is working to implement it.

Although the Canadian Home Foods division does no animal testing, American Home Products does. In a 1990 survey by EthicScan, a spokesperson for AHP said, "virtually all testing is in the US, and almost all of this is for pharmaceuticals". The parent company spent $500,000 (US) in 1989-90 on the development of alternatives to the use of animal testing.

American Home Products maintains some licensing agreements in South Africa, through non-food divisions only.

The Canadian Salt Company Limited

CANSAL

755 boul. St-Jean, Suite 700, Pointe-Claire, PQ H9R 5M9

Founded in Canada: 1893, Windsor, ON
Ownership: Morton International (US), 100%
Operations: BC, AB*, SK*, ON*, PQ*, NS*
Employees: 795

The Windsor Salt Company began as a subsidiary of the Canadian Pacific Railway, but had its name changed to the Canadian Salt Company soon after. Canada's largest manufacturer of salt, it produces over 200 salt products for consumer and industrial purposes. The company owns and operates three rock salt mining operations and four evaporated salt processing plants across Canada.

Making the Grade

CANDOUR: Canadian Salt did not participate in our research, apart from verifying its brands. Members of the Canadian Auto Workers union, who represent some company employees, were our principal source of information.

CHARITABLE GIVING AND COMMUNITY INVOLVEMENT: The company is not pledged to the Imagine campaign and did not disclose the size of its charitable contributions. However, it makes a significant donation to the United Way and other local charities, supports academic scholarships in engineering and allows employees time off for volunteer activities.

PROGRESSIVE STAFF POLICIES: The company offers substance abuse counselling. Newsletters at some sites have been discontinued, while others, like *Salt Licks*, still exist.

ENVIRONMENTAL MANAGEMENT: The union reports that management decisions, including environmental ones, are heavily directed by the parent company in Chicago. However, Canadian Salt has an environmental policy in place and a TQM (Total Quality Management) program that addresses environmental issues among others.

ENVIRONMENTAL PERFORMANCE: A joint union-management recycling committee was started early in 1992, and the company recycles paper, pop cans, glass and cardboard. Canadian Salt has budgeted to reclaim and purify the effluent discharged into the river at its fine salt operations. Similarly, it has allocated money to control the salt dust with an airborne emissions collection system. The com-

BRAND NAMES
Crystal
Half-Salt
Safe-T-Salt
Windsor

pany was assessed two fines in 1991, totalling $3,000, for violations of Ontario's air and water regulations.

MANAGEMENT PRACTICES AND CONSUMER RELATIONS: The company has a written code of ethics.

Notable Facts

Union representatives say there have been two major strikes over the last 20 years: one for eight months in 1975 and another for six months in 1990. The parent company, formerly called Morton-Thiokol, has spun off its Thiokol division, which remains active in the ammunition and nuclear weapons (rocket boosters) markets.

Canbra Foods Ltd.

PO Box 99, Lethbridge, AB T1J 3Y4

Founded in Canada: 1957, Lethbridge, AB
Ownership: Pocklington Financial Corporation (Canada), 72%
Operations: AB*, SK
Employees: 250
Annual sales: $102 million

Canbra is one of Canada's oldest and largest fully integrated oilseed crushing, refining and packaging companies. It produces cooking and salad oil, margarine, shortening and canola meal, which it packages under its own brand name for sale to retailers and food service distributors and sells in bulk to food manufacturers. It has a plant in Lethbridge, Alta., where it is the largest private employer, and grain elevator gathering points in Prince Albert, Sask., and Blackie, Alta.

Making the Grade

Canbra did not participate in the research process. However, the United Food and Commercial Workers union, Canbra employees' collective bargaining agent, took part in an interview, and the company's annual report provided some additional details.

The company has no women in senior management or on its 10-man board of directors. While Canbra is not pledged to the Imagine campaign, it has been operating at a deficit for the past two years, so there are no pre-tax earnings. The union says that the company used to be a good contributor to its communities. It has no record of environmental violations or instances of exceeding discharge limits.

Notable Facts

The union's business representative describes the company as a good employer, although it has become "lean and mean" in order to survive. It had layoffs due to automation and improved efficiencies two years ago that resulted in the loss of 20 jobs. The company has a small operation in Butte, Montana.

> **BRAND NAMES**
> Canola Harvest
> West

Cargill Limited

300-240 Graham Ave., Winnipeg, MB R3C 4C5

Founded in Canada: 1928, Winnipeg MB
Ownership: Cargill Inc. (US), 100%
Operations: BC, AB*, SK*, MB*, ON*, PQ
Employees: 2,000
Annual sales: $1.6 billion
Advertising expenditures: $396,793

This Minnesota-based agribusiness giant, founded by William Wallace Cargill in 1865, is privately held. The Canadian company, active in the meat, grain and fertilizer markets, distributes only one brand name (US-produced Tendercut) in Canadian grocery stores, but hundreds of Canadian products contain Cargill meats. In addition, Cargill produces animal feeds through companies like Nutrina Feeds, and sells fertilizers, chemicals and pesticides to farmers. Cargill is managed by Canadians and reinvests its cash flow in Canada. It has a decentralized management style, with little direction from its US parent.

Making the Grade

CANDOUR: The company was very forthcoming, earning itself a position on our Honour Roll in this category.

WOMEN'S ISSUES: Cargill has an employment equity program and an affirmative action program. While it has no daycare provision, the company does provide extended maternity leave beyond government mandated minimum terms. About 7% of managers and 17% of senior managers are female, and one woman sits on the 10-person board. In general, women have not progressed as rapidly in the grain division as in the meat operations.

CHARITABLE GIVING AND COMMUNITY INVOLVEMENT: A member of this Honour Roll as well, Cargill is pledged to the Imagine campaign and averages donations at approximately 2% of pre-tax earnings. Head office gave $284,000 in 1990 ($4,000 in kind), not including contributions from its 150 facilities, which donate separately. The company matches the donations of head office employees for certain fundraising campaigns. According to its philanthropy report, 60% of donations go to health and human welfare institutions such as the Victorian Order of Nurses (VON), Canadian National Institute for the Blind (CNIB) and various hospitals around the country. It co-sponsors the Manitoba Chamber Orchestra Arts Advocacy Program, which allows inner city students to attend classical music concerts. Cargill sponsors Centen-

BRAND NAMES
Tendercut

nial Farm Awards, to recognize farmers who have maintained the family farm over several generations.

PROGRESSIVE STAFF POLICIES: An employee assistance program is now under development. The company promotes an open-door policy between staff and management and carries out an annual written performance evaluation for all employees.

LABOUR RELATIONS: Cargill has no formal job security program, or methods of addressing layoffs. The company provided health and safety and training data.

ENVIRONMENTAL MANAGEMENT: While the company has a written environmental policy, it has no environmental committees and only three employees with environmental responsibilities, the most senior of these being a manager with full-time duties. Cargill makes monthly reports on its environmental conduct to the board.

ENVIRONMENTAL PERFORMANCE: Cargill is on the Honour Roll in this category as well. The company has completed a comprehensive environmental audit of all operations, using an internal team. Its report, *Cargill and the Environment*, examines some of the positive steps the company is taking in addressing environmental concerns, including new printers which produce computer reports on smaller paper, packaging reformulation and employee education in environmental matters, notably on safety and handling of hazardous materials. Zero effluent discharge is being planned for the new Saskferco fertilizer plant: plants producing granular urea, like this one, typically have carbon dioxide and liquid effluent as byproducts. In 1985 the company was fined $6,500 under the BC Fisheries Act for discharges into the Fraser River. Its High River cattle processing plant has been placed under a control order by the Alberta Environment Pollution Control Division for excessive wastewater discharges and for emitting offensive odour during its start-up period.

MANAGEMENT PRACTICES: Cargill also earned a place on this Honour Roll. The company's code of ethics, which was written before 1970 and revised in 1990, is reinforced through an ethics advisory column in the company's newsletter. Cargill issues a philanthropy report about its donations. It has not been fined in connection with any Competition Act violations.

Notable Facts

Cargill has employment equity programs for minorities and persons with disabilities, and has a specialized training program for Native employees. The new High River, Alta., slaughterhouse and packing plant, opened in 1989 and expanded in 1991, created 625 jobs.

While the Canadian company does not trade with South Africa, its parent sold its South African subsidiary to Omnia, a company licensed to sell Cargill seed and use the Cargill trademark. The Canadian company expects to continue sales to Cuba even if the United States imposes a law to force US companies to halt sales to that country.

Cavendish Farms

100 Midland Dr., PO Box 789, Moncton, NB E1C 8N6

Ownership: K.C. Irving (Canada), 100%
Operations: NB, PE*
Employees: 650 (est.)

Cavendish Farms, one of the two largest potato processors in the country (see also McCain Foods Limited, p. 205), was purchased several decades ago by K.C. Irving. The holdings of the Irving family — one of the wealthiest in Canada — include Irving Oil, pulp and paper mills, timberland in Maine and Canada, media companies and shipbuilding operations. Cavendish Farms owns farms and potato processing plants at New Annan, PEI.

Making the Grade

CANDOUR: This privately-owned company provided virtually no information. Local 1252 of the United Food and Commercial Workers (UFCW) union was also contacted but declined to comment.

CHARITABLE GIVING AND COMMUNITY INVOLVEMENT:
Cavendish Farms is not pledged to the Imagine Campaign.

Notable Facts

In August, 1989, Cavendish Farms was found to have violated the PEI Labour Act by failing to bargain in good faith with the UFCW from November, 1987 to March, 1989. The judgment ordered damages paid to bargaining unit employees and to those no longer employed at the date of union contract ratification.

Cavendish Farms is expanding its New Annan plant. While this could create some 100 to 150 new jobs beyond the existing 530, reports indicate that a Malpeque Bay environmental group was seeking an injunction to keep the plant from expanding until a proposed wastewater treatment facility was completed. Some area residents are concerned that pollution levels in nearby waters are already too high due to farm topsoil run-off, municipal wastes and effluent from the existing plant. Unless the expansion is delayed, production could increase 40% some two years before a new waste treatment facility is completed.

The company has had talks with fishermen, potato farmers and other concerned residents, which it says have reached a "very amiable conclusion." Cavendish Farms knows of no boycott action or injunction against it and says that it has pledged to protect the environment.

BRAND NAMES
Cavendish Farms

Cobi Foods Inc.

PO Box 1000, Port Williams, NS B0P 1N0

Founded in Canada: 1984, Port Williams, NS
Ownership: Minas Group Ltd. (Canada), 79.5%
Operations: ON*, PQ, NS*
Employees: 446
Annual sales: $122 million
Advertising expenditures: $500,000

This publicly-traded, Nova Scotia-based company is a market leader in canned and frozen vegetables, making products under both its own brand and other licensed brand names. The company exports its products to 12 countries worldwide. It is part of the Scotia Investments group of companies. Cobi has plants in Ingersoll and Oakville, Ont.; and Berwick and Hillaton, NS.

Making the Grade

CANDOUR: While the company was very responsive to our surveys, as reflected in its high Candour Quotient, it did not score well in any other category because of a general lack of formal programs and policies.

WOMEN'S ISSUES: Although 25% of its workforce is female, only 2% of management and no senior management positions are occupied by women. There is one woman on the 10-member board of directors. No employment equity, daycare or extended maternity leave programs are offered.

CHARITABLE GIVING AND COMMUNITY INVOLVEMENT: Although not on Imagine's list, it gave $50,500, mostly in kind, to charity in 1990. The company donates equipment and facilities to local groups and provides sports team support.

PROGRESSIVE STAFF POLICIES: Cobi conducts annual written performance reviews of all employees and has scholarship programs for employees and their children.

ENVIRONMENTAL MANAGEMENT/PERFORMANCE: The company has no written environmental policy or environmental committee and does not conduct environmental audits. While it has no full-time environmental affairs officer, either, two Cobi employees have responsibility for environmental issues associated with their jobs. The firm has no record of environmental court cases or fines.

BRAND NAMES
Avon
Cobi
Graves
Hardee Farms
Hi-Lo
Honeydew
Nature's Best
Stokely Van Camp

MANAGEMENT PRACTICES AND CONSUMER RELATIONS: Cobi has no written code of ethics, but has not been fined for any Competition Act infractions.

Notable Facts

The company has had one strike in the past ten years, a short one in January, 1987. Cobi reports two major layoffs over the last three years, affecting 180 workers in total. In 1989, the company closed its Whitby, Ont., plant and gave employees eight weeks' pay in lieu of notice.

Under one of its licensing agreements, Cobi makes Libby's canned and frozen vegetables for Nestlé Canada (see p. 219).

Coca-Cola Beverages

42 Overlea Blvd, Toronto, ON M4H 1B8

Founded in Canada: 1949, Uxbridge, ON
Ownership: Coca-Cola Limited (Canada), approximately 49%
Operations: all provinces and territories
Employees: 4,536
Annual sales: $1 billion
Toll-free number: 800-463-2653

Coca-Cola was first sold in Canada in 1892 and first made here in 1905. The company is responsible for about 97% (by volume) of the Coca-Cola produced in Canada. It has made many acquisitions over the past five years, and bottles Canada Dry, Schweppes (see p. 117) and A&W (see p. 261) beverages under license. Coca-Cola has offices and bottling plants in all provinces, as well as franchise bottlers in the territories.

Making the Grade

CANDOUR: Both majority-owner, Coca-Cola Limited (which provides marketing and advertising services), and Coca-Cola Beverages reviewed our surveys and were quite responsive overall.

CHARITABLE GIVING AND COMMUNITY INVOLVEMENT: The company's exceptional performance earned it a place on our Honour Roll. While Coca-Cola Beverages is not on Imagine's list, it does support the Imagine campaign and it gave 2% of pre-tax earnings to charity in 1990. Community activities include equipment donations, the use of company facilities, paid time off for employee volunteer activity and support for events and organizations like the Special Olympics, United Way and the Canadian Cystic Fibrosis Foundation. Volunteer activity is publicized in the company's employee video magazine, *Wavelength*.

WOMEN'S ISSUES: This was Coca-Cola's lowest score. Women constitute about 11% percent of staff and 7% of management. There are no women in senior management and only one on the 10-person board of directors. The company has no formal employment equity program or daycare provision in place, but does offer extended maternity leave.

PROGRESSIVE STAFF POLICIES: Its employee assistance program provides drug and alcohol abuse counselling while the health promotion plan includes corporate marathons and stop-smoking programs. Communications

BRAND NAMES

caffeine free
  Coca-Cola
cherry Coke
Coca-Cola Classic
Coke
diet Coke
diet Minute Maid
diet Sprite
Fanta
Five Alive
Fresca
Minute Maid
Pure Sun
Sprite
Tab

programs include an employee video and the policy of open-door management.

LABOUR RELATIONS: The company is on this Honour Roll as well. It has a formal job security program and uses methods like retraining, relocation, financial compensation and advance notice of technological change to reduce the impact of downsizing. It also offers a stock purchase plan to its employees. Coca-Cola Beverages was one of the few companies to provide us with health and safety statistics.

ENVIRONMENTAL MANAGEMENT: Coca-Cola's product stewardship code is provided by its industry association, the Canadian Soft Drink Association. The company has no environmental committee although environmental reports to the board are made as needed. There are 12 employees with environmental functions and the majority owner, Coca-Cola Limited, has a vice-president of environmental and corporate affairs who provides support to Coca-Cola Beverages on environmental issues.

ENVIRONMENTAL PERFORMANCE: Since 1988, Coca-Cola Beverages has conducted packaging waste audits for every operation. It has several recycling programs in-house, including ones for paper, manufacturing by-products and packaging. It has been charged on several occasions under Ontario's Environmental Protection Act for failing to meet Ontario's 30% quota for sales in refillable bottles: it was fined $44,950 for 58 violations of the refill quota law in 1990; $3,750 for three violations in 1989; and $1,000 for one conviction in 1988. A company spokesperson for Coca-Cola Limited states that the quota is hard to meet because of consumer preference for non-refillable containers. The company has reduced the amount of metal in its cans (lightweighting), has switched from aluminum to steel cans in Ontario, and has invested in new equipment. It helped develop Ontario's Blue Box program, and funds provincial recycling programs such as OMMRI (Ontario Multi-Materials Recycling Inc.), the Nova Scotia Recycling Fund and the Manitoba Buy Back Program.

MANAGEMENT PRACTICES AND CONSUMER RELATIONS: Coca-Cola Beverages has a written code of ethics, established in 1988. No employee sign-off is required. The company has a toll-free consumer advisory service. In 1988, the company's majority owner, Coca-Cola Limited, was fined (together with other bottlers) $65,000 for its role in a price-fixing conspiracy in Manitoba.

Notable Facts

Employment at the company has risen by about 1,900 over the past five years, primarily because of the acquisition of dozens of independent bottlers across Canada. Seventy-seven percent of these employees are unionized, generally through the Canadian Auto Workers or the United Food and Commercial Workers. Since Coca-Cola Beverages began operations in 1987, there have been no strikes at any of the company's locations.

The company has been consolidating and centralizing its operations for the past few years, resulting in the expansion of some facilities and the closure of others, mostly distribution centres. Coca-Cola Limited retains 49% of Coca-Cola Beverages, which is traded on the stock exchange, as a way to raise capital to build or upgrade plants.

The Atlanta-based Coca-Cola Company, owner of Coca-Cola Limited, sold its South African subsidiaries in 1986. However, it maintains a trademark agreement with South African bottlers. It has a concentrate production facility in Swaziland that supplies South African bottlers.

Colgate-Palmolive Canada Inc.

COLPAL

99 Vanderhoof Ave., Toronto, ON M4G 2H6

Founded in Canada: 1913, Toronto, ON
Ownership: Colgate-Palmolive Co. (US), 100%
Operations: AB*, ON*, PQ*, NB*
Employees: 550

Colgate-Palmolive has been a major presence in Canada's personal care and household products markets since 1913. Its products include toothpaste, soap, shaving cream and laundry detergent, as well as pet foods, which are manufactured and marketed through an associate company, Hill's Pet Foods. In September, 1991, the parent company announced a worldwide corporate reorganization, which led to the closing of a Toronto bar soap and detergent plant. Two other Toronto plants, one bottle making and the other bottle filling, are being merged. All Canadian production of powder detergents, liquid detergents and bar soaps is being transferred to the USA.

Making the Grade

CANDOUR: The company said it was impossible to answer our questions at this time, because of both the major corporate restructuring underway and the acquisition of the bleach, fabric softener and certain household care products from Drackett Canada, a division of Bristol-Myers Squibb Co. (see p. 153). Its Candour Quotient is therefore low, and little information is available on the company. "A significant part of current management activity," explains a company spokesperson, "is dedicated to establishing policies and procedures for the new company that came into being this year."

CHARITABLE GIVING AND COMMUNITY INVOLVEMENT:
The company is not listed among Imagine's Caring Companies.

ENVIRONMENTAL PERFORMANCE: The company has produced a phosphate-free detergent and has significantly reduced the amount of packaging it uses in its fabric softener and dishwashing detergent containers by producing thin pouches as refills rather than formed plastic bottles. The company also uses recycled materials in its cardboard boxes and plastic laundry detergent scoops. Company offices use recycled paper products. One Toronto plant, which has been a source of air emissions

BRAND NAMES

ABC
Ajax
Amex
Arctic Power
Bio-Ad
Cashmere Bouquet
Chanteclerc
Colgate
Fleecy
Glide
HALO
Hill's
Irish Spring
Javex
Mix O Bleaches
Murphy Oil Soap
Nu-Fluff
Palmolive
Perfex
Science Diet
Scrub 'n Shine
Soft Soap
Stainaway
Sunbrite

problems for the surrounding South Riverdale community, is being phased out as part of the new company's "rationalization of operations for future growth."

Notable Facts

The company has many long-serving employees. Union representatives for the Aluminum, Brick and Glass Workers and for two Teamsters locals describe management-labour relations as reasonably positive. As the downtown Toronto plant is closed, the company is providing a training trust fund (co-funded by two levels of government as well) and job-search assistance. Because of the worldwide reorganization now underway, both corporate and union officials predict more than 200 jobs will be lost by 1993. The US-parent company has subsidiary operations in South Africa.

Corporate Foods Limited

CPF

10 Four Seasons Place, Etobicoke, ON M9B 6H7

Founded in Canada: 1969

Ownership: Maple Leaf Foods Inc. (Canada), 67%

Operations: BC*, ON*, NB*, NS*, NF*

Employees: 1,000

Annual sales: $211 million

Corporate Foods is a major Canadian manufacturer of bread and bakery products, with bakeries or plants in 11 locations across five provinces. Founded in 1911 as the Canada Bread Co., it has acquired a number of high-profile subsidiaries over the years, such as Dempster's (1960), Eastern Bakeries (1989), Olivieri Foods Ltd. (1988) and Central Bakery of Toronto Ltd. (1989). It also owns a 25% interest in Multi-Marque Inc., one of Quebec's leading bakeries. All the company's brands are regional; Dempster's bread owns more than a 25% share of the Ontario market.

Making the Grade

WOMEN'S ISSUES: Corporate Foods received a comparatively good score in this area, owing to its formal employment equity program, daycare referral and extended maternity leave. It has two women on its nine-member board, but gave no data about the number of women in management or senior management.

CHARITABLE GIVING AND COMMUNITY INVOLVEMENT:
The company is not part of the Imagine campaign and did not disclose the size of its charitable contributions. However, it provides paid time off for employee volunteer activities, which are publicized in the company newsletter, and it supports arts and cultural causes and provides a mascot for community events. The company has contributed to such sporting events as the Dempsters Fitness Team Display at Ontario Place and the Vancouver Sun Run.

PROGRESSIVE STAFF POLICIES: Corporate Foods received its highest rating in this category. It has an employee assistance program for alcohol and drug abuse, a stop-smoking program, fitness club subsidies, an employee newsletter, rewards for cost-saving ideas and open-door management. In addition, it offers training programs, retirement counselling and parental leave benefits.

BRAND NAMES
Arnold
Bamby
Bon Matin
Brownberry
Butternut
Dempster's
Diana
Durivage
Fun Buns
Gailuron
Grain's
Hollywood
Holsum
Karnes
Olivieri
Pride of Montreal
Sunmaid
Sunny Bee
Sunshine
Toastmaster

LABOUR RELATIONS: The company has a formal job security policy and uses retraining, relocation, early retirement, advance notice of technological change and financial compensation to address the effects of downsizing.

ENVIRONMENTAL MANAGEMENT: Corporate Foods has a written environmental policy, and three staff with environmental responsibilities.

ENVIRONMENTAL PERFORMANCE: The company has no environmental court convictions or instances of exceeding discharge limits. The firm prints its annual report on recycled paper and uses other recycled materials whenever possible. It recycles paper, packaging materials and manufacturing by-products as well as 94% of the solid waste that it generates. It is phasing out disposable cutlery and dishes. The company contributes to OMMRI (Ontario Multi-Materials Recycling Inc.), which among other activities runs the province's Blue Box program. Corporate Foods has environmental education programs for workers and conducts technical research into environmental issues, such as packaging. It has redesigned truck schedules and routes to minimize mileage.

MANAGEMENT PRACTICES AND CONSUMER RELATIONS: Corporate Foods has a written code of ethics, but did not provide enough information for a score in this area.

Notable Facts

The company ceased its manufacturing operations in Toronto in 1989, which caused the partial closure of one facility. The company's unions include the Bakery, Confectionery & Tobacco Workers, and the Teamsters.

Cott Corporation

6525 Viscount Rd., Mississauga, ON L4V IH6

Founded in Canada: 1955, Laval, PQ

Ownership: the Pencer family (Canada), 40%

Operations: AB*, ON*, PQ*, NB*

Employees: 325

Annual sales: $130 million

Cott is becoming a major player in the soft drink market and attracting much attention on the stock market in the process. It exports product to the US and has four representatives working outside Canada. Despite minimal advertising, it fares remarkably well against big name brands.

Making the Grade

CANDOUR: Cott was very forthcoming, as shown in its high Candour Quotient. Most other grades were low, however, because of a lack of formal policies and programs.

WOMEN'S ISSUES: Although 30% of its workforce is female, Cott has no women in management or senior management or on its seven-man board of directors, and it has no formal initiatives for the advancement of women. The company comments that it is still quite young, and hopes to implement employment equity provisions in the near future.

CHARITABLE GIVING AND COMMUNITY INVOLVEMENT: The company is not on Imagine's list, but it donated $25,000, mostly in cash, to charity in 1990. It generally allows paid time off for employee volunteer activities and supports the arts, sports teams and health-related charities.

PROGRESSIVE STAFF POLICIES: Cott subsidizes a stop-smoking program, has an employee assistance program for drug and alcohol abuse and pays the tuition for job-related courses. Communication programs at Cott are few, but it does support a policy of open-door management and provides union bulletin boards. It hopes to set up annual written performance reviews for employees in the near future.

LABOUR RELATIONS: Cott offers employees a share option purchase plan. However, it has neither a formal job security program nor any methods for addressing layoffs, which accounts for its low score in this category.

BRAND NAMES
Allan Denis
Carignan
Cott
Diet Rite
Eau Naturelle
Elite
KIK
RC Cola

ENVIRONMENTAL MANAGEMENT: The company has no written environmental policy or employees with environmental functions, and makes no regular reports to the board.

ENVIRONMENTAL PERFORMANCE: On the other hand, it recycles paper, manufacturing by-products, metals, and packaging and it has upgraded equipment to use less energy and produce less waste. Plastic, reusable shells have replaced cardboard packaging. Cott has not been fined for environmental violations, but notes it does not expect to be able to comply with the Ontario Ministry of the Environment's requirement that 30% of monthly soft drink sales be in refillable containers. The company is working with Peel region to reduce and treat the effluent at its new Mississauga, Ont., plant. In 1991, it received an Award of Excellence for Best Performance by a company for Environmental Protection from the Laval, Que., Chamber of Commerce for its adoption of reusable containers. In addition, Cott supports Ontario's Blue Box recycling program, through OMMRI (Ontario Multi-Materials Recycling Inc.).

MANAGEMENT PRACTICES AND CONSUMER RELATIONS: The company has no written code of ethics, but also no Competition Act litigation on record.

Notable Facts

The company, which is 80% unionized, closed several plants in southern Ontario in 1989. Since that time, a canning and bottling plant has opened in Mississauga and a bottled water plant in Pembroke, both in Ontario. A Calgary bottling plant closed in 1991, but was replaced with another, larger one in that city. Cott has had one strike, which involved 100 employees in Laval, Que., in 1989.

Culinar Inc.

2 Complexe Desjardins, Suite 2700, Box 32, Desjardins Station, Montreal, PQ H5B 1B2

Founded in Canada: 1977, Montreal, PQ
Ownership: Investissement Desjardins (Canada), 55%
Operations: BC, AB, SK, MB, ON*, PQ*, NB, NS, PE, NF
Employees: 3,500 (Canada), 1,300 (US)
Annual sales: $471 million
Advertising expenditures: $3 million

Culinar Inc. is a large, Canadian-owned manufacturer of food products, including a range of baked goods, confectionery, dried bread products, soups and jams. Its cookie products group was founded in 1867 in Montreal under the name Viau, while the bakery products group began in 1923 in Sainte-Marie de Beauce, PQ, with the name Vachon. Various Culinar products own more than a 25% share of their markets, notably Vachon baked goods, Double Fruit jam, Grissol dry bread products and McCormicks' and Viau candies. Since 1986, the company has acquired several food companies, including Granny's Country-Oven Bakery, InterBake, Perfect Endings and Drake Bakeries. In addition to its six plants in Quebec and three in Ontario, the company has US operations in New Jersey and Pennsylvania, which account for 1,300 of its 4,800 employees. Products are imported from, and exported to, the USA.

Making the Grade

CANDOUR: Culinar's highest score was in this area.

WOMEN'S ISSUES: Women comprise 30% of the company's workforce. While Culinar has a formal employment equity program, only 10% of managers and 8% of senior managers are female. Women hold six of 25 positions on its board of directors. No daycare arrangements or extended maternity leave is offered.

CHARITABLE GIVING AND COMMU-NITY INVOLVEMENT: Here the company's score was above average for the *Guide*. Its charitable donations, both cash and product, amounted to al-

BRAND NAMES	
Bear Paws	Meteo
Canadiana	Normandie
Cellini	Old Homestead
Country Harvest	Paulins
Double Fruit	Perfect Endings
Drake's	Rusks
Gallo	Safflo
Granny's	Stuart's
Grenache	Swiss Rolls
Grissol	Tradition
Guest	Unico
1/2 Moon	Vachon
Jos. Louis	Caramel
Lido's	Flaky
Loney's	Viau
Maxi Fruits	Viva Puffs
May West	Wagon Wheels
McCormicks'	Whippet

most one-half of one percent in 1990. Its donation policy has two main emphases: hunger relief and the needs of children and teenagers. Culinar supports cultural events, health-related organizations, and encourages employee participation in host communities through matching gift programs and paid time off for volunteer activities.

PROGRESSIVE STAFF POLICIES: The company provides an employee newsletter, *Transmission*, adoption leave benefits, written annual performance reviews and a scholarship fund for employees' children. As well, it provides confidential counselling to employees and their immediate families for substance abuse, marital difficulties, emotional problems and job-related stresses.

LABOUR RELATIONS: Although without a formal job security policy, the company uses retraining, relocation, early retirement and advance notice of technological change to reduce the impact of layoffs.

ENVIRONMENTAL MANAGEMENT: The company does not have a written environmental policy and did not comment on other aspects of its environmental management.

ENVIRONMENTAL PERFORMANCE: Culinar recycles paper, cartons and corrugated boxes, sells defective products for animal consumption and purchases recycled products. It has no record of environmental court convictions or of exceeding emission guidelines in Canada.

MANAGEMENT PRACTICES AND CONSUMER RELATIONS: Culinar has no written code of ethics, but also no Competition Act convictions.

Notable Facts

Sixty-five percent of the company's employees are unionized. There have been two strikes in the last 10 years, in 1984 and 1989, and two layoffs — one in 1990, affecting 290 employees in Winnipeg, and the other in Montreal in 1991, with 256 employees involved.

Dare Foods Limited

2481 Kingsway Dr., PO Box 1058, Kitchener, ON N2G 4G4

Founded in Canada: 1892, Kitchener, ON
Ownership: C.H. Dare (Canada), 99.8%
Operations: ON*
Employees: 800

Dare Foods is a family-run, privately-held Canadian company.

Making the Grade

CANDOUR: Dare's low rating results from the fact that it chose not to participate in any way. Due to our limited information, scores on the tables are quite low or, in most instances, simply question marks. What little information we could collect on this very private company was, however, relatively positive.

PROGRESSIVE STAFF POLICIES: A union representative reported that Dare offers tuition reimbursement for job-related courses, has an employee assistance program for drug and alcohol abuse, runs an employee newsletter and maintains an open door to managers.

LABOUR RELATIONS: The same union person said the company has seniority recall rights, offers relocation when possible and in some cases provides financial compensation for loss of jobs.

ENVIRONMENTAL PERFORMANCE: Dare has an environmentally inspired product line (Harvest from the Rainforest cookies), uses recycled paper for its letterhead and has had no environmental court convictions nor did it exceed discharge limits. It hopes in future to buy the Brazil nuts and cashews for its Harvest from the Rainforest cookies directly from a new rainforest processing facility. Until the facility can guarantee quality and quantity production standards, Dare is purchasing the nuts for the cookies on the open market — and donating money to Boston-based Cultural Survival, a non-profit group committed to helping aboriginal cultures survive and prosper.

Notable Facts

Approximately 450 of the company's 800 employees are unionized, most of them at the Kitchener, Ont., cookie plant. The union concerned, the Bakery, Confectionery and Tobacco Workers Union (BCTWU), says the company closed a Hamilton candy plant in 1991, relocating about a dozen of the 110 affected workers to the Toronto plant.

BRAND NAMES
Breton
Dare

Despite the plant closure, employment with the company has risen steadily: positions at the cookie plant, for example, have doubled in the last 10 years. The corporate culture is family-oriented, and the union says working conditions are good.

Dial of Canada

Dial Tower, 1850 Central Ave., Phoenix, Arizona, USA, 85077

Founded in Canada: no offices (as of July, 1992)
Ownership: The Dial Corp (US), 100%
Operations: none
Employees: none

Dial of Canada, a division of The Dial Corp, operates from the parent company's head office in Arizona. Dial is a new entrant to the Canadian market, selling its products through distributors rather than Canadian offices. Dial Corp (which changed its name from Greyhound Dial in 1991) is a leading US manufacturer of personal care and laundry products. It also owns Greyhound transportation services and a major ski resort near Banff, Alta.

Making the Grade

Dial has no direct Canadian operations and therefore no staff policies, labour relations or environmental practices in this country. The company provided no information about its charitable giving and community involvement here.

The parent company appointed an environmental officer in 1990, and is doing research and development in the areas of pollution reduction, packaging and employee awareness of environmental concerns. Quarterly reports are printed on recycled paper.

Notable Facts

Dial Corp ended all in-house animal testing six or seven years ago, and all related subcontracting shortly thereafter. The corporation is not involved in South Africa.

BRAND NAMES

Borateem
Borax
Breck
Brillo
Dial
Pure & Natural
Tone

Dover Industries Limited

4350 Harvester Rd., PO Box 10, Burlington, ON L7R 3X8

Founded In Canada: 1940, Hamilton, ON

Ownership: Mrs. K.L. Campbell (Canada), 50.4%

Operations: ON*, NS*

Employees: 600

Annual sales: $106.2 million

Dover Industries' flour products are well known in Canada and each of its Robinson ice cream cone products owns a better than 25% share of its market. Although the majority of Dover's shares are family-owned, it is a publicly-traded company. In addition to manufacturing facilities in Ontario and Nova Scotia, the company operates several corn and soy bean mills. Dover exports products to the United States and Asia.

Making the Grade

CANDOUR: Dover received a low rating because it gave us very little information about policies and procedures in any category, although it did answer some basic questions about ownership, sales and number of employees.

WOMEN'S ISSUES: Dover has one woman (the majority owner) on its 12-member board of directors.

CHARITABLE GIVING AND COMMUNITY INVOLVEMENT: The company has not pledged to the Imagine campaign for charitable giving.

LABOUR RELATIONS: Dover's annual report states, without elaboration, that the company has training programs in place.

ENVIRONMENTAL MANAGEMENT/PRACTICES: Dover manufactures disposable plastic and paper products and frozen food packaging, and it has no written environmental policy.

MANAGEMENT PRACTICES AND CONSUMER RELATIONS: A Dover representative said that the company is in the process of developing a code of ethics. Dover was one of several millers charged under the Competition Act in 1990 with bid rigging and conspiring to lessen competition on wheat sales to the federal government from 1975 to 1987. In a subsequent settlement, the company paid a $100,000 fine.

BRAND NAMES
Carousel
Dover
Hi-Fibre
Robinson
Swan's Down

Notable Facts

Dover has relationships with a number of unions, including the Retail, Wholesale and Department Store union, which represents workers at the Robinson Cone division and has dealt with the company for 20 years. There have been no strikes or lockouts in the last 10 years. Management is hired locally and promoted internally. Changes in a large contract resulted in the loss of a number of Burlington plant jobs, which have dropped from a high of 130 to 85.

DowBrands Canada Inc.

326 Grand River St. N., Paris, ON N3L 3T7

Founded in Canada: 1985, Paris, ON
Ownership: Dow Chemical Canada Inc. (Canada), 100%
Operations: BC, ON*, PQ*
Employees: 114

The company was born in a 1985 merger between Dow Consumer Products in the US and a small Canadian cleaning company, Texize Canada. Today, DowBrands operates as a consumer products company with its own board of directors and operating policies. The company, which manufactures household cleaning products and food wraps, has plants in Paris, Ont., and Varennes, Que.

Making the Grade

CANDOUR: DowBrands was very cooperative, as reflected in its Candour Quotient.

WOMEN'S ISSUES: The company earned a position on the Honour Roll for its comparatively high score in this category. Women constitute 44% of the workforce, hold 27% of management and 20% of senior management positions and one place (of five) on the board of directors. The company provides extended maternity leave, but has no employment equity provision, daycare or daycare referral service.

CHARITABLE GIVING AND COMMUNITY INVOLVEMENT: DowBrands is involved with its communities in a number of ways that include a university matching gift program and support for sports teams and arts and health organizations. The company, not part of the Imagine campaign, donated $21,000 to charity in 1990.

PROGRESSIVE STAFF POLICIES: This was DowBrands' highest rating, placing it on this Honour Roll as well. Its employee assistance program provides counselling for substance abuse, emotional problems and family difficulties. The company offers health education to all employees, plus a fitness club subsidy and a stop-smoking program. Other programs include employee newsletters, suggestion programs, an annual performance review, relocation assistance, scholarship funds for employees and their children and job-search assistance for employees' spouses.

BRAND NAMES
Baggies
Dow
Fantastik
Glass Plus
Handi Wrap
Saran Wrap
Spray 'N Starch
Spray 'N Wash
Stretch 'N Seal
Ziploc

LABOUR RELATIONS: The lack of a formal job security program or method of addressing layoffs accounts for the company's lower score in this area. The company says that it has no need for a formal program, as it has had no layoffs in its seven-year history. A stock option plan is open to all employees; health and safety and training data was provided.

ENVIRONMENTAL MANAGEMENT: The company has a written environmental policy, and makes environmental reports to the board as needed. Three employees have part-time environmental responsibilities. DowBrands has no environmental committee.

ENVIRONMENTAL PERFORMANCE: On this Honour Roll as well, Dowbrands conducts comprehensive environmental audits of all operations, uses recycled paper products in its offices and recycles paper products, plastics by-products, corrugated cardboard and wrapping materials. None of its aerosol products contain CFCs or methyl chloroform. The company has set up an internal pilot project to study the use of recycled plastic and all its packaging is printed entirely with vegetable inks. Its Varennes, Que., plant once exceeded wastewater discharge limits but the problem has been rectified. The company has no record of environmental court cases.

MANAGEMENT PRACTICES AND CONSUMER RELATIONS: DowBrands has a written code of ethics, dated 1991, with an annual sign-off for all management and supervisors. There have been no Competition Act violations.

Notable Facts

This non-unionized company has had no layoffs since its founding seven years ago. As of May 1992, it had had four years of operations with only one lost-time injury. The parent company, Dow Chemical Canada, has been fined a total of $104,000 for numerous environmental violations in the past ten years.

Drackett Canada

111 Gordon Baker Dr., Suite 700, Toronto, ON M2H 3R1

Founding Date In Canada: 1967, Toronto, ON
Ownership: Bristol-Myers Squibb Co. (New York), 100%
Operations: ON
Employees: 31
Toll-free number: 800-267-1448

Drackett Canada is a low-profile company with some big names, such as Drano and Windex, in household cleaning supplies. The company sold all its Laval, PQ, Toronto, Winnipeg, Edmonton and Delta, BC, warehouses and plants to Colgate Palmolive (p. 138) in April, 1990. With no plants in Canada, Drackett now serves this market with a mix of imported goods and contract production from other suppliers. This wholly-owned subsidiary reports to Drackett US, which is the household care products operating unit of Bristol-Myers Squibb.

Making the Grade

CANDOUR: The company did not participate beyond verifying brand names, although spokespersons from the United States provided some help in the final stage of the process.

CHARITABLE GIVING AND COMMUNITY INVOLVEMENT: Drackett contributes to charities and the United Way. Although Drackett Canada is not on Imagine's list, Bristol-Myers Squibb Co. is pledged to the Imagine campaign and contributes to the Alliance for a Drug-Free Canada.

ENVIRONMENTAL MANAGEMENT/PERFORMANCE: The US parent-company provides an environmental policy for all operations, worldwide. It has a vice-president of environmental affairs and occupational health and safety, and has produced several, comprehensive environmental reports.

Notable Facts

This company has no direct links with South Africa although the parent company, Bristol-Myers Squibb Co., does have subsidiary operations there.

The parent states that 99% of all its animal tests are for pharmaceutical and health care products, not household cleaning formulas. Drackett and its sister company, Bristol-Myers Squibb Consumers Products Group (Canada) (see p. 111), do no animal testing in Canada, either directly or through other contractors.

BRAND NAMES
Behold
Drano
Endust
Mr. Muscle
Renuzit
Twinkle
Vanish
Windex

E.D. Smith and Sons, Limited

944 Highway #8, Winona, ON L0R 2L0

Founded in Canada: 1882, Winona, ON
Ownership: the Smith family (Canada)
Operations: ON*
Employees: 200

E.D. Smith and Sons is a small, private Canadian company. For four generations it has produced a range of jams, jellies, pie filling and sauces. The company has employed as many as 425 seasonal and full-time employees during tomato processing season.

Making the Grade

CANDOUR: E.D. Smith chose not to participate in our research and therefore received a low Candour Quotient.

CHARITABLE GIVING AND COMMUNITY INVOLVEMENT: The firm supports sports teams and participates in Niagara Region programs, notably the Winona Peach Festival.

PROGRESSIVE STAFF POLICIES: The company offers training programs and subsidies for external training in safety and skills development. It also encourages workers to spend time in teams working out cost-saving ideas. If the ideas are implemented, the workers may be rewarded.

ENVIRONMENTAL PERFORMANCE: E.D. Smith has no record of exceeding discharge limits and has not been charged with any environmental violations.

Notable Facts

The company's employees are not unionized. The company produces Laura Secord jam under licence for Nestlé Canada Inc. (see p. 219).

BRAND NAMES
E.D. Smith
Habitant (jam)
HP Sauce
Lea & Perrins
Lite 'n Fruity
Staffords
Sun-Ripe

Effem Foods Ltd.

37 Holland Dr., Bolton, ON L7E 5S4

Founded in Canada: 1948, Montreal, PQ
Ownership: Mars Inc. (US), 100%
Operations: ON*
Toll-free number: 800-268-0571

The parent company, Mars Inc. of McLean, Virginia, is a family-owned, private enterprise. Effem Foods has a significant market presence in the rice, candy and chocolate markets, as well as in the pet food industry.

Making the Grade

CANDOUR: Originally the company did not respond to our surveys, other than to provide copies of pamphlets normally available to the public. It subsequently provided some additional information.

WOMEN'S ISSUES: Effem Foods did not provide figures on employment of women. However, it has formal employment equity, affirmative action and minority hiring programs and offers extended maternity leave.

CHARITABLE GIVING AND COMMUNITY INVOLVEMENT: The company is not on Imagine's Caring Company list.

BRAND NAMES
3 Musketeers
Bounty
Exquisine
Kal Kan
M & M's
Maltesers
Mars
Meal Makers
Pedigree
Sheba
Skittles
Snickers
Starburst
Stuff 'n Such
Twix
Uncle Ben's
Whiskas

PROGRESSIVE STAFF POLICIES: Effem Foods has a strong set of policies, which include a formal employee assistance program, a stop-smoking program, retirement counselling, adoption leave and annual written performance reviews for all employees.

ENVIRONMENTAL MANAGEMENT: The company has a written environmental policy, which is not publicly released, and an environmental working committee.

ENVIRONMENTAL PERFORMANCE: Effem Foods recycles paper, glass and pop cans and has made an effort to replace disposable cutlery and dishes in its offices. It has no record of environmental violations.

MANAGEMENT PRACTICES AND CONSUMER RELATIONS: The company has a set of five operating principles which, an official said, it "treats as the Ten Commandments." The principles, written in 1981, do not require an annual sign-off. The company has no record of any Competition Act violations.

Notable Facts

There is no history of layoffs associated with the company. Effem has opened two plants in Ontario in the last six years: a pet food canning facility in Bolton in 1986, and a confectionery plant in Newmarket in 1988.

Everfresh Canada

1030 Walker Rd., PO Box 2230, Windsor, ON N8Y 2N5

Founded in Canada: 1959, Windsor, ON
Ownership: Everfresh Beverages Inc. (US) 100%
Operations: BC, AB, SK, MB, ON*, PQ, NB, NS, NF
Employees: 287
Annual sales: $100 million

The company, founded under the name Holiday Juice Limited, was acquired by John Labatt Limited in 1983 and sold early in 1992 to a newly-formed, US-based company. The company's sparkling mineral water and fruit juice beverage enjoys substantial market share. The US operations consist of two plants, one near Detroit and one in Chicago, both of which produce carbonated fruit beverages.

Making the Grade

CANDOUR: Everfresh was quite responsive to our surveys. However, its overall shortage of formal programs and policies produced low ratings in most other areas.

WOMENS' ISSUES: In this area, though, it had above-average results. Its workforce is roughly 45% female, and women occupy 30% of management and 20% of senior management positions. One woman sits on the seven-member board. Furthermore, Everfresh has an employment equity program.

CHARITABLE GIVING AND COMMUNITY INVOLVEMENT: The company is not on Imagine's Caring Company list and did not supply the amount of its charitable donations. Product donations and involvement in local sporting activities are ways in which the company supports its communities.

PROGRESSIVE STAFF POLICIES: The company offers a stop-smoking program, rewards for cost-saving ideas and annual written performance reviews for all employees.

LABOUR RELATIONS: Everfresh has no formal job security program or methods of addressing layoffs. It did give us training data and health and safety figures.

ENVIRONMENTAL MANAGEMENT: Everfresh has no written environmental policy and one employee with part-time environmental responsibilities.

BRAND NAMES
Cool Down
Everfresh
Mr. Citrus

ENVIRONMENTAL PERFORMANCE: The company conducts partial environmental audits and has invested in such things as product and packaging reformulation and equipment replacement. Everfresh has not been charged with any environmental violations.

MANAGEMENT PRACTICES AND CONSUMER RELATIONS: Though Everfresh has no written code of ethics, its policies and procedures manual does discuss responsible business practices. The company has not been charged with any Competition Act or consumer law violations.

Notable Facts

Everfresh is about 60% unionized, represented by the Teamsters and the Retail, Wholesale and Department Store union. The company has had a few layoffs, affecting four employees at its Windsor, Ont., plant in 1990 and one in Toronto in 1991. Since 1986, employment at Everfresh in Canada has decreased from about 308 to 287.

Fishery Products International Limited

70 O'Leary Ave., PO Box 550, St. John's, NF AIC 5LI

Founded in Canada: 1984, St. John's, NF

Ownership: widely held (largest shareholder is Bank of Nova Scotia, 8%)

Operations: BC, ON, PQ, NF*

Employees: 6,400

Annual sales: $500 million

Fishery Products International (FPI), formed through the integration of eight Newfoundland seafood companies, is the primary private sector employer in most of the 13 communities in which it has operations. In fact, FPI accounts for about 20% of all employment in that province. The company owns two subsidiaries: International Fish Protein Limited (60%) and Clouston Foods Canada Limited (100%). FPI exports products to Japan, the US, Britain, Germany, Switzerland and Sweden.

Making the Grade

CANDOUR: FPI received a low rating, only supplying enough information in one category (Labour Relations) to make a ranking possible.

WOMEN'S ISSUES: All we know is that women make up an estimated 40% of the workforce and that three of the 16 company directors are female.

PROGRESSIVE STAFF POLICIES: The company has an employee assistance program available to both employees and their immediate families. It also offers a quarterly internal news magazine, *Soundings*, and in 1989 won a federal government award for excellence for its emphasis on internal communications.

LABOUR RELATIONS: FPI has two gain sharing plans: a company-wide payroll deduction profit sharing plan for which the company pays all fees and contributes 10% of the share purchase price, and a stock option purchase plan for senior officers. While FPI did not provide detailed health and safety data, a company spokesperson said that new safety training programs and an emphasis on safer working practices resulted in a 55% decrease in accidents between January, 1986 and December, 1991.

ENVIRONMENTAL PERFORMANCE: FPI prints its annual report on recycled paper. The Nova Scotia Department of

BRAND NAMES
Blazin' Redfish
Catch O' the Day
Mirabel
Newfoundland Imperial Cod
Sea Nuggets
Sea Strips
Sea Treasures
Seafood Elites

Fisheries has said that FPI met all environmental standards in 1988.

Notable Facts

Blaming quota restrictions, FPI has closed plants in Galtois, Grand Banks and Trepassey, Nfld., in the last few years, laying off 1,200 workers. (Two of the plants reopened under new operator/ownership.) The company and the government of Newfoundland provided up to $11.1 million over two years to fund advance notice of permanent layoffs. The number of FPI trawlers has dropped from 55 to 38. Even so, production overcapacity is still a problem. The company says it only used roughly 45% of its capacity between 1989 and 1991 and that even with the recent operational cuts, it will still be running at 50% - 55% capacity.

FPI works with several unions, including the United Food and Commercial Workers and the Fishermen's, Food and Allied Workers. There have been several strikes in the last 10 years, primarily over wages. A 1984-85 strike that involved 790 workers caused the loss of over 83,000 person-days worked, and a 1989 strike affected more than 4,000 workers.

Gainers Inc.

12425-66 Street, PO Box 100, Edmonton, AB T5J 2H8

Founded in Canada: 1891, Edmonton, AB

Ownership: Government of Alberta (Canada), 100%

Operations: BC, AB*, SK*, MB, ON*, NS, NF

Employees: 2,500

Annual sales: $468 million

The company was taken over by the Alberta Government after owner Peter Pocklington reportedly defaulted on a government loan. This meat processor was founded in 1891 as Gainer and Co., and today its product lines include Magic Pantry Foods and Superior, Kretchmar and Swift processed meats. It exports Canadian-made products to the US, Japan, Australia and Mexico.

Making the Grade

CANDOUR: Gainers was moderately forthcoming.

WOMEN'S ISSUES: Forty percent of the company's workforce is female but only 20% of management and 1% of senior management positions are occupied by women. There is no board of directors. While the company has a formal employment equity program, it has no extended maternity leave or daycare provisions.

CHARITABLE GIVING AND COMMUNITY INVOLVEMENT: Though not pledged to the Imagine campaign, Gainers donated $53,000, more than half in kind, to charitable organizations in 1990. It did not disclose the value of these donations as a percentage of pre-tax earnings. Gainers' community involvement includes paid and unpaid time off for employee volunteer activity, publicity for these activities in the company newsletter and support for local sports teams, cultural events and health causes.

PROGRESSIVE STAFF POLICIES: The company's highest rating came in this area. It provides drug and alcohol abuse counselling, an employee newsletter, rewards for cost-saving ideas, a policy of open-door management, adoption leave benefits and annual written performance reviews for all salaried employees.

ENVIRONMENTAL MANAGEMENT: Although a written environmental policy exists, Gainers has no environmental committee, no employees with environmental functions and issues no environmental reports.

BRAND NAMES
Kretchmar
Magic Pantry
Sensible
Superior
Swift

ENVIRONMENTAL PERFORMANCE: Gainers does not conduct environmental audits. Its principal environmental programs are paper recycling, an effort to replace disposable dishes and cutlery and the funding of local environment groups. The company has no record of environmental fines or exceeding waste emission guidelines.

MANAGEMENT PRACTICES AND CONSUMER RELATIONS: The company has a written code of ethics, but no ethics advisory or ombudsman. In 1981, prior to the Alberta Government's takeover, the company was one of several Alberta meat companies fined (in its case, $125,000) for fixing the price of hogs. A dispute with the United Food and Commercial Workers union, finally settled late in 1991, began in 1986 over actions concerning pension benefits taken by then-owner Peter Pocklington during a strike in that year.

Notable Facts

In addition to an employment equity program, Gainers has specific hiring policies for minorities, persons with disabilities and Native peoples. Eighty-five percent of its employees are represented by the United Food and Commercial Workers, and there have been no strikes since the Alberta Government took control of Gainers.

Gaines Pet Foods Corp.

GPFC

711 Ontario St., Cobourg, ON K9A 4L3

Founded in Canada: 1946, Cobourg, ON
Ownership: Shato Holdings Ltd. (Canada), 100%
Operations: ON*
Employees: 125 (est.)

Gaines Pet Foods came to Canada in 1946, when General Foods (see p. 195) built its new plant in Cobourg, Ont. General Foods sold the facility to Shato Holdings, a private company owned by West Coast entrepreneur Peter Toigo. The company uses its proprietary technology to manufacture and market its own dog and cat foods, as well as to produce private label products for export to the US, Britain, France and Germany.

Making the Grade

CANDOUR: There was little participation by management in our research but extensive input from the United Food and Commercial Workers union (UFCW), which represents 72% of Gaines' employees.

CHARITABLE GIVING AND COMMUNITY INVOLVEMENT: The company is not on Imagine's list of Caring Companies. The company sponsors a community baseball team, the Gaines Doggers.

ENVIRONMENTAL MANAGEMENT/PERFORMANCE: Gaines does not have a written environmental policy or committee of the board. Soft drink cans are recycled and employees are asked to provide their own mugs to eliminate the use of foam cups. The company has no record of environmental violations.

Notable Facts

Although there have been no strikes or lockouts over the past ten years, a UFCW spokesperson describes a "strained relationship" between the union and management, and says that the company "is threatening to close the plant down if wage reduction demands aren't met."

BRAND NAMES
Cat's Choice
Gaines
Gainesburgers
Master
Me & My Cat
Nuggets & Nibbles
Top Choice

Gay Lea Foods Co-Operative Limited

100 Clayson Rd., Weston, ON M9M 2G7

Founded in Canada: 1958, Weston, ON
Ownership: co-operative (all shares owned by members)
Operations: ON*
Employees: 438
Annual sales: $145 million

Gay Lea is a co-operative, owned by its 3,700 dairy farming members and employees. It has five plants in Ontario (Teeswater, Ottawa, Guelph, Weston and Baden). The co-op provides dairy farmers with a return on investment, a voice in the fluid milk, cheese and yogurt business, and practical information on enhancing operations.

Making the Grade

CANDOUR: The company was very responsive and received a high rating.

WOMEN'S ISSUES: The company's poor rating reflects the fact that, with a workforce that is 14% female, it has almost no women in management (3%) and none in senior management positions or on its nine-man board of directors. There are no formal gender-specific programs or policies.

CHARITABLE GIVING AND COMMUNITY INVOLVEMENT: The company is not on Imagine's list, but did donate $30,000 to charity in 1990, $3,000 of it in cash. It lends equipment and facilities to community organizations and publicizes its employees' volunteer activity in its newsletter, the *Rainbow Gazette*.

PROGRESSIVE STAFF POLICIES: Gay Lea funds an externally provided, once-a-month counselling service for employees with substance abuse problems. Its communications activities include annual written performance reviews for all employees, a newsletter and a policy of open-door management.

LABOUR RELATIONS: Gay Lea has no formal job security program or methods of addressing layoffs, and no gain sharing programs. However, the company did provide 1989 and 1990 health and safety statistics, as well as the figure for dollars spent on training per employee.

ENVIRONMENTAL MANAGEMENT: The company received no marks, since it has no written code, employees with environmental functions or environmental committee.

BRAND NAMES
Gay Lea
Nordica
Oxford Farms

ENVIRONMENTAL PERFORMANCE: The low score here partly reflects the fact that Gay Lea conducts no environmental audit. However, the company has invested an average of $108,000 a year for the last three years to reduce effluent from its plants and replace equipment. It also has an in-office paper recycling program, and prints its annual report on recycled paper. While the company has not been fined for any environmental violations, its Teeswater, Ont., plant exceeded provincial wastewater discharge limits from 1985 to 1988. Recently released 1989 figures show the plant had by then improved its performance and was 92% in compliance with guidelines.

MANAGEMENT PRACTICES AND CONSUMER RELATIONS: The company has no written code of responsible business practices, ethics advisory, social practices report, or toll-free number. On the other hand, it has not been charged with any Competition Act violations.

Notable Facts

Gay Lea has no exports or operations outside Canada. Plant consolidation and the closing of the Woodstock, Ont., cheese cutting operation means that employment has decreased slightly from its 1986 figures of 445, despite the acquisition of the Uniondale Cheese Factory and Longlife Canada in 1989. Fourteen percent of the company's workforce is unionized, and there have been no strikes or lockouts in the past ten years.

General Mills Canada Inc.

1330 Martin Grove Rd., Etobicoke, ON M9W 4X4

Founded in Canada: 1954, Toronto, ON
Ownership: General Mills Inc. (US), 100%
Operations: BC, AB, ON*, PQ, NS
Employees: 350
Annual sales: $200 million

General Mills is probably best known for its cereals, such as Cheerios. However, Betty Crocker, a well-known line of baking mixes, is a central part of General Mills' operations and its Blue Water seafood line has a 25% market share. The company is also the owner of Red Lobster and Olive Garden restaurants (not reported on here). Its one plant, in Etobicoke, Ont., exports product to the US, Holland and Saudi Arabia.

Making the Grade

CANDOUR: General Mills participated in our research process and received an above-average rating.

WOMEN'S ISSUES: While the company's workforce is only 37% female, 50% of its management positions are occupied by women. However, there are no women at the vice-presidential level or higher. While it has no formal employment equity program, the parent company issues a worldwide equal opportunities statement, which is part of employee handbooks and management policy books. There is no provision for extended maternity leave and no daycare service.

CHARITABLE GIVING AND COMMUNITY INVOLVEMENT: General Mills is not pledged to the Imagine Campaign, but reports it donated $75,000 in cash to charity in 1990 and made in-kind donations as well. It provides paid time off to employees who volunteer as teachers for the Junior Achievement organization, runs a matching gift program for the United Way, funds educational materials for various Canadian universities and has corporate positions on the boards of several employer associations and hospitals.

PROGRESSIVE STAFF POLICIES: The company received high marks in this category. It provides an employee assistance program (externally supplied on a case-by-case

BRAND NAMES
Beary Pals
Betty Crocker
Bisquick
Blue Water
Bugles
Cheerios
Cinnamon Toast Crunch
Cocoa Puffs
Count Chocula
Crispy Wheats 'n Raisins
Dinosaur Pals
Fruit Roll-Ups
Garfield
Golden Grahams
Hamburger Helper
Lucky Charms
Nature Valley
Oatmeal Raisin Crisp
Pac-Man
Pop-Secret
Pro*Stars
Shark Bites
Thunder Jets
Trix
Tuna Helper

basis), a health newsletter, bonuses for safety suggestions and open-door management. *Sweet Talker*, the thrice-yearly newsletter, publishes financial information, the results of audits and new product information, among other things. The company also holds small group meetings and management seminars, and provides public notice boards and annual written performance reviews.

LABOUR RELATIONS: General Mills has no formal job security program or methods of addressing layoffs. However, it offers an employee stock option program and pays the brokerage fee for participating employees.

ENVIRONMENTAL MANAGEMENT: The company has a written environmental policy and a waste management policy. It is currently working on a formal recycling policy and on emergency response measures. The company's senior environmental official is a technical services manager. Its environmental committee includes members from head office and the manufacturing and purchasing departments.

ENVIRONMENTAL PERFORMANCE: While the company doesn't yet conduct environmental audits, it is planning one for its head office and manufacturing plant. Recycling programs cover manufacturing by-products, packaging, metals and wooden pallets. The company has changed equipment and reformatted packaging in order to reduce the amount of packaging used, and now has lighter packaging than its US parent. The company has had no environmental fines or charges, and notes that its only effluent is cooling water.

MANAGEMENT PRACTICES AND CONSUMER RELATIONS: General Mills has a worldwide statement of corporate values, which it reinforces with periodic articles on ethical issues in its newsletter (such as conflict of interest guidelines). It has not been charged or fined in connection with any Competition Act violations. Its parent company issues a worldwide social practices report.

Notable Facts

The company sold its Lancia-Bravo facility, one of its two Canadian plants, to Borden Catelli Consumer Products (see p. 109) late in 1990. Cake mix production at the Etobicoke plant is being transferred to Toledo, Ohio, and the union is concerned about the future of the cereals line. A union spokesperson for the American Federation of Grain Millers, which represents all 150 plant workers, says that General Mills is a "good employer," although frequent changes in management since 1986 have caused some problems.

George Weston Limited

22 St. Clair Ave. E., Toronto, ON M4T 2S7

Founded in Canada: 1882, Toronto, ON

Ownership: W. Galen Weston (Canada), 60%

Operations: BC*, SK*, MB*, ON*, PQ*, NB*, NS*

Employees: 14,500 (Weston Foods and Fisheries only)

Annual sales: $10.9 billion (includes Loblaw Companies)

George Weston's is the country's largest Canadian-owned food company. It operates in three main sectors: food processing, food distribution and resource operations. Weston Foods, its food processing division (the subject of this profile), include companies like Weston Bakeries Limited, William Neilson Ltd., Watt & Scott and Rose & Laflamme. In 1987, Neilson acquired the Cadbury confectionery division from Cadbury Schweppes Plc (see p. 117) and now owns seven of Canada's top 25 chocolate bars and holds more than a 30% market share in the confectionery industry.

Weston Resources consists of E.B. Eddy Forest Products (not profiled) and two fisheries operations, Connors Bros. Ltd. and British Columbia Packers Limited. Connors, which operates on the east coast, is the sole producer of canned sardines in Canada and sells 70% of its product outside the country. BC Packers (see p. 113) operates tuna and salmon facilities on the west coast.

George Weston Limited has 13 bakeries, two flour mills, five fish processing plants, five dairy/confectionery plants and five forest product mills in Canada. It also owns dozens of grocery stores across the country under its Loblaw Companies operations (not profiled). Eighty percent of George Weston's sales are in Canada and the other 20% in the US, where it operates 14 bakeries, six fish plants, and one forest products mill.

Making the Grade

CANDOUR: George Weston Limited chose not to respond to our surveys. When its various operating companies were approached, only BC Packers responded to all surveys, while Weston

BRAND NAMES	
Brunswick	Holmes
Burnt Almond	Home Pride
Cadbury's	Hostess (cakes only)
Caramilk	Jersey Milk
Cerises	Malted Milk
Coconut	McNair
Connaisseur	Mr. Big
Connors Brothers	Neilson
Country Harvest	Pep
Cream Eggs	Port Clyde
Crispy Crunch	Rose & Laflamme
Crunchie	Rosebuds
Dairy Milk	Rum and Butter
Danone	Snack Bar
Deli World	Stonehouse Farms
Dietrich's	Sweet Marie
Ellenzweig	Tradition
Fibre Goodness	Virginia
Fruit and Nut	Wasco
Gold	Weston's
Hazelnut	Wonder
Heritage	Wunderbar

Bakeries provided information for the product survey.

WOMEN'S ISSUES: One of the 15 members of George Weston's board of directors is a woman.

CHARITABLE GIVING AND COMMUNITY INVOLVEMENT: George Weston and its subsidiaries are committed to the Imagine campaign goal of contributing 1% of pre-tax profits to charity. The company and its operating units make their donations independently. The Garfield Weston Foundation gave $1 million to the University of Guelph to set up a chair in food packaging technology. The list of other major Foundation recipients includes hospitals, environmental causes (Nature Conservancy), universities (McGill, Acadia) and food banks.

LABOUR RELATIONS: When Neilson sold its ice cream division to Ault Foods (see p. 103), it set up a re-employment centre to help laid-off workers find jobs. It also offered a hiring incentive of $1,000 to any company that hired one of its laid-off workers for a period of at least three months.

ENVIRONMENTAL MANAGEMENT: The company has a written environmental policy and a corporate code of conduct (1986) which applies to all George Weston companies. The companies are otherwise responsible for their own operating policies and decisions. Most operating companies have a senior environmental person on staff, often with multiple responsibilities (such as health and safety and environment). Weston Foods reports that progress is being made in the areas of "effluent limitations, solid waste reduction, spill procedures, hazardous waste management, air emissions controls and pollution abatement." Neilson/Cadbury has reduced its solid waste to landfills by 57% over the past few years. An environmental audit resulted in the 1990 presentation to the board of directors of an impact statement covering all of George Weston's operations, along with a plan for continuous upgrading. The BC Packers subsidiary and an EB Eddy pulp mill (since sold) have both received notices in the past five years for having effluent levels above emission guidelines.

Notable Facts

The company has sold or changed the product line at several plants in the past five years, including three Neilson operations in Ontario. The Neilson layoffs, in Toronto, Oshawa and Whitby, affected more than 300 employees. Technological upgrading caused Weston Bakeries' Montreal plant to lay off 250 workers in 1991. It then offered an in-house literacy course, as needed, to ensure that the remaining workers could read and write well enough to operate the new high-tech machinery. Connors Brothers closed its sardine cannery on Campobello Island, NB. George Weston has no involvement in South Africa, but cannot guarantee that none of its companies import products from that country.

Gerber (Canada) Inc.

56 Brockport Dr., Etobicoke, ON M9W 5N1

Founded in Canada: 1933, Toronto, ON
Ownership: Gerber Products Co. (US), 100%
Operations: ON
Employees: 40
Toll-free number: 800-443-7237

In 1990, the company moved its baby food production from Niagara Falls, Ont., to the US. One hundred and forty jobs, 120 in Niagara Falls and 20 in Toronto, were lost. It now has only marketing, distribution and sales offices in Canada. The company continues to be a major presence in the baby food, baby care and infant safety products markets.

Making the Grade

CANDOUR: Since the company chose to limit its participation in the research process and there are no production jobs in Canada, Gerber received a low Candour Quotient and all other categories bear a question mark or N/A (Not Applicable).

CHARITABLE GIVING AND COMMUNITY INVOLVEMENT: Gerber is not part of the Imagine campaign, and did not comment on its community involvement.

ENVIRONMENTAL PERFORMANCE: There were no environmental violations on record for the company during the time it had a manufacturing presence in Canada.

MANAGEMENT PRACTICES AND CONSUMER RELATIONS: The company offers baby-raising advice on its 24-hour, seven days a week, toll-free help line. As well, the company states, it was the first in Canada to print a "best before" or optimal use date on its baby foods.

Notable Facts

There was a month-long strike at the Niagara Falls plant in 1987. The parent company maintains a licensing agreement for the manufacture and sale of baby food with a South African company, Reckitt & Coleman South Africa (Pty.) Ltd.

BRAND NAMES
Curity
First Foods
Gerber
Nuk

Gillette Canada Inc.

16700 TransCanada Highway, Kirkland, PQ H9H 4Y8

Founded in Canada: 1906, Montreal, PQ
Ownership: The Gillette Company (US), 100%
Operations: ON, PQ
Employees: 200

Gillette is a leader in brand-name personal care and shaving products, as well as office supplies. Worldwide consolidation led the US parent to cease all manufacturing operations in Canada, as of January, 1990. The company maintains a Toronto and a Montreal office for marketing and distribution functions, with sales staff working either from home or from one of the offices. Some hair care products are manufactured in Canada for the company.

Making the Grade

CANDOUR: Gillette did not respond to any of our surveys, but provided some information late in the process. Insufficient data meant it could not be rated in most categories.

WOMEN'S ISSUES: The company did not provide statistics concerning its employment of women. It has no provision for daycare and offers extended maternity leave on a case-by-case basis.

CHARITABLE GIVING AND COMMUNITY INVOLVEMENT: Gillette is not on Imagine's list. A staff committee decides which charitable organizations will receive donations of cash and product. (No figure was provided.)

BRAND NAMES
Aapri
Atra
Dry Idea
Dry Look
Foamy
Good News
Lustrasilk
Oral-B
Right Guard
Sensor
Silkience
Soft & Dri
Tame
Toni
Trac II

PROGRESSIVE STAFF POLICIES: The company has corporate sports teams, a stop-smoking program and, at the Montreal headquarters, an in-house aerobics program. It provides full compensation for tuition costs to employees who successfully complete job-related courses.

MANAGEMENT PRACTICES AND CONSUMER RELATIONS: In addition to an international mission and values statement, the company has a set of key corporate policies that managers must read and sign annually. There is no separate Canadian code of responsible business practices.

Notable Facts

From March, 1989 through March, 1990, Gillette underwent a major downsizing in Canada, closing two plants (in Montreal and Toronto) and eliminating more than 500 jobs. Boston-based Gillette Company is on the boycott list of an organization called PETA (People for the Ethical Treatment of Animals) for its continued use of animal testing. The Canadian company did not comment on whether its parent has conducted or funded research into alternative test methods. The parent company has subsidiary operations in South Africa.

Hershey Canada Inc.

200 Ronson Dr., Etobicoke, ON M9W 5Z9

Founded In Canada: 1962, Smiths Falls, ON
Ownership: Hershey Foods Corp. (US), 100%
Operations: BC, AB, SK, MB, ON*, PQ*, NS*
Employees: 1,500
Annual sales: $244 million
Advertising expenditures: $9.5 million

Hershey Canada owns a significant share of the Canadian markets for nuts, confectionery and baking products. Twelve of its 50 national brands (including the five Planters snack nut brands and some of the Moirs boxed chocolate brands) maintain a more than 25% market share.

When Hershey acquired Planters in a 1987 takeover of Nabisco's (see p. 213) confectionery division, it nearly tripled its employees in Canada — from approximately 550 in 1986 to 1,700 in 1990. However, consolidation and plant closures then eliminated some jobs, resulting in the 1991 employment total of 1,500. Hershey's major plants are located in Montreal, Dartmouth, NS, and Hamilton and Smiths Falls, Ont., where it is the largest private employer.

Making the Grade

CANDOUR: Hershey's high rating is a reflection of the company's willingness to provide full, detailed answers to the majority of our questions.

WOMEN'S ISSUES: Women make up approximately 50% of its employees, 28% of its managers and 10% of its senior managers. The firm offers extended maternity leave but has no provision for daycare.

CHARITABLE GIVING AND COMMUNITY INVOLVEMENT: Hershey Canada donated $100,000 in cash to charity in 1990. The company runs a scholarship fund and supports children's hospitals and the Children's Miracle Network.

BRAND NAMES	
All Nuts	Nibs
Almondillos	Nut Milk
Beaver	Oh Henry!
Beech-Nut	Ovation
Breath Savers	Planters
Bridge Mixture	Pot of Gold
Brown Cow	Reese
Caravan	Reese's Pieces
Cherry Blossom	Selection
Chipits	Skor
Eat-More	Special Crisp
Glosette	Special Dark
Golden Caramels	Strawberry Cow
Goodies	Temptation
Hershey	Top Scotch
Life Savers	Tradition
Lowney	Twizlets
Moirs	Twizzlers

PROGRESSIVE STAFF POLICIES: Hershey received a relatively high score in this category. The company emphasizes communication with an open-door management policy and has both a suggestion program with reward incentives for cost-saving ideas and an employee newsletter. Other staff policies include corporate marathons, employee training programs, tuition aid, adoption leave and written annual performance reviews.

LABOUR RELATIONS: There is an employee share option purchase plan. Hershey provided health and safety statistics, as well as training data.

ENVIRONMENTAL MANAGEMENT/PERFORMANCE: Four members of staff have environmental responsibilities. The company has completed a comprehensive environmental audit and environmental engineering studies. It runs an environmental awareness program for facility management, recycles paper, packaging and manufacturing by-products and has been active in package reformulation and efforts to increase energy efficiency. According to the Ontario Ministry of the Environment, in 1990 Hershey was found guilty of replacing equipment without the required Certificate of Approval and was fined $5,000. Also in 1990, Hershey was fined $15,000 under the Pesticides Act for the improper discharge of pesticide.

MANAGEMENT PRACTICES AND CONSUMER RELATIONS: Hershey has a written statement of corporate philosophy, but no written code of ethics. The company has no record of violations of the Competition Act.

Notable Facts

The company works with a total of six unions and approximately 50% of all employees are unionized. There have been no strikes or lockouts within the last 10 years. Two plants were closed when the Nabisco facilities were amalgamated: the Planters Nuts operation in Toronto in 1987, and a Sherbrooke, PQ, plant in 1989, affecting 141 and 544 employees respectively. When the company closed the Toronto plant, it gave employees six months' advance notice and set up an employment counselling service. The firm offered all 119 United Food and Commercial Workers union employees jobs at the Smith Falls, Ont. plant, and $5,000 for moving expenses. It also pledged to try to find positions for 27 salaried non-union employees. Most employees did not accept the relocation.

H.J. Heinz Co. of Canada Ltd.

5650 Yonge St., 16th floor, North York, ON M2M 4G3

Founded in Canada: 1909, Leamington, ON
Ownership: H.J. Heinz Company (US), 100%
Operations: AB, ON*, PQ, NS
Employees: 2,000
Toll-free number: 800-268-6641

Heinz of Canada is known primarily as a manufacturer of baby food, ketchup, tomato juice and other canned and bottled foods. Its processing plant in Leamington, Ont., is the town's largest employer. The company owns 100% of Weight Watchers Canada.

Making the Grade

CANDOUR: Heinz answered most questions concerning progressive staff policies, charitable giving and environmental performance, but left many other categories largely unanswered.

WOMEN'S ISSUES: The company's low score reflects the fact that despite its many progressive staff policies, Heinz has no provisions for daycare or extended maternity leave. The firm supplied no data for numbers of women in management or senior management positions. However, the company did institute a formal employment equity program in October, 1991.

CHARITABLE GIVING AND COMMUNITY INVOLVEMENT: Although not pledged to the Imagine campaign, Heinz donated $675,000 to charity in 1991. The company provides time off for employee volunteer activity, runs a charitable foundation and supports cultural events. It donated land for a sports complex in Leamington, and gave $50,000 for the purchase of sports equipment. In addition, Heinz is a United Way supporter, worked with UNICEF Canada on a $50,000 fundraising campaign and supported the Variety Club's 1990 Children's Christmas Extravaganza. In 1989, Weight Watchers in Canada co-sponsored National Nutrition Month with the Canadian Dietetic Association.

PROGRESSIVE STAFF POLICIES: Heinz earned a place on this Honour Roll. It offers fitness subsidies and an employee assistance program that includes financial planning assistance and counselling for alcohol, drug abuse and marital difficulties. It also provides newsletters, suggestion programs, training programs, adoption leave, scholarship funds and more.

BRAND NAMES
9-Lives
Alphagetti
Envirogetti
Heinz
Omstead
Scarios
Shady Maple
StarKist
U.F.O.'s
Weight Watchers

LABOUR RELATIONS: The company offers an employee stock option plan to all employees, and supplied us with complete health and safety data. Despite the lack of a formal job security policy, Heinz has a reputation for harmonious labour relations and low turnover rates.

ENVIRONMENTAL MANAGEMENT: Heinz has a written environmental policy.

ENVIRONMENTAL PERFORMANCE: The company has invested in product research and development, reformatted packaging, reduced its energy consumption, and set up an ongoing program to monitor pesticides and chemical residues. It recycles paper and packaging, co-generates its own electricity and funds local environmental groups.

Notable Facts

In 1991, 75% of the Leamington plant's union members (United Food and Commercial Workers) voted for a wage freeze. The UFCW maintains that its members did so unwillingly, after the company president warned that the plant would close and all remaining production move to Michigan or Ohio unless costs could be reduced to compete with the US. The company noted in response that the freeze was accompanied by a cost of living adjustment.

Heinz subsidiary StarKist Canada no longer produces tuna in Canada, though the company currently markets StarKist here, supplied from the US. In 1985, 20 million cans of the tuna were recalled by the StarKist cannery in New Brunswick: they had been rejected by inspectors from Canada's Department of Fisheries and Oceans, but approved for sale in Canada by the then-Minister, John Fraser. The StarKist cannery, which employed 400 workers, closed in 1985. Heinz reopened the cannery in 1988, still using the StarKist brand, but ended this effort in 1990, as costs made the plant uncompetitive with production from the Far East.

The Earth Island Institute, based in California, led a boycott against StarKist for using tuna caught by methods that kill dolphins. In 1990, StarKist became the first company to adopt a worldwide "dolphin-safe" policy. It states that it refuses to buy any tuna caught with gill or drift nets, which capture dolphins as well as tuna. The parent company has two trademark licences in South Africa.

The Hostess Frito-Lay Company

6700 Century Ave., Suite 300, Mississauga, ON L5N 6A4

Founded in Canada: 1988, Toronto, ON
Ownership: PepsiCo Inc. (US), 100%
Operations: AB*, ON*, PQ*, NS*
Employees: 825

Hostess Frito-Lay is the leading producer of salted snacks in eastern Canada (Ontario and east), with an estimated 30%-45% of the potato chip market. It was the result of an October, 1988 merger between former competitors Hostess (owned by General Foods Canada Inc., see p. 195) and Frito-Lay (owned by PepsiCo Foods International, a division of PepsiCo Inc., see p. 228). In June, 1992, Kraft sold its half-interest to PepsiCo. Hostess Frito-Lay's four plants are located in Taber, Alta., Cambridge, Ont., Lauzon, PQ, and Kentville, NS.

Making the Grade

CANDOUR: Hostess Frito-Lay did not participate in the survey process, although it provided some limited information during final fact-checking. We received some information about the company's Cambridge, Ont., plant from a spokesperson for the Retail, Wholesale and Department Store union, one of the two unions representing Hostess Frito-Lay employees.

CHARITABLE GIVING AND COMMUNITY INVOLVEMENT: The company, which is not pledged to the Imagine campaign, has a charitable donations budget set by the president. It matches employee contributions to the United Way and at each plant location regularly supports local charities with cash and product donations.

PROGRESSIVE STAFF POLICIES: The company plans to introduce an employee assistance program by 1993. It provides smoke-free areas, staff sports teams and corporate marathons. There are in-house training programs and lectures, and the company provides paid external training.

LABOUR RELATIONS: Because production is seasonal, the number of jobs fluctuates. The company gives advance notice of the introduction of new machinery, and relocation is used where possible. A union representative said that workers at the Cambridge plant have a good relationship with Hostess Frito-Lay.

ENVIRONMENTAL PERFORMANCE: With the goal of achieving a 65% carton return rate, the company pays a bonus

BRAND NAMES
Chee-tos
Crunch Tators
Doritos
Fritos
Gibney's
Hostess (chips)
Rold Gold
Ruffles
Smartfood
Sunchips
Tostitos

to sales staff who bring back packaging for recycling. Soft drink cans are recycled at several plants. The firm has no environmental fines on record.

MANAGEMENT PRACTICES AND CONSUMER RELATIONS: Old Dutch Foods Limited (see p. 226), supported by several Toronto area store owners, claims Hostess had been buying up their potato chips in an attempt to keep the product off Ontario store shelves. A Consumer and Corporate Affairs Spokesperson says that the Federal Bureau of Competition Policy looked into the claims. The Bureau found that, while the practice was limited, there was some basis for the allegations. According to Consumer and Corporate Affairs, Hostess says the practice has been stopped. The Bureau found no need for further action.

Notable Facts

The company, which is reported to have spent over $900,000 in 1991 to advertise a single brand (Doritos), won an award in that same year for the best Canadian advertisement. The parent company, PepsiCo Inc., has Pepsi-Cola and Pizza Hut franchises in South Africa.

Humpty Dumpty Foods Limited HUMPTY

2100 Norman St., Lachine, PQ H8S 1B1

Ownership: Borden Inc. (US), 100%

Operations: ON*, PQ*, NB*

Humpty Dumpty, a wholly-owned division of Chicago-based Borden Inc., owns an estimated 20%-35% of the salty snacks market in eastern Canada. Borden operates several other divisions in Canada, including pasta giant Borden Catelli Consumer Products (p. 109) and Sunworthy Wallcoverings.

Making the Grade

Humpty Dumpty did not complete any of our surveys, referring us to Borden in Columbus, Ohio. The parent expressed interest in our *Guide*, but did not participate in the research process, nor did anyone for the Retail, Wholesale and Department Store union, which represents workers at Humpty Dumpty's Toronto plant.

The company is not on Imagine's list of Caring Companies. Employees participate in a retirement savings plan provided by the parent, with the parent matching eligible contributions.

Notable Facts

The parent company has one subsidiary operation and a holding company in South Africa.

BRAND NAMES
Humpty Dumpty

Hunt-Wesson Canada

1 Concord Gate, Don Mills, ON M3C 3N6

Ownership: ConAgra (US), 100%
Operations: ON
Employees: 11

The company is owned by Nebraska-based ConAgra, one of the five biggest food companies in the United States. Hunt-Wesson is a market leader in canned tomato products, sauces and popcorn. The company ceased manufacturing operations in Canada when it closed its Tilbury, Ont., plant in 1991, laying off 57 people. Now 96% of Hunt-Wesson's products are imported, with the rest produced by Canadian manufacturers under license. Product sales are handled by brokers; Hunt-Wesson has no sales staff.

Making the Grade

CANDOUR: Though the company provided some information, much of our survey was not applicable, since Hunt-Wesson has only 11 employees here. Most areas in the Tables are therefore marked N/A (Not Applicable).

CHARITABLE GIVING AND COMMUNITY INVOLVEMENT: Hunt-Wesson is not pledged to the Imagine campaign and did not disclose its charitable giving figures. However, it says that it provides some low-profile support to charities in the Toronto area.

OTHER: The company uses its parent's international code of ethics. The company had no record of environmental violations at its Tilbury, Ont., plant while it was in operation.

BRAND NAMES
Healthy Choice
Hunt's
Manwich
Orville
  Redenbacher's

Industries Lassonde Inc.

170-5th Avenue, Rougemont, PQ J0L 1M0

Founded in Canada: 1918, Rougemont, PQ
Ownership: Pierre-Paul Lassonde (Canada), 51%
Operations: PQ*, NS*
Employees: 500
Annual sales: $103.7 million

This third-generation, Quebec-based company, originally called A. Lassonde & Fils Inc., exports fruit juices and drinks to more than 10 countries around the world, including the US, Mexico, Hong Kong and countries in Europe and the Caribbean. There are two plants, one in Rougemont, Que., and the other in Nova Scotia.

Making the Grade

CANDOUR: Lassonde's exceptionally high level of disclosure earned it a place on our Honour Roll. However, it has relatively few formal programs or policies, and this was reflected in its grades in other categories.

WOMEN'S ISSUES: The company, whose workforce is 50% female, has an estimated 13% women in management and 8% in senior management. It has no women on the nine-man board of directors and no formal employment equity program.

CHARITABLE GIVING AND COMMUNITY INVOLVEMENT: Though not pledged to the Imagine campaign, it gave $50,000, half in cash and half in kind, to charity in 1990. The only community activities it reported were sports team support and occasional paid time off for employee volunteer activity.

PROGRESSIVE STAFF POLICIES: Lassonde's policies include training programs, retirement counselling, annual written performance reviews, a company newsletter, and an open door to managers policy. There are no formal employee assistance or health promotion programs.

LABOUR RELATIONS: The company has no formal job security program, but would use retraining and relocation to ease the impact of any layoffs. It established an annual performance bonus system for all employees in 1991 and offers a share purchase plan to top managers. The company provided some health and safety statistics, and partial figures on training.

BRAND NAMES
Fruite
Mont-Rouge
Oasis
Oasis Del Sol
Rougemont

ENVIRONMENTAL MANAGEMENT: Lassonde has no written environmental policy, environmental committee of the board or full-time environmental affairs official. On the other hand, it does have an environmental working committee, which has just started making regular reports to the board, and two staff with environmental responsibilities, the most senior being the vice-president of production and engineering.

ENVIRONMENTAL PERFORMANCE: The company plans to begin its first environmental audit in the near future. Current environmental programs include paper and packaging recycling and an effort to eliminate disposable cutlery and dishes in the office. The company contributes to a Quebec recycling association, and has invested in package reformulation and energy efficiency (by switching from oil to natural gas). It has just started monitoring wastewater discharges and plans to invest in equipment replacement and environmental promotion over the next few years. Lassonde has no environmental court cases on record.

MANAGEMENT PRACTICES AND CONSUMER RELATIONS: Lassonde has no written code of ethics or ethics advisory service for employees. However, it has not had any Competition Act violations.

Notable Facts

Lassonde, which is 60% unionized, had a three-day strike in 1990. It reports no layoffs in the past ten years: in fact, employment is up overall, from 300 in 1986 to about 500 now.

J.M. Schneider Inc.

321 Courtland Ave. E., PO Box 130, Kitchener, ON N2G 3X8

Founded in Canada: 1890, Berlin (now Kitchener), ON
Ownership: Schneider Corporation (Canada), 100%
Operations: BC, AB*, MB*, ON*, PQ, NB
Employees: 3,333
Annual sales: $617.5 million

J.M. Schneider is primarily known as a producer of popular meat, grocery and cheese products. Many of its brands, including Schneider Bologna, Fried Chicken, Meat Pies and Schneider's Old Fashioned Ham, own more than a 25% share of their respective markets.

Making the Grade

CANDOUR: Schneider's high rating reflects its willingness to provide information about its policies and procedures.

WOMEN'S ISSUES: Women comprise up to 25% of the total workforce, but only 5% of Schneider's senior managers and 10% (one person in 10) of the board of directors. The company offers no daycare or formal employment equity policies, and only grants extended maternity or parental leave "on an individual basis, based on merit."

CHARITABLE GIVING AND COMMUNITY INVOLVEMENT: Schneider participates in the Imagine campaign.

PROGRESSIVE STAFF POLICIES: The company is a member of the Honour Roll in this category. Policies include employee assistance programs (on-site Alcoholics Anonymous, for example), stop-smoking programs, a sports team, training programs, employee newsletters, open-door management, adoption leave and written annual performance reviews for salaried employees. An employee suggestion program was instituted in 1964: since 1984 it has attracted more than 20,500 suggestions, resulting in savings of approximately $21.9 million, and awards to employees of $2.3 million.

LABOUR RELATIONS: Schneider addresses job security issues in its collective agreements and offers early retirement. The company also provided us with some health and safety data.

ENVIRONMENTAL MANAGEMENT: Schneider has a written environmental policy and produces environmental reports to the board of directors as needed.

BRAND NAMES
Breakfast Tyme
Casa Italiana
Cheese Eeze
Deli Bulk
Handi Meals
Lifestyle
Lunch Tyme
Mini-Sizzlers
Oktoberfest
Red-Hots
Schneiders
Schneider's Old Fashioned

ENVIRONMENTAL PERFORMANCE: Schneider has not done an environmental audit and was cited in a 1990 environmental court case under the Ontario Water Resources Act, resulting in a $8,000 fine. The firm also exceeded wastewater discharge limits in 1985, 1986 and 1987: since 1989, however, it has no longer been on the list of operations most closely monitored by the Ontario government. A company spokesperson says that the company created a waste management department to promote environmental programs throughout the firm, including water conservation through recovery and recycling, a paper recycling program, a recycled can unit, an annual Environmental Day and exhibits and contests for employees. The company makes a non-chemical fertilizer product from rendering by-products that otherwise would go into the trash.

MANAGEMENT PRACTICES AND CONSUMER RELATIONS: The firm has a written code of ethics with an annual employee sign-off, and has not been charged with any Competition Act violations.

Notable Facts

Seventy-five percent of the workforce is unionized. The company has had three strikes in the last 10 years, the largest of which (in 1988) involved more than 2,000 employees at the firm's Kitchener, Ont., operation. Layoffs in 1989 and a plant closure in 1990 resulted in the loss of about 300 jobs.

Johnson & Johnson (Canada) Inc.

J&J

2155 boul. Pie IX, Montreal, PQ H1V 2E4

Founded in Canada: 1919, Montreal, PQ
Ownership: Johnson & Johnson (US), 100%
Operations: BC, AB, PQ*
Employees: 770
Annual sales: $149.9 million
Toll-free number: 800-361-8068

The company is a major presence in the health care, feminine hygiene, oral hygiene and personal care markets. The parent company, New Jersey-based Johnson & Johnson, was founded in 1885 and today has a workforce of 82,000 in dozens of countries worldwide. It operates several other subsidiaries in Canada, including Ortho Pharmaceuticals (a world leader in birth control), Ortho Diagnostic Systems, MacNeil Pharmaceutical and Janssen Pharmaceutica. The Canadian company, with a plant in Montreal and distribution centres in Alberta and British Columbia, exports to 25 countries.

Making the Grade

CANDOUR: The company was very responsive to our surveys and received a high rating this area.

WOMEN'S ISSUES: Forty percent of Johnson & Johnson's workforce is female, but only 20% of its managers and 10% of its senior managers. There is one woman on the six-member management board (equivalent to a board of directors). The company has no daycare provision, extended maternity leave or formal employment equity program. When asked about the lack of a formal employment equity program, the spokesperson replied that Johnson & Johnson complies with government regulations and therefore has no need for formal programs.

CHARITABLE GIVING AND COMMUNITY INVOLVEMENT: Johnson & Johnson has committed itself to the Imagine campaign, although the 1990 corporate donations of $48,000 totalled only about one-tenth of the target 1% mark. The company donates both dollars and product, with each Johnson & Johnson Canadian subsidiary (consumer, professional and pharmaceutical) making its own contributions. Community involvement includes support for health-related organizations and cultural events. Employee volunteer activity is publicized in the company newsletter, *Express*.

BRAND NAMES
Assure
Carefree
Johnson's
Johnson & Johnson
K-Y
o.b.
Prevent
Reach
Serenity
Shower to Shower
Stayfree
Sundown
Sure and Natural
Prima

PROGRESSIVE STAFF POLICIES: It scored well in this category, since it provides an employee assistance program, on-site fitness facilities and a fitness club subsidy, rewards for cost-saving ideas and an annual social report for employees. The parent company has established an education and conference centre in New Jersey to provide training for employees from around the world.

LABOUR RELATIONS: The company did not say whether it has a formal job security program or methods of addressing layoffs. It does have an employee share option plan, which allows all employees to invest in the company.

ENVIRONMENTAL MANAGEMENT: While the parent company has an environmental code, there is none specifically for the Canadian operations. Johnson & Johnson Canada has no senior environmental affairs official or environmental committee and makes no regular reports to its management board on this subject.

ENVIRONMENTAL PERFORMANCE: The company conducted an environmental audit of all its operations in 1992. About 95% of product packaging is derived from recycled fibres, and much of it is recyclable. The company upgraded equipment at its Montreal plant to make the operation safer and more efficient, and has no record of environmental court cases.

MANAGEMENT PRACTICES AND CONSUMER RELATIONS: Rather than a formal code of ethics, Johnson & Johnson has a one-page outline of its corporate responsibilities called the *Credo*. There is no annual employee sign-off for the document.

Notable Facts

The size of the company's workforce has fallen over the past five years from about 900 to 770. Closing some Montreal operations in 1989 and the Toronto distribution centre in 1991 resulted in layoffs of 72 and 16 people respectively. About 35% of the company's workforce is unionized, all of them at the Montreal plant.

Johnson & Johnson Canada does not engage in any animal testing. Its parent company does, and has been asked by PETA (People for the Ethical Treatment of Animals) to reduce its use of animals in testing and provide a public report on the number of animals involved. However, the parent company is conducting extensive in-house tests on alternatives to animal testing.

The parent company earned considerable consumer support and loyalty when it quickly and voluntarily recalled all Tylenol capsules after a few were suspected of being laced with cyanide. This action helped it maintain a strong market presence despite the tragedy. Johnson & Johnson Canada exports dental floss to South Africa and the parent company has subsidiary operations there.

Kellogg Canada Inc.

6700 Finch Ave. W., Etobicoke, ON M9W 5P2

Founded in Canada: 1914, Toronto, ON
Ownership: Kellogg Company (US), 100%
Operations: AB, ON*, PQ, NS
Employees: 1,291
Annual sales: $321 million

Kellogg Canada, like its parent in the US, is best known for its line of breakfast cereals. The parent company, established in 1906 in Battle Creek, Michigan, set up operations in Canada in 1914. The Canadian company now exports some products to the United States.

Making the Grade

CANDOUR: The company was very open in discussing its operations and policies, earning a place on our Honour Roll. In addition to completing all three of our surveys, it gave us copies of its code of ethics and social practices report.

WOMEN'S ISSUES: This was the company's lowest score by far. While women account for 30% of management positions, they make up only 8% of senior management and hold one position (of nine) on the board of directors. Furthermore, Kellogg has no formal employment equity program or provision for daycare or for maternity leave beyond the legislated minimum.

CHARITABLE GIVING AND COMMUNITY INVOLVEMENT: The company's scores were high overall, particularly in this category, where it also joined the Honour Roll. Kellogg has not made a pledge to the Imagine campaign but it was included in Imagine's 1991 list. Its charitable contributions, both cash and in kind, amount to well over Imagine's 1% goal and are administered through the Kellogg Canada Community Involvement Fund. Its community involvement includes equipment donations, the loan of company facilities, educational funding and paid time off for United Way activities.

BRAND NAMES	
All-Bran	Honey Nut Corn
Bran Buds	Flakes
Common Sense	Just Right
Corn Flakes	Kellogg's Raisin
Corn Pops	Bran
Cracklin' Oatmeal	Kenmei
Crispix	Mini Wheats
Cruncheroos	Mrs. Smith's
Eggo	Muslix
Frosted Flakes	Nutri-Grain
Fruit Loops	Pop Tarts
Fruitful Bran	Rice Krispies
Fruity Marshmallow	Shirriff
Krispies	Special K
Fun Pack/Variety	Strawberry Squares
Pak	

PROGRESSIVE STAFF POLICIES: The company also scores highly in this category, for it offers the workforce a high level of support through such measures as an employee assistance program, written annual performance reviews for employees, an on-site fitness facility and retirement counselling.

LABOUR RELATIONS: Yet another Honour Roll position. Kellogg earned a perfect score for its employee share option plan and its comprehensive formal job security program, which includes retraining, relocation and provisions for early retirement. The company spent a significant amount on employee training in 1990, and it gave us health and safety figures.

ENVIRONMENTAL MANAGEMENT: The company has a written environmental policy and an environmental working committee. While 25 Kellogg employees have environmental responsibilities, there is no full-time senior environmental affairs member on staff.

ENVIRONMENTAL PERFORMANCE: Kellogg is also on this Honour Roll. It recycles paper, manufacturing by-products, steel and other metals, oils and packaging. It has invested in product research and development, package reformulation and equipment replacement. It conducted a partial environmental audit, which examined packaging, solid waste, wastewater discharge and air emissions. The company has no record of environmental court cases.

MANAGEMENT PRACTICES AND CONSUMER RELATIONS: Kellogg appears on this Honour Roll as well. The company has a written code of ethics, last updated in 1979, that requires an annual employee sign-off. It is one of the few companies in this *Guide* to publish a social practices report (outlining how the Kellogg Canada Community Involvement Fund distributes monies to the numerous charities in which it is involved). Although Kellogg has no toll-free number, it accepts all collect calls from consumers. It has not been charged with any Competition Act violations.

Notable Facts

Eighty-one percent of employees at the London plant are unionized, represented by the American Federation of Grain Millers. Only one strike has been recorded, with 540 workers involved in a brief stoppage there in 1988. The company closed its Etobicoke, Ont., plant in early 1992, letting 300 workers go in the process. The parent company has subsidiary operations in South Africa.

Kimberly-Clark Canada Inc.

90 Burmanthorpe Rd. W., Mississauga, ON L5B 3Y5

Founded in Canada: 1925, Toronto, ON
Ownership: Kimberly-Clark Corporation (US), 100%
Operations: ON*, PQ*
Employees: 1,600 (consumer products only)
Toll-free number: 800-668-0495

The company is a major name in the paper products and feminine hygiene markets. The US-based parent coined the brand name, Kleenex, a word now almost synonymous with facial tissue. The Canadian company began as Cellucotton Products Co. Ltd., which made bandaging for wounds. Its consumer products division (profiled here) makes such products as sanitary tissue, disposable diapers and paper towels.

Making the Grade

CANDOUR: Kimberly-Clark Canada, in conjunction with its US parent, provided a considerable amount of information late in our research process. We also approached four unions and received additional information from representatives of the International Brotherhood of Electrical Workers (IBEW).

WOMEN'S ISSUES: Women comprise 33% of the company's workforce but only 20% of management, and have no representation in senior management or on the three-member board of directors. Kimberly-Clark offers flexible working hours at its head office, but has no provisions for daycare, extended maternity leave or employment equity.

CHARITABLE GIVING AND COMMUNITY INVOLVEMENT: Though the company is not part of the Imagine campaign, its charitable donations have averaged 1% of its pre-tax earnings for each of the past five years. (No dollar figure was provided.) It donates products and equipment to charitable organizations, offers the use of company facilities in small communities and gives employees paid time off for volunteer activity. Its community involvement includes support for sports teams, the Children's Miracle Network, the United Way and a home for battered children.

PROGRESSIVE STAFF POLICIES: Kimberly-Clark received its highest score in this category and is on the Honour Roll. The company's employee assistance program in-

BRAND NAMES

Anyday
Delsey
Depends
Hi-Dri
Huggies
Kleenex
Kotex
Lightdays
Pull-Ups
New Freedom
Profile

cludes counselling on legal matters and for substance abuse and psychological, family and eldercare difficulties. It funds a quarterly employee newsletter, *The Updater*, and has a policy of open-door management. It also offers tuition reimbursement, annual performance reviews and team-building programs.

LABOUR RELATIONS: Although the company has no formal job security program, it mitigates the impact of layoffs and downsizing with retraining, relocation and early retirement. There are no gain sharing programs. The company provided health and safety data.

ENVIRONMENTAL MANAGEMENT: The Canadian company follows a written environmental policy provided by its parent. There is no environmental committee, although the Canadian management team does address environmental issues. Similarly, there is no full-time senior environmental affairs official, but each mill has a full-time worker with environmental responsibilities.

ENVIRONMENTAL PERFORMANCE: Kimberly-Clark does not conduct environmental audits of its operations. However, the company recycles manufacturing by-products and packaging, and is working on changes to the paper bleaching process. It has no record of environmental fines or wastewater discharges above emissions guidelines, although its Terrace Bay operation was one of nine Ontario kraft mills placed under a control order to reduce emissions into waterways. It has invested a considerable sum to reduce effluent, improve waste treatment and reduce packaging, particularly at its Terrace Bay, Ont., mill, where it spent $25 million on a lagoon to remove various chemicals from its wastewater.

MANAGEMENT PRACTICES AND CONSUMER RELATIONS: Kimberly-Clark had a relatively good score in this area. The company follows the written code of conduct provided by its parent, which was written in 1988 and requires sign-off by all managers. It has not been charged with any Competition Act violations, and provides a toll-free number.

Notable Facts

The company, which is about 65% unionized, has had at least three layoffs over the past few years, some of which may be attributed to what the IBEW spokesperson called an industry-wide downturn, that have left several hundred employees out of work. The company has one strike on record, a June, 1988 stoppage that involved 480 timber workers. The sale of older plants, such as the Kapuskasing, Ont. mill (sold to employees) and one in Quebec, have also reduced employment totals. The parent company has minority interests in a South African affiliate company.

Kitchens of Sara Lee

SARLEE

379 Orenda Rd., Bramalea, ON L6T 1G6

Founded in Canada: 1963, Bramalea, ON
Ownership: Sara Lee Corporation (US), 100%
Operations: ON*
Employees: 208
Advertising expenditures: $50,000

The Sara Lee Corporation, a Chicago-based consumer products giant, makes dozens of products, including panty hose, shoe polish, underwear, leather gloves, lingerie, coffee, processed foods, lunch meats and baked goods. It has operations in more than 30 countries, with 110,000 employees around the world and net sales of $12.4 billion (US). The Canadian company, Kitchens of Sara Lee, has a plant in Bramalea, Ont. and makes frozen bakery products, some of which are exported to the United States. It is the only division of Sara Lee Corporation with manufacturing operations in Canada.

Making the Grade

CANDOUR: Kitchens of Sara Lee was very forthcoming, earning a position on our Honour Roll.

WOMEN'S ISSUES: The company's workforce is 57% female. With a comparatively high percentage of women in management (44%), senior management (20%) and on the management committee (17%), the company was awarded a place on the Women's Issues Honour Roll as well. However, there is no employment equity program, extended maternity leave or provision for corporate daycare.

CHARITABLE GIVING AND COMMUNITY INVOLVEMENT: In 1990, Kitchens of Sara Lee donated $16,200 to charity, most of it as cash donations. It supports Junior Achievement and has matching gift programs. It is not pledged to the Imagine campaign.

PROGRESSIVE STAFF POLICIES: The company offers annual performance reviews, a policy of open-door management, a scholarship program for employees' children and an employee newsletter, *Kitchen Talk*.

LABOUR RELATIONS: A stock option plan is offered to all employees, with the company contributing 15% of the purchase price. Health and safety statistics were supplied.

ENVIRONMENTAL MANAGEMENT: Kitchens of Sara Lee is a small operation, with no full-time environmental affairs

> **BRAND NAMES**
> Sara Lee

position or any environmental committees. It uses the worldwide environmental code provided by its parent.

ENVIRONMENTAL PERFORMANCE: The company has invested in packaging and product reformulation and it recycles paper, manufacturing by-products and packaging. No environmental violations are on record.

MANAGEMENT PRACTICES AND CONSUMER RELATIONS: The company uses its parent's written code of ethics, revised in July of 1991, but does not require an annual employee sign-off. The company has not been charged with any Competition Act violations.

Notable Facts

Seventy percent of Kitchens of Sara Lee's workers are unionized. It has had no strikes in the past 10 years, but there has been an increasing number of seasonal layoffs in the last couple of years.

The parent company's subsidiary, Douwe Egberts Ltd., manufactures pipe and cigarette tobacco in Holland and Ireland, its brand names including Amphora, Irish Mead and Drum. Sara Lee Corporation maintains trademark and licensing agreements in South Africa.

Kraft General Foods Canada Inc.

95 Moatfield, Don Mills, ON M3B 3L6

Founded in Canada: 1921, Montreal, PQ
Ownership: Philip Morris Companies Inc (US), 100%
Operations: BC*, AB, SK*, ON*, PQ*, NB, NS, NF
Employees: 4,600
Annual sales: $1.3 billion (US)
Toll-free number: 800-561-7131

Owned by one of the world's largest tobacco and food products companies, Kraft General Foods is a formidable presence on supermarket shelves. Prior to 1989, Kraft General Foods operated as two separate companies: Kraft, in Canada since 1921, and General Foods, here since 1929. The original brands of General Foods (such as Baker's Chocolate, Jell-O and Post) have roots in Canada that go back to the end of the 19th century.

Making the Grade

CANDOUR: The company was quite forthcoming overall.

WOMEN'S ISSUES: Kraft is on the Honour Roll. Forty percent of its workforce are women, as are nearly one-third of its company managers — an impressive figure when compared to most of the other companies in this *Guide*. It has a formal employment equity program, a daycare referral program, and provides six months of extended maternity leave. On the other hand, the three-member senior management team is entirely male. (There is no Canadian board of directors.)

CHARITABLE GIVING AND COMMUNITY INVOLVEMENT: Kraft is not on the Imagine campaign list and did not supply any information under the charitable giving section of our survey. However, it is involved with the community in a variety of ways, including equipment donations, the loan of company facilities and a university matching gift program.

PROGRESSIVE STAFF POLICIES: The company earned a place on this Honour Roll for its comprehensive list of programs and policies. Its employee assistance program in-

BRAND NAMES	
Alpha-bits	Kraft Pure
Baker's	Lunchables
Cheese Pot	Magic Moments
Cheese Whiz	Maxwell House
Cool Whip	Milka
Country Time	Minute Rice
Cracker Barrel	Miracle Whip
General Foods	Parkay
International	Philadelphia
Coffee	Post Raisin Bran
Grape-Nuts	Shake 'n' Bake
Honeycomb	Snackeroos
Jell-O	Stove Top
Kool-Aid	Tang
Kraft	Toblerone
Kraft Free	Velveeta

cludes health, finance, substance abuse and eldercare counselling. Other programs, such as on-site medical services and referral, weight-loss counselling and an on-site fitness facility, are all part of the health promotion plan. The extensive list of communication programs includes surveys concerning quality of life in the workplace and employee exchange forums. The company also offers regular written performance reviews, adoption leave, multi-level training programs and retirement counselling.

LABOUR RELATIONS: Kraft is also on this Honour Roll. It reports an employee share option plan open to all employees and a formal job security program, which provides for retraining, relocation and job reassignment in the event of any layoffs or downsizing.

ENVIRONMENTAL MANAGEMENT: Kraft is a member of this Honour Roll as well. It uses the written environmental policy developed for Kraft North America. However, it has an engineer with full-time environmental responsibilities and a green task force that reports to both the president of the Canadian company and the parent.

ENVIRONMENTAL PERFORMANCE: Despite the small number of employees with environmental responsibilities, relative to the size of the workforce, the company's environmental performance is good. This is due in part to its adoption of TQM (Total Quality Management), which addresses environmental issues along with other policies. The company conducts environmental audits of some of its operations. It seeks to reduce packaging and it recycles fine paper, manufacturing by-products and packaging. When the inadequate capacity of the sewage system near its Ingleside, Ont., plant caused plant effluent to exceed emission guidelines, the company joined with the municipality to upgrade the system.

MANAGEMENT PRACTICES AND CONSUMER RELATIONS: A member of this Honour Roll, the company operates under an international code of ethics provided by its parent, with a quarterly sign-off required by each department. It also has an ethics ombudsman. It maintains a consumer toll-free number and has no Competition Act violations.

Notable Facts
Only 15% of the company's workforce is unionized and there have been no strikes since the 1989 merger with General Foods. A 1989 downsizing of General Foods operations resulted in the loss of 200 jobs, although many affected employees chose the early retirement option that was offered to them. The parent company, Philip Morris Companies, has a trademark and licensing agreement with a South African company.

Lantic Sugar Limited

1 Westmount Square, Westmount, PQ H3Z 2P9

Founded in Canada: 1915, Montreal, PQ
Ownership: BC Sugar Refinery, Limited (Canada), 100%
Operations: ON, PQ*, NB*
Employees: 644

Lantic Sugar Limited, formerly called Atlantic Sugar Refineries Ltd., has been selling sugar in eastern and parts of central Canada since 1915. The company owns more than a 25% share of its market.

In addition to the company's plants in St. John, NB, and Montreal, Lantic has a Yonkers, NY, plant with 400 employees. Plants in Oshawa, Ont., and Ferrier, Que., closed in 1988 and 1989 respectively. In July, 1992, industry consolidation led then-parent Jannock Limited to sell its remaining 50% of the company's shares to BC Sugar Refinery, Limited (see p. 105).

Making the Grade

CANDOUR: Lantic answered most of the questions about progressive staff policies and women's issues, but left sizable gaps throughout the rest of the survey.

WOMEN'S ISSUES: Women represent 22% of employees but only 4% of managers. There are no female senior managers or board members. The firm has no employment equity, daycare, or extended maternity leave programs.

CHARITABLE GIVING AND COMMUNITY INVOLVEMENT: Lantic publicizes employee volunteer activities in *Horizons*, the employee newsletter, and supports sports teams. The company has recently established a charitable donations committee, but is not part of the Imagine campaign.

PROGRESSIVE STAFF POLICIES: The company earned its highest score in this area. Its employee assistance program includes alcohol and drug abuse counselling and financial counselling. There are also training programs, an employee newsletter, a suggestion program with reward incentives and a policy of open-door to management. The company once offered interest-free loans to employees buying computers, but has ended the program.

ENVIRONMENTAL MANAGEMENT: Lantic has a written environmental policy and has included environmental is-

BRAND NAMES
Lantic

sues in the mandate of its TQM (Total Quality Management) committee of managers.

ENVIRONMENTAL PERFORMANCE: The company has a program to recycle paper and is replacing disposable cups with ceramic mugs. Lantic has no environmental court convictions or record of exceeding discharge limits.

MANAGEMENT PRACTICES AND CONSUMER RELATIONS: Lantic has a written code of ethics.

Notable Facts

Sixty-eight percent of all employees are unionized. Represenatives for one of the unions, the Bakery, Confectionery & Tobacco Workers, claim that the company is generally receptive to working with the union. Collective agreements include seniority recall rights and some retraining. The union at the Saint John facility says that mechanization and attrition have caused the number of refinery jobs there to drop somewhat.

Lyons Tetley Canada Limited

6725 Airport Rd., Suite 704, Mississauga, ON L4V 1V2

Founded in Canada: 1991, Mississauga, ON
Ownership: Allied Lyons PLC (UK), 100%
Operations: BC, ON, NS
Employees: 8
Annual sales: $48 million
Advertising expenditures: $2 million

This major tea and coffee company is wholly owned by one of the world's six largest wine and spirits producers. Allied Lyons owns such names as Dunkin' Donuts, Baskin Robbins and the Canadian alcohol giant, Hiram Walker. Shares of Allied Lyons PLC are traded on the Toronto Stock Exchange. Lyons Tetley has only eight employees in Canada, up from three in 1986, but it indirectly employs about 600 Canadians. Its iced tea products are manufactured under licence by five independent plants across Canada, while three advertising agencies provide marketing assistance to head office. Products are distributed through six independent sales/distribution companies, who sell the products to the retail food trade and mass merchandisers. Lyons Tetley owns roughly 30% of the tea bag market in Canada, due in part to the effective promotion of its round tea bag.

Making the Grade

CANDOUR: With only eight employees and no plants in Canada, many of the questions on our surveys were inappropriate, so many scores in the Tables read N/A (Not Applicable). The company chose instead to furnish us with information in a less structured form and was quite forthcoming overall.

WOMEN'S ISSUES: Of Tetley's eight employees, three are women. No special policies or programs, such as daycare referral or extended maternity leave, are in place.

CHARITABLE GIVING AND COMMUNITY INVOLVEMENT: It is not part of the Imagine campaign, and charitable contributions, both cash and product, are provided directly by the independent distributors and brokers. However, Lyons Tetley participates in its parent's support for the Save the Children Fund, a development agency.

PROGRESSIVE STAFF POLICIES: With such a small number of employees, some of the programs in our survey, such as an on-site fitness facility, are not feasible. However, the company offers a pension plan, counselling referral serv-

BRAND NAMES
Amore
Gold Roast
Lyons
Tetley

ice and training programs. In 1990 it spent $700 on training per employee.

LABOUR RELATIONS: All employees may purchase Allied Lyons shares, with the company contributing half the purchase price. There is no formal job security policy for the eight, non-unionized employees of Lyons Tetley Canada.

ENVIRONMENTAL MANAGEMENT: The Canadian company follows policies outlined in Allied Lyons' environmental policy.

ENVIRONMENTAL PERFORMANCE: While it does not conduct environmental audits of its office operations, it carries out partial audits of its licensed manufacturers. The company president deals with environmental concerns, should they arise.

MANAGMENT PRACTICES AND CONSUMER RELATIONS: Lyons Tetley uses its parent's code of ethics. It has not been involved in any consumer court cases. The company did not have much information on the practices and policies of its licensed manufacturers, marketers or distributors.

Notable Facts

The parent company sells some brands in South Africa through distributors, and some products are made there under license.

Maple Leaf Foods Inc.

30 St. Clair Ave. W., Toronto, ON M4V 3A2

Founded in Canada: 1991, Toronto, ON
Ownership: Hillsdown Holdings Plc (UK), 56%
Operations: BC*, AB*, SK*, MB, ON*, PQ*, NB*, NS*, PE*, NF*
Employees: 10,000
Annual sales: $3 billion

Maple Leaf Foods, one of Canada's largest food processing companies, was created in a 1990 merger of meat processing giant Canada Packers and Maple Leaf Mills, a milling and baking conglomerate. Canada Packers and Maple Leaf Mills operations together control 56% of Canada's rendering (meat and poultry processing) market. The company has three major businesses: consumer foods, agribusiness and milling, with exports to more than 50 countries. Assets include Corporate Foods Limited (see p. 140), McGavin Foods, Bunsmaster Bakery, Country Style Donuts, Prime Poultry Products, Shur-Gain and Northam Food Trading Co.

Making the Grade

CANDOUR: Maple Leaf Foods participated fully in our research process, and therefore received a high score in this area. However, with the merger, many former corporate activities — such as the newsletter and annual performance appraisals — were either discontinued or left a matter of individual operating unit discretion. As a result, the company received low scores in all other areas.

CHARITABLE GIVING AND COMMUNITY INVOLVEMENT: The company is not pledged to the Imagine campaign. It gave slightly more than $600,000 to charity in 1991, well down from its 1990 total of $1,520,000 (both in kind and cash). Prior to 1991, Canada Packers had made sizable contributions to the National Ballet, Youth Employment Skills, the United Way and the National Conservancy of Canada. The new company is attempting to diversify its philanthropy, albeit in a more modest way, beyond the earlier focus on the arts.

BRAND NAMES	
Added Touch	Micro Marvels
Bon Appetit	Monarch
Burns Flakes of	Nutriwhip
Ham	Prime
Burns Flakes of	Purity
Meat	Red River Cereal
Burns (lard)	Sherwood Farms
Buttercup	Sno'Flake
Citadel	Spork
Cream of the West	Stillmeadow
Domestic	Tea-Bisk
Homestead	Tend-R-Fresh
Jolly Miller	Tenderflake
Kam	Thirst ade
Klik	Vienna Sausages
Maple Leaf	York
McGavin	

PROGRESSIVE STAFF POLICIES: Company policies include substance abuse and retirement counselling, and an open-door management policy. Maple Leaf Foods is continuing pay equity and employment equity programs for women, people with disabilities, minorities and Native peoples.

LABOUR RELATIONS: Although not structured into a formal job security program, provisions for retraining, relocation, early retirement and financial compensation are all used by the company to assist employees affected by layoffs and downsizing.

ENVIRONMENTAL MANAGEMENT: There is no corporate environmental committee. Although the environmental department has been eliminated, regular reports that include environmental topics are made quarterly to the Board.

ENVIRONMENTAL PERFORMANCE: Although Maple Leaf has no regular audit program, it recycles paper, manufacturing by-products, cardboard and plastics in plants and offices, uses more recycled content packaging and works with suppliers to develop more environmentally friendly packaging. It has undertaken a continuing process of energy efficiency and equipment upgrading. Both Maple Leaf Mills and Canada Packers had numerous environmental violations, some involving fines, prior to the 1991 merger.

MANAGEMENT PRACTICES AND CONSUMER RELATIONS: Maple Leaf Foods has no written code of ethics, although many specific policies exist, some of which require regular sign-off by key personnel. The Canada Packers - Maple Leaf Mills merger went ahead without approval from the Bureau of Competition Policy, ignoring a Bureau order to run the two operations separately during its investigation. The merger was retroactively approved by a competition tribunal in February, 1992. While still a separate company, Maple Leaf Mills and several other millers were charged with bid rigging on sales to the Canadian government of wheat for export purposes, including famine relief in Ethiopia and Sudan. Maple Leaf Mills pleaded guilty and paid a $1-million settlement.

Notable Facts

In the decade prior to the merger, Canada Packers was involved in ten strikes, most of them in 1984. Maple Leaf Mills had two strikes, both in 1987: one in Windsor at a Monarch plant, and one at a McGavin plant in Calgary. The large number of strikes reflects in part the large number of collective agreements (75), unions and sites involved. Over the last two years, the company has let go 2,500 employees and closed 18 to 20 plants, primarily in its meat processing segment.

Maple Leaf Foods operates a Shur-Gain animal research centre near Brantford, Ont., and is the largest privately owned agribusiness research centre in Canada. The Canadian company is not involved in South Africa, nor is its parent.

Maple Lodge Farms Ltd.

RR 2, Norval, ON L0P 1K0

Founded in Canada: 1955, Norval, ON
Ownership: the May family (Canada), 100%
Operations: ON*, NB*
Employees: 1,200
Annual sales: $201.3 million

Maple Lodge Farms is a family-owned poultry processor that has created a significant niche market for itself by producing meat products from chicken that are traditionally made from beef and pork. Chicken wieners, pepperoni, sausage and "ham" are a few of the more than dozen packaged meats the company makes at its Norval, Ont., plant. The company also has a meat processing plant near Edmonston, New Brunswick.

Making the Grade

CANDOUR: The company completed our product survey, but did not participate further. However, a spokesperson for the United Food and Commercial Workers union, which represents company employees, provided some information about the company's Norval operations.

CHARITABLE GIVING AND COMMUNITY INVOLVEMENT: The company is not on Imagine's list, but shareholders meet to determine corporate donations.

ENVIRONMENTAL MANAGEMENT/PRACTICES: Maple Lodge has no written environmental policy, but no record, either, of environmental prosecutions or exceeding wastewater discharge guidelines.

MANAGEMENT PRACTICES AND CONSUMER RELATIONS: It has no written code of ethics.

Notable Facts

The Norval processing plant's 620 unionized employees have not had a strike in the past 10 years. However, the union spokesperson comments that management-labour relations have been difficult for the last few years, with 80 to 100 grievances outstanding at any given time. Quarterly meetings between shareholders, union and management are held in order to resolve problems.

```
BRAND NAMES
Maple Lodge Farms
```

McCain Foods Limited

Florenceville, NB E0J 1K0

Founded in Canada: 1956, Florenceville, NB
Ownership: the McCain family (Canada), 100%
Operations: BC, AB*, MB*, ON*, PQ, NB*, NS, PE*
Employees: 5,300
Annual sales: $2.7 billion (worldwide)

The company, which began producing frozen french fries in Florenceville in 1957, has grown from thirty employees to 12,500 worldwide, almost half of whom are in Canada. McCain Foods is now just one part of the McCain Group of companies, which includes Day & Ross Inc. and Thomas Equipment Limited, a manufacturer of farm and construction machinery. McCain Foods is a major producer of juice, meats, cheese, frozen vegetables and frozen prepared foods, and has over 45 production facilities on three continents.

Making the Grade

CANDOUR: The company is a private, family-run business that typically does not release much information. However, McCain participated in our survey and provided considerable data about its environmental and community initiatives.

CHARITABLE GIVING AND COMMUNITY INVOLVEMENT: McCain made our Honour Roll because of its impressive contributions. The company has committed itself to the Imagine target and in 1990 donated $5 million of cash and product to such charities as the World Wildlife Fund, the Alliance for a Drug Free Canada and the Atlantic Alliance of Food Banks. The company is an active participant in its host communities, providing equipment donations, the use of company facilities and both paid and unpaid time off for employee volunteer activity. Each year McCain grants a number of agricultural scholarships: the list includes scholarships at New Brunswick Community College, bursaries to graduating high school students in Portage la Prairie, Man., and an annual $2,500 McCain Award for dietetics to a graduate student in that field.

PROGRESSIVE STAFF POLICIES: The company earned high marks in this category as well. Its health promotion plan includes stop-smoking programs, a fitness facility at its Florenceville office and various company athletic competitions (golf, curling, hockey and softball). McCain encourages internal communications by supporting a company newsletter, the *McCain Star*, suggestion programs,

BRAND NAMES
Caterpac
Kent
McCain
Picnic
Valley Farms

rewards for cost-saving ideas and an open-door management policy. It hosts annual picnics for employees and their families at most major locations worldwide, and runs a scholarship fund for employees and their children.

LABOUR RELATIONS: McCain has a formal job security program for its employees, and uses retraining, relocation and early retirement to reduce the impact of downsizing. On the other hand, it has no gain sharing programs.

ENVIRONMENTAL MANAGEMENT: The company received a low score because it has no full-time environmental affairs person or environmental committee of the board. However, it does have an internal environmental committee, led by the executive vice-president and general manager, which reports to the board four times a year. Although without a formal environmental policy, McCain has a brochure, *McCain Foods and the Environment*, which provides a detailed description of the company's commitment to the environment.

ENVIRONMENTAL PERFORMANCE: The company does not conduct environmental audits, but it demonstrates environmental stewardship through its investments in new equipment, less packaging, energy efficiency, improved pollution control systems, use of recycled materials and research into organic alternatives to chemical pesticides. McCain's recycling and other waste reduction initiatives have diverted a considerable amount of solid waste from landfill sites in PEI and New Brunswick. Potato peels are sold for animal feed, while unused vegetable remnants are given to local farmers for use as cattle feed. Steel drums, batteries, copper wire, polystyrene, and steel from obsolete machinery are all recycled. The McCain Green Ideas preschool program teaches children about environmental responsibility. The company was charged in 1982 for water discharge violations at its Florenceville facility, and was fined $1,000. It was also fined $3,500 in 1984, again for water discharge violations.

MANAGEMENT PRACTICES AND COMMUNITY RELATIONS: McCain has no written code of ethics, but has not on been charged with any Competition Act violations.

McCormick Canada Inc

316 Rectory St., London, ON N5W 3V9

Founded in Canada: 1883, London, ON
Ownership: McCormick & Company Inc. (US), 100%
Operations: AB* MB ON* PQ
Employees: 425
Toll-free number: 800-265-2600

McCormick, established as Gorman Dyson Co. in 1883, holds a significant part of the spices, seasonings and flavourings market. Its US parent dominates the spice business in North America and imports ingredients from around the world.

Making the Grade

CANDOUR: The US parent company completed our surveys and was very forthcoming.

WOMEN'S ISSUES: McCormick is on this Honour Roll. Women represent 45% of employees, 62% of management and 20% of senior management. One of ten directors is female. The company has no formal employment equity program, although it says that it has written procedures in place to ensure non-discrimination in hiring and promotion practices. It offers maternity leave beyond the government minimum, but has no daycare programs in place.

CHARITABLE GIVING AND COMMUNITY INVOLVEMENT: The company is not pledged to the Imagine campaign, but it gave $53,000 ($3,000 in kind) to charity in 1991. Community activities include the loan of company facilities, equipment donations, paid and unpaid time off for employee volunteer efforts and the publicizing of such efforts in the company newsletter.

PROGRESSIVE STAFF POLICIES: On this Honour Roll as well, McCormick provides substance abuse, family and career counselling under its employee assistance program. It offers a stop-smoking program and sponsors corporate sports events. Communications programs include an employee newsletter, rewards for cost-saving ideas, an open-door management policy and regular employee meetings. In addition, it provides adoption leave and annual written performance reviews, and offers summer employment opportunities for employees' children.

BRAND NAMES
Cake Mate
Club House
Gardenfare
McCormick
Spice Cargo
Spice Classics
Stange

LABOUR RELATIONS: McCormick has a place on this Honour Roll also. Although without a formal job security program, it uses retraining relocation, early retirement and advance notice of technological change to address layoffs. The company has both a stock option plan and a profit sharing program for all employees. We were provided with 1990 and 1991 health and safety statistics as well as training data.

ENVIRONMENTAL MANAGEMENT: McCormick has a written environmental policy and an environmental working committee and makes an environmental report to the board each year. It has three employees with environmental functions, the most senior of them a director of engineering and facilities management.

ENVIRONMENTAL PERFORMANCE: The company does not conduct environmental audits. However, it has replaced equipment, improved energy efficiency and reformatted packaging to reduce waste. In addition, McCormick recycles cans, bottles, paper, packaging and manufacturing byproducts. It has no record of environmental court fines or instances of exceeding wastewater discharge guidelines.

MANAGEMENT PRACTICES AND CONSUMER RELATIONS: The company has a written code of ethics, revised in 1989, which requires an annual sign-off by employees. It has a toll-free number and sends regular mailings to customers who are part of its Dinner Club. McCormick has no record of violations of the Competition Act.

Mead Johnson Canada

333 Preston St., Suite 700, Ottawa, ON KIS 5N4

Founded in Canada: 1923, Montreal
Ownership: Bristol-Myers Squibb Co. (New York), 100%
Operations: ON*, PQ
Toll-free number 800-263-7464

Mead Johnson is a world leader in nutritional supplements and infant formula, although the company name itself is not as well-known as the products it sells. The company has one manufacturing facility in Belleville, Ont., that produces an extensive line of nutritional products for both Canadian and export markets. The company is wholly-owned by Bristol-Myers Squibb Co., as are Bristol-Myers Squibb Consumer Products Group (see p. 111) and Drackett Canada (see p. 153). It reports as a part of a North American division to its US parent. That parent company is realigning its management and production worldwide.

Making the Grade

CANDOUR: The company did not participate beyond completing the initial product survey. US parent-company officials provided some further information late in the process.

CHARITABLE GIVING AND COMMUNITY INVOLVEMENT: While Mead Johnson Canada is not pledged to the Imagine campaign, Bristol-Myers Squibb Co. is. For the last 10 years it has sponsored an annual series of symposia for health care workers on nutrition at the University of Toronto. It loaned a director and donated $25,000 to the Alliance for a Drug Free Canada.

ENVIRONMENTAL MANAGEMENT: Mead Johnson has a worldwide written environmental policy and has a full-time director of environmental and government affairs in Canada. The parent company's environmental committee, which reports to a member of the board, has Canadian representatives from Mead Johnson and Bristol-Myers Squibb Consumer Products Group.

ENVIRONMENTAL PERFORMANCE: The company seeks to have environmentally suitable packaging and has an internal technical group that conducts environmental audits. The company has not been charged with any environmental violations.

BRAND NAMES
Alactamil
Boost
Enfalac
Isocal
Nutramigen
Pablum
Pregestimil
Prosobee
Sustacal

Notable Facts

Mead Johnson Canada, in conjunction with the Canadian Infant Formula Association, has agreed to market its infant formula only to health professionals. The parent company is on a consumer boycott list for the way it markets infant formula in developing countries. The parent company has subsidiary operations in South Africa. Mead Johnson Canada says it conducts no animal testing. The parent company continues to do animal testing on new compounds, although it has been involved in developing non-animal tests. Ninety-nine percent of all of its animal testing is for pharmaceutical and health care products.

Melitta Canada Inc.

75 Westmore Dr., Rexdale, ON M9V 3Y6

Founded in Canada: 1960, Toronto, ON
Ownership: Melitta Haushaltprodukte Gmbh & Co., Kommanditesellschaft (Germany), 100%
Operations: BC, ON, PQ
Employees: 50
Annual sales: $39 million
Advertising expenditures: $1.9 million

Melitta runs a vertically integrated operation. Canadian activities are limited to sales, with coffee, coffee filters, coffee makers and coffee maker cleaning products all being marketed under the Melitta brand name. The Canadian operations became a sales-only arrangement in 1991, when the company's filter-making operations moved south to Melitta North America's head office in New Jersey. Melitta's $1.9-million advertising strategy has paid off in sales 20 times that amount, giving the company more than 25% of the coffee filter market in Canada.

Making the Grade

CANDOUR: Melitta Canada cooperated with our process, although the surveys were primarily completed in the United States by Melitta North America's public relations department. Nonetheless, all spokespersons were open and helpful, earning Melitta Canada a place on our Honour Roll. A number of the survey items were not appropriate because the company no longer has manufacturing operations in Canada.

WOMEN'S ISSUES: Melitta earned a place on the Honour Roll because of the comparatively high percentage of women in management (50%) and senior management (33%). The company has an equal opportunity program and provides six months of maternity leave for Canadian employees.

CHARITABLE GIVING AND COMMUNITY INVOLVEMENT: Although Melitta is not part of the Imagine campaign, in 1990 it contributed $10,000 in cash and product to charity, which it notes as the equivalent of 1.25% of its pre-tax earnings. Its community involvement includes corporate equipment donations and contributions to Wild-Care, a Toronto-based organization.

PROGRESSIVE STAFF POLICIES: The corporate health promotion plan involves a fitness club subsidy and a stop-

---

BRAND NAMES
Melitta

smoking program. Melitta provides regular written performance reviews and an employee newsletter.

LABOUR RELATIONS: A profit-sharing program is in place for all employees. While the company has no formal job security program, it provided severance benefits in excess of government requirements to the 50 employees laid off when manufacturing operations were shut down in 1991.

ENVIRONMENTAL MANAGEMENT: The company scored poorly here, because of its lack of policies aimed at preventing environmental problems. It has no environmental working committee and no environmental affairs personnel. Melitta does have a written environmental policy, determined by Melitta North America, which is reprinted in part on filter paper packages.

ENVIRONMENTAL PERFORMANCE: Because the company no longer does any manufacturing in Canada, it could not be scored in this area. However, there are no environmental violations on record for the period of time when it did manufacture products here. Also, the parent company no longer uses chlorine in the production of white paper coffee filters and now produces brown filters as another option.

MANAGEMENT PRACTICES AND CONSUMER RELATIONS: The code of ethics, written in 1985, does not require an annual sign-off. The company has not been charged in connection with any Competition Act infractions.

Nabisco Brands Canada Ltd.

Royal Bank Plaza, South Tower, Suite 2700, PO Box 165, Toronto, ON
M5J 2J4

Founded in Canada: 1982
Ownership: RJR Nabisco Inc. (US), 100%
Operations: ON*, PQ*
Employees: 5,000 (est.)
Toll-free number: 800-668-2253

Nabisco Brands Canada Ltd. is one of the country's primary producers of cereals, canned fruits and vegetables and snack foods, holding approximately 50% of the Canadian cookie market. The company has two major divisions: groceries (Del Monte, Alymer) and cookies and biscuits (Christie Brown). Nabisco's parent company owns RJ Reynolds Tobacco Co., one of the largest tobacco companies in the US.

Making the Grade

CANDOUR: Nabisco refused to respond to surveys for this *Guide* or to comment upon any of the information collected from other sources. The company has therefore received a low Candour Quotient, and question marks in all categories but Progressive Staff Policies. Union representatives were our main source of information, but the picture they presented of the company was not entirely consistent.

PROGRESSIVE STAFF POLICIES: According to union representatives, the company offers both alcohol abuse and retirement counselling and pays tuition for job-related courses. The company has an employee newsletter and, reportedly, a policy of open-door management.

Notable Facts

Nabisco works with at least these three unions in Canada: the International Brotherhood of Firemen and Oilers (IBFO), the United Food and Commercial Workers (UFCW), and the Canadian Auto Workers (CAW). A CAW official says that relations between man-

BRAND NAMES	
100% Bran	Mr. Christie's
Aylmer	Nuts 'n Crunch
Balance	Oreo
Barnum's Animals	Pantry
Bits & Bites	Peek Freans
Chips Ahoy!	Pirate
Christie	Premium Plus
Coffee Breaks	Ritz
Cream of Rice	Shredded Wheat
Cream of Wheat	Shreddies
Dads	Snacking Crackers
Del Monte	Sultana's
Fig Newtons	Team
Fruit Wheats	Teddy Grahams
Fudgee-O	Triscuit
Honey Bran	Twigs
Crunchies	Uneeda
Honey Maid	Wheatsworth
Milk Bone	Wright's
Mister Salty	

agement and workers are better than ever since Nabisco took over the Dresden, Ont. plant: "Managers are recruited locally, the number of jobs has increased, layoffs are shorter and the seniority list is growing by leaps and bounds." Some of this may be due to the fact that the company relocated production lines to Dresden when it closed a canning plant in Simcoe, Ont. and another in Leamington, Ont.

The UFCW is also basically satisfied with the relationship between the company and the union, noting that the company cooperated with the union during plant closures, and went beyond government minimums in its retraining, relocation and early retirement packages. However, IBFO representatives in Niagara Falls describe the management/labour situation as "terrible at present, because of the company's continuous violations of our contract." The union has 259 members at the plant, all of whom were on strike from January 6 to April 7, 1991. Strike issues included seniority, mandatory overtime and recall rights.

RJR Nabisco's subsidiary, R.J. Reynolds Tobacco Co., has a licensing agreement with a South African company.

Nabob Foods Limited

PO Box 2170, Vancouver, BC V6B 3V6

Founded in Canada: 1896, Vancouver, BC
Ownership: Klaus Jacobs (Switzerland), 100%
Operations: BC*, ON
Employees: 212
Annual sales: $113 million
Advertising expenditures: $5 million
Toll-free number: 800-661-4063

The company was founded in 1896 in Vancouver as the Kelly Douglas Co. Ltd. Grocer Robert Kelly's major brand, Nabob, became a separate food company in 1911. The company changed hands in 1976, when Swiss-owned Jacob Suchard Co. purchased it from George Weston Limited (see p. 168), owner of the Kelly Douglas Co. Philip Morris Company bought Jacob Suchard Co. in 1991, but Swiss businessman Klaus Jacobs kept Nabob Foods, which continues as an independent Canadian operation. A major producer of coffee and tea, Nabob roasts coffee in its BC plant for sale in Canada.

Making the Grade

CANDOUR: Nabob was very responsive to our surveys and gained a place on this Honour Roll.

WOMEN'S ISSUES: Thirty-six percent of the company's workforce is female, and 23% of its management. There are no women in senior management or on the seven-man board of directors. Despite the lack of a formal employment equity program, women have filled 50% of all entry-level positions over the past five years. Nabob offers maternity leave beyond the regulatory minimum.

PROGRESSIVE STAFF POLICIES: Nabob has an extensive range of programs, earning a place on this Honour Roll. Its employee assistance program includes drug and alcohol abuse counselling, psychological counselling for employees and dependents and retirement counselling, as well as fitness and nutrition seminars. In addition, the company holds an annual "stakeholders" meeting for all employees.

LABOUR RELATIONS: Nabob is also on this Honour Roll. It has a formal job security program and uses early retirement and advance notice of technological change to reduce the impact of any downsizing. All employees receive a financial performance award when profit targets are met.

BRAND NAMES
Deluxe
Kettle Chips
Nabob
Lifestream
Summit
Tradition

The company gave us training figures and health and safety data.

ENVIRONMENTAL MANAGEMENT: Again on the Honour Roll, the company has a written environmental policy and a full-time environmental affairs manager, one of two employees at the company with environmental responsibilities. It also has an environmental working committee, but has no such committee at board level, and there are no regular environmental reports to the board.

ENVIRONMENTAL PERFORMANCE: The company is one of the few in this *Guide* to conduct a comprehensive environmental audit of all of its facilities, one of the many factors explaining its presence on this Honour Roll. It's actively involved in developing more environmentally friendly packaging, and has upgraded equipment and improved energy efficiency at its plants. It already recycles paper and packaging and is studying ways to recycle manufacturing by-products as well. Nabob has no environmental fines or record of exceeding discharge guidelines.

MANAGEMENT PRACTICES AND CONSUMER RELATIONS: Nabob has no written code of ethics, but it is currently reviewing company policy in this area, and may produce a written code within the next few years. The company has a toll-free consumer advisory service and has had no consumer or Competition Act prosecutions.

National Sea Products Limited

1959 Upper Water St., PO Box 2130, Halifax, NS B3J 3B7

Founded in Canada: 1899, Halifax, NS
Ownership: Scotia Investments Ltd. (Canada), 28%
Operations: BC, AB, MB, ON, PQ, NS*, NF*
Employees: 4,800
Annual sales: $607.9 million

National Sea Products began as W.C. Smith and Co., a family fishing firm. Companies controlled by the Sobey and Joudrey families hold 47% of its common shares. NatSea is a primary producer and distributor of seafood products in Canada. The company has six national brands, three of which — High Liner, Light Tonight and Captain's Chicken — are aggressively marketed and hold more than a 25% share of their markets. The company has six plants, three each in Nova Scotia and Newfoundland.

Making the Grade

CANDOUR: NatSea gave us complete information in some categories but very little in others.

WOMEN'S ISSUES: NatSea is on the Honour Roll. Women make up approximately 50% of the total workforce and 25% of management (though less than 1% of senior management). There is one woman on the 13-member board of directors. The company offers extended maternity leave and time-sharing for jobs, and has contributed to the expansion of a daycare facility in Lunenburg, NS, that is used by NatSea employees.

CHARITABLE GIVING AND COMMUNITY INVOLVEMENT: NatSea is not pledged to the Imagine campaign, and did not provide specific information about its charitable donations. The company contributes cash and product to some charitable organizations and some secretarial services to groups like the United Way. It gives both paid and unpaid time off for employee volunteer activities, runs a scholarship fund and supports local sports.

PROGRESSIVE STAFF POLICIES: The company did reasonably well in this area, with employee assistance programs for alcohol and drug abuse and retirement counselling, as well as sports and social programs and company-wide performance awards.

BRAND NAMES
Captain's Chicken
High Liner
Light Tonight
SeaFresh
Treasure Isle

LABOUR RELATIONS: NatSea gave us very little information in this category, but does have an employee share purchase plan.

ENVIRONMENTAL MANAGEMENT: NatSea has a written environmental policy, an environmental committee of the board of directors, which provides regular environmental reports to the board, and an environmental working committee. The company has completed a comprehensive environmental audit.

ENVIRONMENTAL PERFORMANCE: The company prides itself on its strong environmental commitment, and is on our Honour Roll in this category. It has recycling programs for paper, packaging materials and manufacturing by-products, and it funds local environmental groups. It has no record of environmental fines or of exceeding discharge guidelines.

MANAGEMENT PRACTICES AND CONSUMER RELATIONS: The company has a service quality policy, and an ethics code that is currently under review.

Notable Facts

Within the last year NatSea has divested itself of all non-North American operations, and in the last five years has eliminated more than 2,200 jobs worldwide (400 in Canada). Since 1989, the number of the company's plants has declined from nine to five, and the number of vessels from 40 to 22.

NatSea works with three unions. Since 1985 the company has had three strikes in Newfoundland, affecting some 1500 employees.

Nestlé Canada Inc.

1185 Eglinton Ave. E., Don Mills, ON M3C 3C7

Founded in Canada: 1918, Chesterville, ON
Ownership: Nestlé S.A. (Switzerland), 100%
Operations: BC, AB, SK, MB*, ON*, PQ*, NS, NF
Employees: 4,720
Annual sales: $1 billion
Advertising expenditures: $25 million

Nestlé, a leader in the Canadian processed food industry, makes dozens of products, including frozen entrees, drink mixes, infant formula and pet food, and has licensed many more products for manufacture by other Canadian companies. It has nine plants in Ontario, two in Quebec and one in Manitoba.

Making the Grade

CANDOUR: Nestlé was very responsive to our surveys, provided an extensive amount of additional information and is on our Honour Roll in this category.

WOMEN'S ISSUES: Again a member of the Honour Roll, Nestlé has women in 22% of both its management and senior management po-

BRAND NAMES

Aero	Fussell's	Nescafé
After Eight	Goodhost	Nestea
Big Turk	Grand Gourmet	Nestlé
Black Magic	Grifo	Nutchos
Buitoni Fresco	Hills Bros	Perugina
Cailler	Jelly Tots	Quality Street
Capri	Kit Kat	Quik
Carnation	Laura Secord	Raisinettes
Chew-Eez	Lean Cuisine	Rich Blend
Coffee Crisp	Libby's	Rolo
Coffee Mate	Mackintosh	Rossana
Columbia	Maggi	Smarties
Crosse & Blackwell	Maple Buds	Stouffer's
Dairy Box	McKay	Super 8
Dr Ballard	Mint Patties	Taster's Choice
Elegante	Mint Royale	Toll House Morsels
Encore	Minuet Cherries	Turtles
Fancy Feast	Mirage	Viva
Fiesta	Miss Mew	Wagtime
Friskies	MJB	Yorkie

sitions and in one of the eleven positions on its executive committee. It has a formal employment equity program and supports alternative working arrangements like flex-time.

CHARITABLE GIVING AND COMMUNITY INVOLVEMENT: A member of this Honour Roll as well, Nestlé's charitable donations of more than 2% of its pre-tax profits far exceed its 1% pledge to the Imagine campaign. Although the exact figures were not disclosed, the company gives cash to charitable organizations and product donations to food banks. It allows both paid and unpaid time off to employees for community volunteer activities, and contributes to Canadian universities and to two organizations of which it is a founding member, the Canadian Children's Foundation and the National Institute of Nutrition.

PROGRESSIVE STAFF POLICIES: Once again on the Honour Roll, the company provides on-site fitness classes and supports numerous sports activities. It has a policy of open-door management, and a range of communications programs that includes a company newsletter, suggestion programs and rewards for cost-saving ideas. Although it does not have an internal employee assistance program, Nestlé provides a counselling referral service with all costs covered by the company. As well, it offers nutrition counselling and quarterly written performance reviews, and pays tuition costs for external training programs.

LABOUR RELATIONS: Nestlé is on this Honour Roll as well. While it has no formal job security program, it uses retraining, relocation, early retirement and advance notice of technological change to reduce layoffs to a minimum. In addition, it has an employment adjustment committee to assist in relocation or in finding new jobs. While it has no formal gain sharing plans, it runs a bonus program based on the whole company's performance. Nestlé spent $1,000 per employee on training in 1990, and it provided us with health and safety statistics.

ENVIRONMENTAL MANAGEMENT: Nestlé has a Canadianized environmental policy based on its parent's worldwide code. It has an environmental committee (composed of representatives from technical services, packaging and quality assistance), which makes quarterly reports to the executive committee. There is no full-time environmental affairs officer for the Canadian company.

ENVIRONMENTAL PERFORMANCE: Although its score in Environmental Management is low, Nestlé is on the Environmental Performance Honour Roll for its significant number of environmental initiatives, including a comprehensive environmental audit of all of its operations, investments in packaging reductions and improvements in the treatment of emissions. Nestlé recycles paper, manufacturing by-products and packaging, and contributes to recycling programs in Quebec and Nova Scotia. It has been burning spent coffee grounds as fuel for over 30 years. The company has not been fined for any environmental violations, but its Chesterville, Ont., plant was operating under a Certificate of Approval pending improvements to the plant to reduce wastewater emissions (now completed).

MANAGEMENT PRACTICES AND CONSUMER RELATIONS: Nestlé's *Code of Responsible Business Practices*, written in 1978 and revised in 1991, does not require annual employee sign-off. The company has different toll-free numbers for its various product lines. It has not been charged with any Competition Act violations.

Notable Facts

Considerable downsizing has cut the company's unionized workforce (50% of the total) by more than 700 over the past five years. Most of these layoffs were the result of plant closings: production from the closed facilities was typically transferred to other Canadian locations.

Nestlé has licensing agreements, with Cobi Foods (see p. 133), E.D. Smith and Sons, (see p. 154) and Cadbury Beverages (see p. 117) among others.

Nestlé, along with several other companies, has been the subject of an international boycott because of the way it markets infant formula in the developing world. The company reports that it has renewed its pledge to stop providing free and low-cost supplies of infant formula to maternity wards and hospitals in developing countries by the end of 1992. It neither sells nor donates infant formula to maternity wards anywhere in Canada.

The parent company has subsidiary operations in South Africa.

Ocean Fisheries Limited

2215 Commissioner St., Vancouver, BC V5L 1A8

Founded in Canada: 1962, Vancouver, BC
Ownership: the Safarik family (Canada), 100%
Operations: BC*
Employees: 125 (1,400 seasonal)
Annual sales: $39 million

The company is a family-run business, with fish product sales to more than 20 countries worldwide. Countries like Japan, Australia, New Zealand, the UK and Europe in general account for 65% of its total annual sales of over $150 million. In addition to its 125 full-time staff, 500 shore workers and 900 fishermen and vessel staff are employed seasonally. Despite turbulent times for the North American fishing industry, the company has never closed a plant, although it sold its operations in the United States in May, 1992. Ocean Fisheries has a 15% share in the canned salmon and tuna markets of Ontario and western Canada.

Making the Grade

WOMEN'S ISSUES: While women constitute 50% of all Ocean Fisheries employees, they occupy just 5% of management and no senior management positions. The board of directors consists of Safarik family members — all sons. The company offers one month of extended maternity leave beyond the legislated minimum.

CHARITABLE GIVING AND COMMUNITY INVOLVEMENT: Ocean Fisheries is not on the Imagine campaign list and did not provide any details about the size of its charitable donations. However, it donates to food banks and has supported Simon Fraser University, the University of British Columbia and the British Columbia Children's Hospital in Vancouver. As well, it provides paid time off for employee volunteer activities, runs a matching gift program, supports local sports teams, and makes donations to local community centres.

PROGRESSIVE STAFF POLICIES: Ocean Fisheries provides staff with a fully subsidized referral to an external employee assistance program, which offers legal, marital, financial and substance abuse counselling. An employee suggestion program and a policy of open-door management help maintain lines of communication internally. Fishing crew members are offered support services ranging from accounting to legal advice and help in arranging financing. Adoption leave is available, and the employees' extended benefits package is almost completely funded by the company. Ocean Fisheries emphasizes training in

BRAND NAMES

North Pacific
Ocean's
Royale

quality control and is in the process of implementing a system of written performance reviews.

LABOUR RELATIONS: The company has a formal job security program and uses attrition for downsizing. It offers a performance-based profit sharing program to all employees.

ENVIRONMENTAL MANAGEMENT: The company has a written environmental policy, but no environmental committee, system of reports to the board or full-time environmental affairs officer. However, the company has ten employees with environmental responsibilities.

ENVIRONMENTAL PERFORMANCE: Ocean Fisheries conducts environmental audits of some of its operations. Its initiatives in this area include equipment replacement, energy efficiency improvements and recycling programs for paper and packaging. It uses all solid by-products for fish meal, fish food or animal feed and operates a system of filters to screen liquid waste before it is returned to waterways and inlets. The company requires its Far East suppliers to catch tuna in ways that do not kill dolphins, and puts a "dolphin friendly" seal on its tuna cans. It noted that it was the first company to receive an endorsement from the California-based Earth Island Institute for its dolphin policy. No environmental court cases or violations of limits are recorded for any of its BC plants.

MANAGEMENT PRACTICES AND CONSUMER RELATIONS: The company has no written code of ethics or ethics advisory for employees. It has no toll-free number, either, but it does have a policy of responding to all complaints or queries within 24 hours and will provide full cash refunds to dissatisfied customers. The company has not been involved in any Competition Act cases.

Notable Facts

The company has an informal Native peoples hiring program and provides cash support for Native trade shows to Europe. The 10% of the company's workforce that is unionized all work at the Prince Rupert plant. The company had an eight person reduction in staff at its head office in 1990-91.

Ogilvie Mills Ltd.

1 Place Ville Marie, Suite 2100, Montreal, PQ H3B 2X2

Founded in Canada: 1801, Montreal, PQ
Ownership: John Labatt Limited (Canada), 100%
Operations: AB*, MB*, ON*, PQ*
Employees: 950
Annual sales: $300 million

Ogilvie Mills, Canada's largest flour miller, owns plants in Midland and Strathroy, Ont., Montreal and Medicine Hat, Alta. It is among the world's leading producers of wheat starch and gluten, with operations in Quebec, Ontario, Iowa (USA) and Bordeaux, France. In May, 1992, owner John Labatt Limited reached an agreement in principle to sell the company to Archer Daniels Midland Co., a big US conglomerate that has been building its share of the Canadian milling market over the past two years.

Making the Grade

CANDOUR: Ogilvie Mills was exceptionally forthcoming, earning a spot on our Honour Roll.

WOMEN'S ISSUES: Women make up 25% of the workforce and 12% of management personnel. There are no women in senior management; one of the seven board members is a woman. Ogilvie offers formal employment and pay equity programs and some of its plants provide on-site or nearby daycare facilities.

CHARITABLE GIVING AND COMMUNITY INVOLVEMENT: Ogilvie Mills is not part of the Imagine campaign, yet in 1990 it gave 1% of its pre-tax earnings to charity, a total of $142,000. It gives employees paid time off for volunteer activities, publicizes such activities in the *Ogilvie News* and runs a matching gift program.

PROGRESSIVE STAFF POLICIES: Noteworthy policies include counselling for drug and alcohol abuse, retirement counselling, adoption leave, a stop-smoking program, rewards for cost-saving ideas and open-door management. The company also provides the *Ogilvie News* newsletter, annual written performance reviews for each employee and an annual report for employees.

LABOUR RELATIONS: Its strong showing in this category gave Ogilvie a spot on this Honour Roll, despite the lack of a formal job security program. The company uses retraining, relocation, early retirement, financial compen-

Brand Name:
Five Roses
Ogilvie

sation and advance notice of technological change to reduce the impact of layoffs or downsizing. As well, it has tested a number of quality of working life initiatives (e.g. job redesign) at specific work sites. The company not only runs an employee share ownership purchase plan, it pays all associated brokerage fees. In 1990, the company spent $500 per employee on training.

ENVIRONMENTAL MANAGEMENT: The company received a low score in this area. It has a written environmental code but no environmental committee, and makes no regular reports to the board. While at least five employees have environmental responsibilities, none has full-time duties. No environmental audits are conducted.

ENVIRONMENTAL PERFORMANCE: Another low score, although the company recycles paper in its offices and has invested in product research and development, equipment replacement and packaging reformulation. Its Envirostrip product, a starch abrasive used for blasting surfaces and stripping paint, is more environmentally-friendly than traditional chemical methods. The company has been featured in a Quebec Government film on the transformation of effluent into methane gas. However, its Thunder Bay plant is operating under an Ontario Government environmental control order directed at reducing wastewater discharges.

MANAGEMENT PRACTICES AND CONSUMER RELATIONS: Ogilvie Mills has a written code of ethics but no annual employee sign-off and no ethics advisory service. It was one of several millers fined in 1990 for bid rigging on wheat flour sold to the Canadian government, some of it destined for famine relief in developing countries.

Notable Facts

The company, which is 80% unionized, has had two strikes, one in 1987 and another in 1988. The former lasted only one week and affected 70 Thunder Bay, Ont., employees; the latter lasted eight weeks and affected 70 Candiac, PQ workers. The company sells its Envirostrip paint stripper to the military for airplane maintenance. In addition to employment and pay equity, Ogilvie has hiring and promotion programs for minorities, people with disabilities and Native peoples.

Old Dutch Foods Limited

100 Bentall St., Winnipeg, MB R2X 2Y5

Founded in Canada: 1951, Winnipeg, MB
Ownership: Vernon G. Aanenson (US), 100%
Operations: BC, AB*, SK, MB*, ON
Employees: 625
Annual sales in Canada: $100 million

Old Dutch Foods, a wholly-owned private company, has its roots in a Minneapolis firm founded in 1935. Its snack food products are expanding from its stronghold in western Canada, where it has a 56% share of the potato chip market. The company has offices in Manitoba and Ontario, and plants in Winnipeg, Calgary, and Airdrie, Alta.

Making the Grade

CANDOUR: Old Dutch Foods was fairly responsive to our surveys. However, most of its scores were low, as it has relatively few formal programs.

WOMEN'S ISSUES: Old Dutch earned a place on our Honour Roll. Women represent 50% of the workforce, and 20% and 37% of management and senior management positions respectively. Two of the company's three board members are female. On the other hand, Old Dutch has no formal programs for the advancement of women.

CHARITABLE GIVING AND COMMUNITY INVOLVEMENT: Old Dutch is not on Imagine's Caring Company list and did not provide any charitable donation figures. However, it is involved with its local communities: it donates equipment, provides unpaid time off for employee volunteer activity and supports numerous local civic groups.

LABOUR RELATIONS: The company's formal job security program includes retraining, relocation, early retirement and advance notice of technological change.

ENVIRONMENTAL MANAGEMENT: While Old Dutch makes reports to the board as needed, it has no environmental policy, full-time environmental affairs officer or environmental committee.

ENVIRONMENTAL PERFORMANCE: The company's highest score was in this area. It conducts audits of some of its operations, recycles paper, packaging and manufacturing byproducts and has invested in equipment upgrades and package reformulation. It has no record of environmental infractions.

Brand Name
Old Dutch

MANAGEMENT PRACTICES AND CONSUMER RELATIONS: The company has no written code of ethics, but it has not been charged with any Competition Act or consumer law transgressions, either.

Notable Facts

The United Food and Commercial Workers Union represents 35% of employees. There have been no strikes in the past 10 years.

Pepsi-Cola Canada Ltd.

1255 Bay St., Toronto, ON M5R 2A9

Founded in Canada: 1934, Montreal, PQ
Ownership: PepsiCo Inc. (US), 100%
Operations: bottling operations in all provinces and territories except NWT
Employees: 3,000

Pepsi-Cola is a leading bottler and marketer of carbonated beverages across Canada. It consists of 3,000 people who work in company-owned operations and another 1,500 to 2,000 who work in franchised bottling plants. In a streamlining process begun in 1988, the number of independent bottlers has been reduced from 60 to fewer than 10.

Making the Grade

CANDOUR: Pepsi-Cola Canada and its public relations counsel, Hill and Knowlton, provided us with some information late in our process.

WOMEN'S ISSUES: Two of seven members of the executive committee (which serves as the company's board of directors) are women.

CHARITABLE GIVING AND COMMUNITY INVOLVEMENT: The company is not part of the Imagine campaign and did not disclose the amount of its charitable donations. However, through the Pepsi Substance Abuse Foundation, the company has either developed or sponsored a wide variety of local and national substance abuse programs. While this is the main focus of the company's community involvement, it also supports the United Way, sporting events and a youth development program. Bottlers support local activities in their own communities.

LABOUR RELATIONS: An employee share option plan, called Pepsi Share Power, is offered to all full-time employees, with part-time employees eligible after working for the company for 24 months.

ENVIRONMENTAL MANAGEMENT: Pepsi-Cola is on our Honour Roll in this category. It has a written environmental policy, provided through the Canadian Soft Drink Association, and a vice-president of environmental and government affairs. It also has a staff environmental committee and makes monthly environmental reports to the executive committee.

BRAND NAMES

7UP
Diet 7UP
Diet Mountain Dew
Diet Pepsi
Mountain Dew
Pepsi

ENVIRONMENTAL PERFORMANCE: The company has reduced the weight of its containers, removed CFCs from its foam labels, modified the plastic liners in bottle caps so they can be removed during recycling and minimized the amount of secondary packaging (one means being the adoption of reusable shells). In Quebec, the company has started using bottles manufactured in part with recycled plastic. In Ontario, it helps fund the Blue Box recycling program. In 1988, Pepsi was fined $1,000 under Ontario's Environmental Protection Act (EPA) for a 1987 violation of beverage container advertising regulations.

MANAGEMENT PRACTICES AND CONSUMER RELATIONS: Pepsi-Cola's written code of ethics comes from its US parent company. It was fined $2,000 for misleading advertising in a 1987 contest, when it falsely advertised the number of eligible entries. It has no toll-free number or social practices report.

Notable Facts

Shareholders in the United States have asked the parent company to stop its use of animal testing and surgical stapling. The Canadian company does no animal testing. The parent has no direct involvement in South Africa, although it maintains certain franchise rights in that country.

PepsiCo Foods International, also a subsidiary of PepsiCo Inc., owns 100% of Hostess Frito-Lay Company. (see p. 178). Pepsi-Cola Canada produces C-Plus, Crush, Hires (see Cadbury Beverages Canada Inc. profile, see p. 117), Pure Spring and Dr. Pepper under licence for other soft drink companies.

Pillsbury Canada Ltd.

675 Cochrane Dr., Suite 700, Markham, ON L3R 0M7

Ownership: Grand Metropolitan Plc (UK), 100%

Operations: BC*, AB, ON*, PQ*, NS

Employees: 1,236

The British parent company, one of the six largest alcohol manufacturers in the world, acquired US-based Pillsbury in 1988. Pillsbury has introduced North Americans to brand-name characters such as the chubby Pillsbury Dough Boy and the towering Green Giant, mascot for Green Giant frozen and canned vegetables.

Making the Grade

CANDOUR: The company provided us with a fairly substantial amount of information.

WOMEN'S ISSUES: Forty-four percent of the company's workforce is female, and 25% of both management and senior management positions are filled by women. There are no women on the 10-man board of directors. Pillsbury has no formal employment equity program and does not offer extended maternity leave, but provides a daycare referral service and has flexible working hours.

CHARITABLE GIVING AND COMMUNITY INVOLVEMENT: The company is not on Imagine's list, and did not disclose the percentage of pre-tax earnings donated to charity. The 1990 total, however, was $67,000. Its community involvement includes a university matching gift program, sports team support and an annual picnic to benefit the Children's Aid Society.

PROGRESSIVE STAFF POLICIES: Pillsbury offers staff flexible benefits, a stop-smoking program, annual written performance reviews of all employees and various activities co-ordinated through a staff social committee. The comments gathered through attitiude surveys are reviewed regularly and help shape subsequent management actions. Twice yearly, plant and head office operations are closed for a half-day employee communications meeting.

LABOUR RELATIONS: Pillsbury is on the Honour Roll in this category. It has a formal job security program, and uses financial compensation and advance notice of technological change to address downsizing issues. The company has two incentive programs (one for plant workers and one for head-office staff) and a gain sharing program for management and non-unionized employees. The com-

BRAND NAMES
FraserVale
Green Giant
Jeno's
Le Sieur
Pillsbury
Pizza Pops
Totino's

pany spends $2,500 annually on training per employee, not including wages. Health and safety figures were provided.

ENVIRONMENTAL MANAGEMENT: The company scored poorly in this area because it has no formal policy, committee or personnel dedicated to addressing environmental concerns.

ENVIRONMENTAL PERFORMANCE: This score was only slightly higher. The company conducts no environmental audits, and its environmental programs are limited to in-house recycling efforts and the replacement of disposable cutlery and dishes. Pillsbury has not been charged with violation of any environmental laws.

MANAGEMENT PRACTICES AND CONSUMER RELATIONS: Although Pillsbury has no written code of ethics, the parent company has provided conflict of interest guidelines, updated in 1992, which Canadian employees are required to read and sign annually. No ethics ombudsman, social practices report or toll-free number exist. The company has not been charged with any Competition Act violations.

Notable Facts

Employment is up 50% from six years ago, when the company had 800 workers, despite the fact that it closed a Niagara Falls, Ont., plant in 1987. Over 70% of the employees are unionized and there have been no strikes or lockouts in the past 10 years. The parent company owns three alcohol-related South African operations.

Playtex Ltd.

6363 Northam Dr., Mississauga, ON L4V 1N5

Founded in Canada: 1953, Arnprior, ON
Ownership: Playtex Family Products Corporation (US), 100%
Operations: ON*
Employees: 200

The company had its origins as a bandaging and tampon plant in Arnprior, Ont., in the early 1950s. In 1988, the breakup of the parent company resulted in the formation of two separate operations in Canada: Playtex Ltd. and Playtex Apparel. Playtex Ltd.'s non-unionized workforce makes tampons, baby feeding systems and latex gloves.

Making the Grade

Playtex Ltd. did not complete any of the EthicScan surveys but did provide some comments during the final fact-checking. The company is not on Imagine's Caring Company list and does not have a large involvement in the community. No environmental violations are on record.

Notable Facts

The US parent is involved in court cases concerning Toxic Shock Syndrome (TSS). The Canadian company chose not to comment on this subject.

BRAND NAMES
Cherubs
Jhirmack
Playtex

Primo Foods Limited

3700 Steeles Ave. W., Suite 1100, Woodbridge, ON L4L 8M4

Founded in Canada: 1952, Hamilton, ON
Ownership: Pet Incorporated (US), 100%
Operations: BC, AB*, ON*, PQ*
Employees: 1,000

Originally a Canadian-owned operation, Primo Foods was acquired by US-based Pet Incorporated in 1988. Pet, a leading food manufacturer in the US, became an independent, publicly-traded company in 1991 when it was sold to shareholders by the then parent, Whitman Corporation. Primo is a major presence in the pasta, processed meats, and Mexican foods markets. Restructuring in 1991 involved four plant closures (three in Quebec and one in Ontario) and the relocation of processing lines to other facilities. It has plants in Cottam, Ont., Toronto, Edmonton and Montreal.

Making the Grade

CANDOUR: After being reviewed by Primo, our surveys were sent on to Pet Incorporated in Missouri. While Pet expressed interest, it did not return any information to us. Primo provided some details on its operations late in the process, but the overall lack of data meant we could not provide scores in most categories.

CHARITABLE GIVING AND COMMUNITY INVOLVEMENT: The company is not part of the Imagine campaign and did not provide any figures for charitable donations. However, it often contributes cash, food and organizational help to community events, particularly in host communities. Primo also supports the Canadian Spitfires, a paraplegic basketball team. Employees in the firm's many retail and food service facilities can participate in a matching gift program.

LABOUR RELATIONS: Staff who successfully complete a range of job-related retraining programs have their expenses reimbursed by the company.

ENVIRONMENTAL PERFORMANCE: While environmental policy decisions are made by the parent company, an environmental program is being developed and implemented by a Canadian subcommittee. The program calls for a 50% reduction in waste by the year 2000, the use of more recyclable packaging and container materials and a reduction in the weight and number of layers in plastic containers. Primo was fined $7,000 for a 1987

BRAND NAMES
Ac'cent
Bittner
Coorsh
Old El Paso
Primo
Sugar in the Raw
Sweet 'n Low
Underwood

violation of the Ontario Water Resources Act when food wastes and starches were found in the drainwater.

MANAGEMENT PRACTICES AND CONSUMER RELATIONS: Primo is directed in Canada by a management team, rather than a board of directors. It has a code of ethics, modelled on that of the parent company but adapted for Canadian conditions.

Notable Facts

Primo has no record of strikes over the past 10 years. The company announced that it was providing severance packages and job search assistance to the 150-250 workers laid off during the 1990-91 restructuring.

Procter & Gamble Inc.

PO Box 355, Station A, Toronto, ON M5W 1C5

Founded in Canada: 1952, Toronto, ON
Ownership: The Procter & Gamble Company (US), 100%
Operations: AB*, ON*, PQ*
Employees: 3,500
Annual sales: $1.4 billion

Procter & Gamble is the leading manufacturer of disposable diapers in Canada and the market leader in laundry detergent. It is involved in virtually every part of the personal care products market, with a strong presence in soap, shampoo and toothpaste. Acquisitions like Max Factor (Cover Girl, Clarion) and Facelle (paper products) in 1991 have further strengthened the company's dominance in the consumer products industry both here and abroad. P&G exports to 24 countries worldwide.

Making the Grade

CANDOUR: The company participated in our research, although some information gaps remain.

WOMEN'S ISSUES: The company did not provide figures on the employment of women. It offers staff a daycare referral program, adoption leave and extended maternity leave (on a case-by-case basis).

BRAND NAMES

Always	Duncan Hines	Old Spice
Attends	Facelle	Oxydol
Bain de Soleil	Facettes	Pampers
Bold	Fasteeth	Pantene
Bounce	Festival	Pert
Camay	Fixodent	Pringles
Cascade	Florelle	Pronto
Cheer	Fluffo	Royale
Citrus Hill	Hawaiian Punch	Safeguard
Clearasil	Head and Shoulders	Scope
Coast	Ivory	Secret
Comet	Ivory Snow	Spic 'n Span
Crest	Joy	Sunny Delight
Crisco	Lestoil	Tide
Dash	Luvs	Vidal Sassoon
Dove (sanitary tissue)	Mr. Clean	Wondra
Downy	Noxema	Zest
Dreft	Oil of Olay	

CHARITABLE GIVING AND COMMUNITY INVOLVEMENT: The company is not part of the Imagine campaign and did not disclose its 1990 charitable giving information. However, in a 1990 issue of the *Corporate Ethics Monitor*, P&G said the company gave $500,000 to charity in 1989, with employees contributing another $100,000. This total amounted to 0.5% of corporate pre-tax earnings for that year. The company participates in the United Way's loaned executive program and supports the Canadian Special Olympics, the Women's National Basketball team and Block Parents. The President of P&G helped establish the Alliance for a Drug Free Canada, a group organized to combat drug abuse in the workplace.

PROGRESSIVE STAFF POLICIES: P&G is on this Honour Roll. Its employee assistance program includes personal and family counselling, while the health promotion program includes an on-site fitness facility at head office and company-supported health and self defense classes. The company provides service awards to employees with outstanding achievements and runs a scholarship fund for employees and their children. All employees receive an annual written performance review.

LABOUR RELATIONS: P&G has no formal job security program, but has provided severance benefits and job-search assistance to laid-off employees. The company has a share ownership purchase plan and a profit-sharing plan that acts as a retirement benefit.

ENVIRONMENTAL MANAGEMENT: The Canadian subsidiary has a written environmental policy and an environmental committee made up of senior managers.

ENVIRONMENTAL PERFORMANCE: Over the last three years, solid wastes have been reduced more than 50% overall and more than 85% at the Belleville, Ont., plant. The weight and volume of P&G diapers have been cut by 50% over the past six years and the amount of packaging by 90 percent. Consumer and environmental organizations charge that disposable diapers damage the environment largely because of the space they occupy in landfill sites. On the other hand, two life cycle studies commissioned by parent P&G suggest that cloth and disposable diapers each have associated benefits and costs. P&G is spending $23 million worldwide, $3.5 million of it in Canada, on experimental diaper composting centres. One of P&G's Ontario plants was fined $4,000 in 1986 for a violation of the Environmental Protection Act (EPA). Its new Grande Prairie, Alta., operation, which makes pulp for tissue products, was put under a control order after a December 1991 fish test revealed levels of toxins (furans) in the plant effluent that exceeded discharge guidelines.

MANAGEMENT PRACTICES AND CONSUMER RELATIONS: Procter & Gamble has a written code of ethics, but does not require an annual employee sign-off. The Recycling Council of Ontario filed a complaint against the company for claiming that its disposable diapers are 80% compostable: the Council argues that the claims are misleading because no facilities in Canada are currently producing compost from disposable diapers, while P&G defends its advertising as an accurate vision of future diaper composting initiatives. The company has different toll-free numbers for its various product lines.

Notable Facts

The P&G workforce is not unionized. The company has closed three plants in the past five years and carried out layoffs in Hamilton, Ont. (in 1987) and Grande Cache, Alta. (in 1991). However, the company expects the Free Trade Agreement to create between 200 and 400 jobs for Procter & Gamble in Canada.

While the Canadian company does not conduct any animal tests, its US parent does. In 1991, the parent company announced a joint research agreement with Marrow-Tech Incorporated to help P&G further reduce its use of animals in safety and efficacy testing. Noxell, one of P&G's US-based subsidiaries, is a founding member of the Centre for Alternatives to Animal Testing.

The parent company retains a trade mark licensing agreement with a former South African subsidiary.

The Quaker Oats Company of Canada Limited QUAKER

Quaker Park, Peterborough, ON K9J 7B2

Founded in Canada: 1901, Peterborough, ON
Ownership: Quaker Oats Company (US), 100%
Operations: BC, AB, ON*, PQ, NS
Employees: 1,000
Annual sales: $282 million

The parent company, founded in 1888, began milling and selling oats in Canada at the turn of the century. Since that time, the name has become virtually synonymous with oatmeal. In addition to breakfast cereals, the company produces frozen foods, syrup, pet foods, granola bars and baking mixes, and has a 25% share in many of those markets. Its plants, one in Peterborough and two in Trenton, Ont., are major employers in their communities.

Making the Grade

CANDOUR: Quaker and its two independent unions were responsive to our surveys and provided fairly comprehensive information.

WOMEN'S ISSUES: Quaker did not disclose the percentages of women in management and senior management positions, so it could not receive a score in this category. However, 40% of its workforce are women, and one member of the 10-person board of directors. Quaker has no formal employment equity program and no daycare provision, but does offer extended maternity leave.

**CHARITABLE GIVING AND COMMU-
NITY INVOLVEMENT:** While not pledged to the Imagine campaign, Quaker donated $150,000 (0.5% of pre-tax earnings) to charity in 1990. It lends corporate facilities to charitable organizations and gives employees paid time off for volunteer activities, which it also publicizes in the company newsletter, *Quaker Update*. As well, it supports health-related charities and funds both the arts and youth programs. In 1990, the company contributed $375,000 toward the construction of an environmental sciences centre at Trent University.

BRAND NAMES	
Aunt Jemima	OH's
Cap'n Crunch	Pamper
Chicken Cuts	Pep
Chocolate Coated	Pounce
Dips	Puss 'n Boots
Corn Bran	Quaker
Cycle	Rice-A-Roni
Harvest Crunch	Rover
Ken-L-Ration	Savoury Classics
Kibbles 'N Bits 'N	Snausages
Bits 'N Bits	Society
Kretschmer Wheat	T-Bone
Germ	Tender Chunks
Life	Total Diet
Oat Squares	Treats

PROGRESSIVE STAFF POLICIES: Quaker is on the Honour Roll in this category. It recently revamped its employee assistance program to include drug and alcohol abuse counselling and funds a health promotion program that offers stop-smoking support and a fitness facility (at the Peterborough, Ont., head office). Communication activities include one company and one union newsletter, an open-door management policy and an annual written performance review. The company provides a wage bonus plan.

ENVIRONMENTAL MANAGEMENT: The company received a high grade in this area, earning a place on this Honour Roll as well. Quaker issues a five-page environmental responsibility policy, has an environmental committee of the board (which makes reports to the Board as needed) and an environmental working committee. Two staff work full-time at Peterborough on waste reduction.

ENVIRONMENTAL PERFORMANCE: Quaker is also on this Honour Roll. It conducts environmental audits of some of its operations, and investments and in-house programs over the last few years have resulted in a better than 80% reduction of landfill-bound waste — as well as savings of $1 million. Much of its packaging is now made from recycled materials and various packaging improvements have been introduced, including a change of glue on its boxes so that underfilled containers can be returned to the production line instead of being thrown away. The company runs a waste-reduction training program for employees and provides all 250 staff at head office with individual recycling bins at their desks. The no-waste policy extends to manufacturing by-products: 28% of all food-based waste is sold to other companies for use in the production of animal feed. The company has not been charged with any environmental violations.

MANAGEMENT PRACTICES AND CONSUMER RELATIONS: The company has no written code of ethics, and did not comment on whether or not it has been involved in any Competition Act litigation. It provides a toll-free number for consumers in southern Ontario only.

Notable Facts

The company and its unions are committed to building a cooperative relationship, using such mechanisms as flex-time and flex benefits, pay for knowledge and joint management-union committees to deal with hiring and promotion issues. The union offers bursary programs to children of members, and counselling on benefits and pensions, as well as bereavement counselling.

Ralston Purina Canada Inc.

2500 Royal Windsor Dr., Mississauga, ON L5J 1K8

Founded in Canada: 1928, Mississauga, ON
Ownership: Ralston Purina Company (US), 100%
Operations: BC, AB*, MB, ON*, PQ, NS
Employees: 1,000
Toll-free number: 800-268-5384

This company is wholly-owned by the Missouri-based Ralston Purina Company. Its checkerboard trademark has been its symbol since the parent company began operations in 1894. In Canada, the company is a leader in the pet food industry and owns one of the two biggest names in batteries, Eveready. It also has an agricultural feeds division, which is not included in this *Guide*.

Making the Grade

CANDOUR: Ralston Purina provided us with a considerable amount of information.

WOMEN'S ISSUES: Women represent 30% of the company's workforce, and occupy 25% of management and 33% of senior management positions. All three members of the board of directors are male. There is a daycare referral service available to employees, but no employment equity program or extended maternity leave benefits.

CHARITABLE GIVING AND COMMUNITY INVOLVEMENT: Ralston Purina is not on Imagine's Caring Company list and did not disclose the amount of its charitable contributions. However, it donates product to charitable organizations, has a matching gift program and supports hearing ear and seeing eye dog programs. As well, the company strongly supports education programs aimed at responsible pet ownership.

PROGRESSIVE STAFF POLICIES: The company received a good grade in this area, partly because of its comprehensive employee assistance program, which includes parental and eldercare, financial, substance abuse, and stress counselling for employees, their dependents and retirees. Suggestion programs, an employee newsletter (*Grocery Notes*) and a policy of open-door management are among its communications initiatives.

ENVIRONMENTAL MANAGEMENT: The company has a written environmental code and the pet foods division

BRAND NAMES
Butcher's Blend
Grrravy
Happy Cat
Kibbles and Chews
Meow Mix
O.N.E.
Pro Plan
Purina
Tender Vittles

240

has an environmental task force consisting of four senior managers. While each of its three divisions has an employee with environmental duties, none is a full-time environmental affairs position.

ENVIRONMENTAL PERFORMANCE: Although Ralston Purina conducts environmental audits of some of its operations, its grade in this category was low because of the small number of environmental initiatives. The company recycles paper in all of its offices and has a green products line: its 99.9% mercury-free Encore batteries. No other environmental programs or practices were noted. It has had no environmental violations in the past 10 years.

MANAGEMENT PRACTICES AND CONSUMER RELATIONS: The score in this category is comparatively good. Ralston Purina uses its parent's worldwide *Business Practices and Standards of Conduct* policy, reissued in 1991. This policy does not require annual employee sign-off. The company has not been charged with any Competition Act violations.

Notable Facts

The unionized 20% of its workforce belong to the Energy and Chemical Workers union. No layoffs have been reported over the past ten years. One prolonged strike, from September 1980 to February 1981, is on record, which affected 100 workers. It is company policy not to use irradiated ingredients or processes in its food products and animal feed.

Redpath Sugars

95 Queen's Quay E., Toronto, ON M5E 1A3

Founded in Canada: 1854, Montreal, PQ
Ownership: Tate & Lyle PLC (UK), 100%
Operations: ON*, PQ
Employees: 320
Annual sales: $222.5 million

Redpath Sugars was founded in Montreal in 1854. In 1989, parent company Tate & Lyle, which had held 50% of Redpath's shares, purchased all the outstanding shares. Redpath operates one refinery on the Toronto waterfront and is the largest remaining commercial user of the Port of Toronto. The company recently established a division called Redpath Specialty Products to launch the artificial sweetener Splenda.

Making the Grade

CANDOUR: Redpath was more forthcoming in certain areas of our survey (for instance, Progressive Staff Policies) than in others, and this difference is reflected in the Tables.

WOMEN'S ISSUES: Women compose 35% of Redpath's total workforce but hold only 17% of its management positions. There are no women in senior management. The firm has no formal employment equity program or provision for extended maternity leave.

CHARITABLE GIVING AND COMMUNITY INVOLVEMENT: In 1991, Redpath donated a total of approximately $30,000 in cash to some 75 charitable recipients. The company is not pledged to the Imagine campaign, although it was mentioned in the *Recent Imagine Activities* newsletter for printing the Imagine logo on sugar packets to be distributed throughout eastern Canada. Redpath also donates sugar in bulk, supports local sports teams and operates a sugar museum that draws 15,000 visitors each year.

PROGRESSIVE STAFF POLICIES: This was the company's highest-rated category. Redpath offers retirement and alcohol and drug abuse counselling, an on-site fitness facility, training programs and scholarship funds for employees' children (24 awards were made in 1989). As well, the company has a long-standing written policy of paying tuition for employees' night school courses and contributing financially to educational upgrading. Communication is a priority at Redpath, with an employee newsletter (*Communique*), a suggestion program and annual performance reviews.

Brand Names
QuickSet
Redpath
Splenda

242

LABOUR RELATIONS: Redpath does not have a formal job security policy, although it does use seniority in cases of layoffs. The company has a stock purchase plan for all employees. All workers are eligible for cardiopulmonary resuscitation and St. John's Ambulance training.

ENVIRONMENTAL MANAGEMENT: Redpath has a written environmental policy and provides environmental reports to the board as needed. The company did not say how many of its employees have an environmental function, although at least one senior engineer has some environmental responsibilities.

ENVIRONMENTAL PERFORMANCE: The company's initiatives include a staff environmental committee and in-office recycling. The company recycles the heat produced in its plant (which is powered by natural gas) and has no environmental court convictions or instances of exceeding discharge limits.

Notable Facts

Redpath works with two unions, the Chemical Energy and Allied Workers and the Canadian Conference of Teamsters, Local 1688. Approximately 45% of the workforce is unionized. The company has had one strike in the last 10 years, which was over wages and involved 156 employees. Redpath exports Canadian-made product to several countries.

The parent company has one subsidiary in South Africa.

Reynolds Aluminum Company of Canada

1420 Sherbrooke St. W., Suite 802, Montreal, PQ H3G 1K9   REYNLD

Founded in Canada: 1955, Cap-de-la-Madeleine, PQ
Ownership: Reynolds Metals Co. (US), 100%
Operations: BC, AB, SK, MB, ON*, PQ*, NS
Employees: 990
Annual sales: $678 million (US) (total for Canadian Reynolds Metals Company Limited)

Reynolds Aluminum Company of Canada operates four plants: two in Quebec (Cap-de-la-Madeleine and Anjou) and two in Ontario (Rexdale and Weston). Reynolds Aluminum of Canada is one of three divisions of Canadian Reynolds Metals Company Limited, the others being Reynolds Extrusion and Reynolds Cable. The division makes an average of 79,000 tons of aluminum each year. Though its principal product is aluminum sheet and foil, it also makes car radiator fins, packaging materials, construction materials and containers.

Making the Grade

CANDOUR: Canadian Reynolds Metals, referred to here as the Canadian parent company, completed our surveys. Despite waiting until late in the process, the company received a high rating. Some information was also provided by the Federation of Metals Trades, one of the unions representing Reynolds employees.

WOMEN'S ISSUES: Reynolds has a formal employment equity program and in 1991 received an Equal Opportunity Award from Employment and Immigration Canada for its program to hire women in non-traditional jobs. Although women represent only 15% of the company's workforce, 27% of its managers are women. Only 1% of senior officers are women, however, and there are no women on the 13-member board of directors.

CHARITABLE GIVING AND COMMUNITY INVOLVEMENT: Canadian Reynolds Metals, which does not belong to the Imagine campaign, made charitable donations of $68,200 in 1991. It also donates equipment and in some plant locations provides scholarships for employees' children.

PROGRESSIVE STAFF POLICIES: The company's highest score was in this category. It offers counselling for alcohol and drug abuse, retirement planning and family and financial issues. It also provides training programs, publicizes health issues in employee publications, runs a suggestion program with reward incentives for cost-saving

BRAND NAMES
Baker's Choice
Brown-In-Bag
Diamond
Presto
Reynolds

ideas and offers scholarship funds for both employees and their children.

LABOUR RELATIONS: Reynolds has a formal job security policy and five specific methods of addressing job security issues (retraining, relocation, early retirement, financial compensation and advance notice of technological change). It provided health and safety figures for its Cap-de-la-Madeleine plant.

ENVIRONMENTAL MANAGEMENT: Canadian Reynolds Metals has a written environmental policy, a working environmental committee made up of various layers of management, and 10 staff members with environmental responsibilities.

ENVIRONMENTAL PERFORMANCE: The Canadian parent company has done a comprehensive environmental audit in some of its operations, and has no environmental convictions or record of exceeding discharge limits. In the last 10 years, Canadian Reynolds Metals has devoted some $200 million to environmental expenditures, much of it used to upgrade plants in Quebec and the Baie-Comeau smelter. (The company acknowledges that the Baie-Comeau smelter had been identified as one of the 50 most serious industrial polluters along the St. Lawrence.)

In 1989, Canadian Reynolds Metals signed a pollution abatement program agreement with the Quebec ministry of the environment as part of the St. Lawrence Action Plan. Reynolds Aluminum's Cap-de-la-Madeleine plant is covered under a different provincial pollution control plan. The Canadian parent says that soil contaminated by PCBs at the Baie-Comeau smelter is being stored in compliance with ministry of the environment guildelines. US-based Reynolds Metals Co., owner of Canadian Reynolds Metals, has now developed a process for the non-hazardous treatment of spent potlinings (an industrial by-product).

Reynolds supports curbside recycling programs, including a pilot project with the City of Scarborough in Ontario to recycle aluminum foil and foil containers. The company recycles both scrap aluminum and process scrap at the Cap-de-la-Madeleine plant, and the recycled material accounts for almost 15% of its metal supply.

MANAGEMENT PRACTICES AND CONSUMER RELATIONS: Reynolds has a written code of ethics which employees periodically review. A company spokesperson says the code has been revised in the last two years. Reynolds has had no convictions under the Competition Act.

Notable Facts

The Ontario ministry of the environment stated in a 1990 press release that fluoride levels in vegetation on Cornwall Island (part of the Mohawk reserve at Akwesasne) were higher than Ontario government guidelines permit. The ministry identified the Massena, NY plant of Canadian Reynolds Metals' US parent company, Reynolds Aluminum Co., as the source of the emissions. In 1992, a ministry spokesperson stated that, because the plant meets New York state environmental legislation, the company has been "slow to act on the problem." The same spokesperson said that, to its credit, Reynolds moved quickly to address problems with water emissions as soon as they were discovered. The company is now actively involved in PCB cleanup around the site, and has agreed to fund research into environmental sampling and other programs to help alleviate some of the reported problems.

Robin Hood Multifoods Inc.

RHOOD

60 Columbia Way, Markham, ON L3R 0C9

Founded in Canada: 1909, Moose Jaw, SK
Ownership: International Multifoods Corporation (US), 100%
Operations: BC, SK*, MB, ON*, PQ*, NB
Employees: 1,400
Annual sales: $396 million
Toll-free number: 800-268-3232

Originally named Robin Hood Flour Mills Ltd., the company began its operations in Canada as a miller and has since expanded into the condiment market by purchasing well-known brands such as Bick's and Habitant. Two plant closures (in Newfoundland and Toronto) and the sale of its Stafford Food division have dropped employment totals over the past five years from 1,775 to the current 1,400.

Making the Grade

WOMEN'S ISSUES: Women are 23% of Robin Hood's workforce but only 15% of its management. There are no women in senior management. The company did not report on the number of women on the board. Robin Hood has a formal employment equity program and offers extended maternity leave.

CHARITABLE GIVING AND COMMUNITY INVOLVEMENT: The company received a low rating in this category. It is not pledged to the Imagine campaign and did not reveal donations figures. However, it has a high level of involvement in the communities in which it operates. Among other things, it runs a university matching gift program, donates equipment and gives employees paid time off for their volunteer activites.

PROGRESSIVE STAFF POLICIES: Policies and services include drug and alcohol abuse counselling, adoption leave, a scholarship fund for employees' children, open-door management and an employee newsletter.

LABOUR RELATIONS: Robin Hood received a low rating, despite offering an employee stock option purchase plan to all employees. It has no formal job security program.

ENVIRONMENTAL MANAGEMENT: While the company has a written environmental policy, its lack of environmental committees or any senior environmental affairs officials led to a poor rating.

BRAND NAMES
Bick's
Celebration
Gattuso(condiments)
Habitant(condiments
McLarens
Old Mill
Palm
Robin Hood
Rose

ENVIRONMENTAL PERFORMANCE: The rating here was somewhat better. Robin Hood conducts audits of some of its operations, and has redesigned product packaging to make use of recycled materials in its boxes, bags and glass containers. It has no record of environmental violations or fines.

MANAGEMENT PRACTICES AND CONSUMER RELATIONS: Robin Hood is on the Honour Roll in this category. It has both a written code of ethics, revised in 1991, which requires annual sign-off by managers, and an ethics advisory section in the company newsletter. Robin Hood was one of several millers fined in 1990 under the Competition Act for rigging prices for wheat sold to the federal government, some of which was designated as famine relief for Africa.

Notable Facts

Approximately 43% of Robin Hood employees are unionized. A five-month strike at the Port Colborne, Ont., plant involved 130 workers who were concerned about the loss of 16 jobs due to technological change. No other strikes have been reported.

The company makes Gattuso-brand condiments, while Borden Catelli Consumer Products (see p. 109) and Campbell Soup Company (see p. 119) make Gattuso pasta and sauces and soups respectively. Similarly, Campbell Soup Company owns the Habitant soup label, while Robin Hood Multifoods makes condiments under that brand name.

Neither the company, nor its parent is involved in South Africa.

S.C. Johnson & Son, Limited

I Webster St., Brantford, ON N3T 5RI

Founded in Canada: 1920, Brantford, ON
Ownership: S.C. Johnson & Son, Inc. (US), 100%
Operations: ON*
Employees: 370

The company was founded in 1886 in Wisconsin and now has operations in more than 48 countries worldwide. It is a private, family-controlled enterprise that began as a manufacturer of parquet flooring and expanded into floor care products. Samuel C. Johnson, great-grandson of the founder, serves as president and chairman of the board. In addition to a well-established leadership in floor care products, the company makes insect repellant (launched in 1956), shampoos (dating from the 1970s), laundry stain remover and shaving cream. It has brands with significant market share in furniture polish, floor finish, air deodorizers and insecticides. Its one Canadian plant is located in Brantford, Ont.

Making the Grade

CANDOUR: The company provided considerable information about its environmental performance and completed the product survey, but did not answer questions about other aspects of its operations. Its Candour rating was therefore quite low.

CHARITABLE GIVING AND COMMUNITY INVOLVEMENT: S.C. Johnson has not joined the Imagine campaign. However, the company supports its Brantford, Ont., community through donations to a wide variety of cultural activities, such as the Capital Theatre Building Foundation, and to such community services as the YMCA and Nova Women's Shelter. It also supports a host of environment-related causes, including the Apps Mill Nature Centre and the Greening of Brant project, which involves school presentations and a tree-planting program.

PROGRESSIVE STAFF POLICIES: Through the Johnson Employees Association, all permanent employees can use the on-site fitness facility and the Lake St. Joseph vacation resort.

LABOUR RELATIONS: Like its parent, the Canadian company has a no-layoff policy for full-time workers: the company keeps full-time staff at levels that can be maintained

BRAND NAMES
Agree
Aveeno
Bon Ami
Bravo
Clubman's
Deep Woods
Edge
Favor
Fine Wood Buffing Wax
Freedom
French Formula
Future
Glade
Glory
Halsa
Johnson
Klear
Mop Magic
Off!
Pledge
Raid House and Garden
Shout
Skintastic
Soft Sense
Toilet Duck
Wax-Strip

year-round and hires part-time help to cover heavy production periods. A performance-based profit sharing program is provided for all full-time staff.

ENVIRONMENTAL MANAGEMENT: The company has a written environmental policy.

ENVIRONMENTAL PERFORMANCE: It has an energy conservation program and, having worked on machinery to make aerosol can recycling possible, opened a Brantford aerosol can recycling depot in 1991. Johnson eliminated CFCs from its aerosol products in 1975 and is already following packaging guidelines that will facilitate the recycling of plastics when recycling programs become more comprehensive. The company is in the third year of a program with the Grand River Conservation Authority to plant one million trees over a 10-year period. Its other programs include the recycling of pop cans and fine paper and a significant reduction in packaging volume through design innovations. S.C. Johnson has no record of environmental violations or wastewater discharges above emission guidelines. In 1990-91 it reduced its solid waste by 13% despite a 15% increase in production.

MANAGEMENT PRACTICES AND CONSUMER RELATIONS: The company has a written code of ethics, *This We Believe*.

Notable Facts

The parent company is implementing a strategy of reassigning production so that individual plants make certain products for all of North America. The US company has a subsidiary operation in South Africa. The Canadian operation did not comment on whether it conducts any animal testing.

The company's environmental efforts have won two awards, both in 1991: a Certificate of Honour from Environment Canada as one of three finalists in the Corporate Environmental Achievement Awards and, in Ontario, a Lieutenant Governor's Conservation Award.

Scotsburn Co-Operative Services Ltd.

PO Box 340, Scotsburn, NS B0K 1R0

Founded in Canada: 1900, Scotsburn, NS

Ownership: owned and controlled by co-op members

Operations: NB*, NS*, NF*

Employees: 740

Annual Sales: $145 million

Advertising expenditures: $1 million

The company began in 1900 as Scotsburn Creamery Co., when its major product was butter. In 1946, it became the Scotsburn Co-Operative through the consolidation and amalgamation of several smaller dairies and dairy co-ops, such as the Farmers Co-Op, Eastern Dairyfoods, Brookfield Dairy Products and Tatamagouche Creamery. The company also distributes feed for livestock and petroleum fuel to farms.

Making the Grade

CANDOUR: The company's exceptional level of disclosure gave it a position on the Honour Roll in this category. Union officials provided us with considerable information as well.

WOMEN'S ISSUES: Women comprise 25% of the company's workforce and hold 10% of its management and 20% of its senior management positions. One of the 11 members of its board of directors is female. Scotsburn has a formal employment equity program and provides extended maternity leave.

CHARITABLE GIVING AND COMMUNITY INVOLVEMENT: The company, which is not pledged to the Imagine campaign, donated $100,000 (half cash, half in kind) to charity in 1990. It supports its communities with equipment donations, the use of company offices, paid time off for employee volunteer activities and a university matching gift program. Scotsburn also provides free space on the side panel of its milk cartons for messages from community or health-related organizations.

PROGRESSIVE STAFF POLICIES: The company offers a formal employee assistance program for substance abuse, retirement and financial counselling. It also provides adoption leave, training programs, employee suggestion programs and an employee newsletter, *Dairy Diary*. It has a policy of open-door managment.

BRAND NAMES
Bluenose
Cape Breton
Dairymen
Scotsburn
Sydney Sandwich
Tatamagouche

LABOUR RELATIONS: Scotsburn is on this Honour Roll as well. It has a formal job security program and uses retraining, relocation and advance notice of technological change to reduce the impact of lay-offs. It has no gain sharing programs and says it does not keep statistics on health and safety or on the amount spent on employee training.

ENVIRONMENTAL MANAGEMENT: Scotsburn has a written environmental code and an environmental committee of the board, making environmental reports to the board as needed. It has four employees with environmental responsibilities, the most senior being a vice-president.

ENVIRONMENTAL PERFORMANCE: The company earned a place on this Honour Roll for its wide range of activities: it conducts a comprehensive environmental audit of all operations and has invested in equipment replacement, packaging reformulation and energy efficiency improvements. In addition, it recycles paper and packaging and has reduced the cruising speed for all company trucks to 90 km/h to save gas and maintenance costs. It has had no environmental fines within the last 10 years.

MANAGEMENT PRACTICES AND CONSUMER RELATIONS: Scotsburn does not have a written code of ethics, although it has various related policies in place. It has not been charged with any Competition Act violations.

Notable Facts

There are no strikes in the company's history and its layoffs have been minor in nature and typically seasonal. Through a relationship with Ault Foods (see p. 103), Scotsburn is the licensed manufacturer of Sealtest and some other ice cream products for Atlantic Canada. The company buys nuts for its new Rainforest Brittle ice cream from the Xapuri co-op, a Brazilian rainforest town of 3,500.

Scott Paper Limited

PO Box 3600, 1111 Melville St., Vancouver, BC V6B 3Y7

Founded in Canada: 1922, New Westminster, BC
Ownership: Scott Paper Company (US), 50.1%
Operations: BC*, AB, MB, ON, PQ*, NS
Employees: 2,460
Annual sales: $435 million

Scott Paper Limited, originally called Westminster Paper, is a publicly traded company, majority-owned by the Philadelphia-based Scott Paper Company. Unlike its American majority-owner, the company has a good environmental record in Canada and is not on any consumer boycott lists. It is the largest producer of sanitary tissue from recycled materials in Canada and exports products to several countries. With the recent purchase of E.B.Eddy's White Swan division, the company has an even stronger national presence. It has four mills, one in Westminster, BC, and three in Quebec (Crabtree, Hull and Lennoxville).

Making the Grade

CANDOUR: The company and its union were very responsive, winning Scott Paper a place on the Honour Roll.

WOMEN'S ISSUES: The company received its lowest score in this area. At the mills, women tend to do the lighter work and are given regular hourly jobs rather than long weekend shifts. The company's workforce is only about 16% women. Management is 11% female but there are no women either in senior management or on the 10-man board of directors. Scott has no formal employment equity program, but notes that it hires on the basis of qualifications needed for the job, regardless of sex. It does not offer either daycare or extended maternity leave.

CHARITABLE GIVING AND COMMUNITY INVOLVEMENT:
Scott is on this Honour Roll as well, for it contributes significantly to the communities in which it operates. Its charitable donations almost double its Imagine campaign commitment to donate 1% of pre-tax earnings to charity — and the figure is even higher with product donations included. The company provides paid time off for employee volunteer activities, makes company officers available to help with not-for-profit campaigns (including the BC Access Ability Program) and runs several matching gift programs. It is a continuing donor to Ronald Mac-Donald Children's Charities of Canada and the Canadian

BRAND NAMES
Baby Fresh
Cashmere
Cottonelle
Cut-Rite
Purex
Scotowels
Scott Family Napkins
Scotties
Viva
White Swan

Foundation for the Physically Disabled, among other organizations.

PROGRESSIVE STAFF POLICIES: Scott Paper is again on the Honour Roll. Its confidential family assistance program offers substance abuse, financial and grief counselling. In addition it has training programs, written annual performance reviews, stop-smoking programs, an employee newsletter, a suggestion program and open-door management.

LABOUR RELATIONS: The company is also on this Honour Roll. Although it has no formal job security program, it has kept layoffs to a minimum in the past 10 years through the use of relocation, retraining and early retirement. It is committed to building a long term relationship with staff members and offers a stock purchase plan to all employees.

ENVIRONMENTAL MANAGEMENT: Again a member of the Honour Roll, Scott Paper has a written environmental code and three separate environmental committees: one responsible for communications with the public and industry groups, one that deals with marketing and product evaluation, and one to co-ordinate environmental audits and ensure compliance with governmental laws. Environmental reports are delivered to the board of directors at least once a year. Senior environmental responsibilities are shared by two vice-presidents, who handle these issues along with their other duties.

ENVIRONMENTAL PERFORMANCE: Scott is on this Honour Roll as well, making six mentions in all. It has committed no environmental violations or discharges above permitted limits — an impressive record, given the nature of its business. All four of the company's facilities meet wastewater regulations and have been independently audited in 1991. Scott conducts an annual, comprehensive environmental audit of all its operations, and has invested a sizable sum over the past three years in the environment. These expenditures include the expansion of a recycled-paper plant and more than a decade of developing deciduous tree farms for high-yield fibre production. The company recycles paper in its office and a number of its products contain from 50% to 90% recovered waste.

MANAGEMENT PRACTICES AND CONSUMER RELATIONS: Scott Paper has a written code of ethics, updated annually, but it does not require a yearly sign-off and has no ethics advisory service. While Scott has wide-ranging community involvement, it does not produce a social practices report.

Notable Facts

Union representatives speak of a positive management-labour relationship, especially at the BC mill, which continues to have the "family" feeling of its early days. The US majority-owner, Scott Paper Company, owns a kraft pulp mill in Pictou, NS, which has had a series of environmental problems. This mill makes no tissue products for the Canadian market.

SmithKline Beecham Consumer Brands Inc.　　　　SKB

2 Norelco Drive, Weston, ON M9L 1R9

Ownership: SmithKline Beecham PLC (UK), 100%
Operations: BC, ON*, PQ
Employees: 300

SmithKline Beecham Consumer Brands is a leading Canadian marketer of personal care products and non-prescription medications. The name of the original Canadian company was Beecham Canada Inc. The company has one Toronto-area plant and reports to its British parent through the parent's American subsidiary. The parent company also maintains Canadian operations in pharmaceuticals and animal health.

Making the Grade

SmithKline declined to participate in our research (beyond verifying brand names) and was one of the few companies that we could not score in any category. The company is not pledged to the Imagine campaign, although sister company SmithKline Beecham Pharma Inc. is on the Imagine list. The firm has no Canadian written environmental policy, but also has no environmental fines or records of exceeding discharge limits.

Notable Facts

SmithKline Beecham Consumer Brands Inc. is not unionized.

The parent company states in the 1991 Beecham annual report: "We embrace open and non-discriminatory recruitment, training and promotion policies for all employees, including those who are, or become, disabled." It also says: "We strive to find alternative methods but reluctantly conclude that animal testing will continue to be a component of pharmaceutical research and development. We wish to keep their use to an absolute minimum and to conduct required studies with every consideration for their comfort and well being."

SmithKline Beecham issued a social practices report entitled *Shared Visions: A Transnational Report on Giving in the 1990's*. However, this report concentrates on activities in the UK and the US. The parent company has four wholly-owned subsidiaries in South Africa.

BRAND NAMES

Aqua Velva

Aquafresh

Baby's Own

Horlicks

Lectric Shave

Macleans

Massengil

Orafix

Ribena

Specialty Brands (Canada)

65 International Blvd., Toronto, ON M9W 6L9

Founded in Canada: 1986, Toronto, ON
Ownership: Burns Philp Group (Australia), 100%
Operations: BC, SK*, ON, PQ*
Employees: 268
Annual sales: $28 million

Specialty Brands Canada, a division of Fleischmann's Yeast Limited, is part of California-based Specialty Brands (US), which in turn is part of a conglomerate owned by Australia's Burns Philp Group. The Canadian company makes and markets a variety of baking supplies, including yeast, cake decorations, spices and vinegar. All of its spices and dried fruit are imported from the United States. Canadian operations consist of two business offices and three plants: two in LaSalle, Que (yeast, vinegar) and one in Saskatoon, Sask. (vinegar)

Making the Grade

CANDOUR: All our surveys were directed to Specialty Brands' head office in San Francisco (US) and then on to Australia. The Canadian head office answered some further questions in the fact-checking stage. As shown by the company's Candour Quotient and the number of categories marked "?", not all questions were answered.

WOMEN'S ISSUES: While 27% of Speciality Brands' employees are female, there are only eight female managers (out of an unspecified total number of management positions). The Canadian company has no board of directors. It also has no employment equity program, but the parent company says it has a strongly enforced equal opportunity program. The Canadian company does not provide daycare support services or extended maternity leave benefits.

CHARITABLE GIVING AND COMMUNITY INVOLVEMENT: There is no separate budget allocation for Canadian philanthropy, nor information on the size of the company's charitable contributions. It is not part of the Imagine campaign, but it lends facilities to community groups and supports country fairs and various other charitable organizations. The parent company has a charitable foundation, which makes most of its disbursements within Australia.

PROGRESSIVE STAFF POLICES: The company has no employee assistance or health promotion programs but

BRAND NAMES
Allen's
Blue Ribbon
Dromedary
Fleischmann's
French's (spices only)
Schwartz (spices only)
Spice Islands
Winston House

does provide a scholarship fund for employees' children, a company newsletter called *Food for Thought* and annual written performance reviews for all employees.

LABOUR RELATIONS: Senior executives are eligible for a share option plan, and a share purchase plan is under consideration for all Canadian employees.

ENVIRONMENTAL PERFORMANCE: The parent company has no environmental policy other than one that applies to Timber Resources, a division which does not operate in Canada (but which imports North American and Malaysian timber into Australia). No environmental court cases or instances of exceeding discharge guidelines are on record.

MANAGEMENT PRACTICES AND CONSUMER RELATIONS: A worldwide ethics statement, just introduced in the parent company's 1991 annual report, is too new to be familiar to North American staff.

Notable Facts

Only the Fleischmann's Yeast plant in LaSalle, Que., is unionized. The parent company spent $20 million (Aus.) on waste treatment in 1990-91, and prints its annual report on recycled paper.

Tambrands Canada Inc.

255 Consumers Rd., Suite 280, Willowdale, ON M2J 1R4

Founded in Canada: 1935, Brantford, ON
Ownership: Tambrands Inc. (US), 100%
Operations: ON
Employees: 50 (est., upon completion of 1992 plant closure)
Annual sales: $237 million (US)
Toll-free number: 800-268-3448

Originally a Canadian-owned business called Canadian Tampax Corporation, the company is a market leader in feminine protection products. Tambrands Inc., the US-based parent, is making major adjustments to its worldwide operations and in 1992 closed its only Canadian manufacturing plant (in Barrie, Ont.) with the loss of 190 jobs.

Making the Grade

CANDOUR: Tambrands Canada provided a significant amount of information late in the process.

WOMEN'S ISSUES: While not high, Tambrands' score was good enough in this low-scoring area to rank near the top of the Honour Roll. Forty percent of management, 20% of senior management and 25% of board positions (one of four) are occupied by women — on the other hand, 70% of the company's employees are female. Tambrands offers extended maternity leave but has no daycare provisions or formal employment equity program.

CHARITABLE GIVING AND COMMUNITY INVOLVEMENT: The company is not part of the Imagine campaign and did not disclose the size of its charitable contributions. However, Tambrands does contribute to the community in several ways, including equipment donations, paid time off for employee volunteer activity and support for health-related causes. In 1991, the company promised to contribute 20 cents for every box of tampons sold (or $45,000, whichever is greater) to support Toronto-area shelters for battered women. The campaign was accompanied by company-sponsored promotions aimed at generating independent contributions to the shelters.

PROGRESSIVE STAFF POLICIES: The company is on this Honour Roll as well. It offers numerous programs, including drug and alcohol abuse counselling, weight loss clinics, CPR (cardiopulmonary resuscitation) classes, a "Smoke Enders" program, suggestion programs, incentives for cost-saving ideas and a scholarship fund for employees' children. As well, it conducts an annual written performance review

BRAND NAMES
Compak
Maxithins
Tampax

of each employee and maintains a policy of open-door management.

LABOUR RELATIONS: Although Tambrands does not have a formal job security policy, it has used retraining, early retirement and financial compensation to ease the impact of layoffs. It offers an employee share option purchase plan and a bonus incentive program to all employees.

ENVIRONMENTAL MANAGEMENT: The company is on the Honour Roll in this category. It has a written environmental policy and an environmental working committee. Four of its approximately 50 employees have environmental responsibilities but there is no full-time environmental affairs officer.

ENVIRONMENTAL PERFORMANCE: While Tambrands does not conduct an environmental audit, during the years it had manufacturing operations in Canada it invested in equipment replacement, energy efficiency and packaging reformulation. The primary packaging redesign was the elimination of plastic wrapping around the paperboard box. Tambrands recycles paper, uses some recycled paper products in its offices and has made an effort to replace disposable cutlery and cups with reusable ones. It also scrutinizes all purchasing practices for environmental impact, choosing, for example, to launder cloth towels in phosphate-free soap rather than purchase paper towels. The company had no environmental violations or fines while it had production here. Because it no longer has manufacturing operations in this country, it was not scored in this area.

MANAGEMENT PRACTICES AND CONSUMER RELATIONS: The company is first on this Honour Roll by a wide margin. Not only does it have a written code of ethics, established in 1988 and requiring an annual employee sign-off, it has an ethics ombudsman. Tambrands issues a Canadian social practices report, and has not been charged with any Competition Act violations.

Notable Facts

The US parent company has been named in product liability lawsuits concerning Toxic Shock Syndrome. The Canadian company did not comment on the issue, but its tampon products contain information about the signs and symptoms of the condition, and a full-time nurse is available for consultation on this and other tampon-related issues through the company's toll-free advisory service.

Unilever Canada Limited

160 Bloor St. E., Suite 1500, Toronto, ON M4W 3R2

Founded in Canada: 1903, Toronto, ON
Ownership: Unilever PLC (UK), 100%
Operations: BC*, AB, SK, MB, ON*, PQ*, NB, NS, PE, NF*
Employees: 7,588
Annual sales: $1.2 billion
Advertising expenditures: $59 million

The parent company was founded in 1888 and began selling products in Canada that same year. Fifteen years later, the company set up offices and production facilities in Canada. The parent company has an astounding 304,000 employees around the world. Unilever companies included in this profile are Chesebrough-Pond's, Thomas J. Lipton, Unox Meats Canada, Monarch Fine Foods and Lever Brothers Limited. In addition, Unilever owns other well-known companies, such as A&W Food Services, Calvin Klein Cosmetics and Elizabeth Arden (the latter two managed directly from the US). The company has 10 manufacturing plants in Canada.

BRAND NAMES

Aim	Golden Girl	Pears
Amaze	Good Luck	Pepsodent
Aqua Net	Hygrade	PG Tips
all	I Can't Believe It's	Pond's
Baseball	Not Butter	Puritan
Bavarians	Imperial	Q-Tips
Becel	Impulse	Ragu
Blue Bonnet	Knox	Red Rose
Brut	Krona	Regal
Caress	La Belle Fermiere	Salada
Chicken Tonight	Lawry's	Shopsy's
Chipolettes	Lever 2000	Snuggle
Close-Up	Lifebuoy	Sunkist Fun Fruit
Country Crock	Lipton	Sunlight
Cutex	Lux	Surf
Deli-Fresh	McGarry's	Teenage Mutant Ninja
Deli-Lean	Meister	Turtles Pizza Sticks
Deli-Stik	Mexicasa	Timotei
Dove	Microchef	Vaseline
Egg Beaters	Mir	Vim
Essense Magique	Mom's	Wet Soap
EverSweet	Monarch	Wisk
Excel	Overlander	
Fleischmann's	Oxo	

Making the Grade

CANDOUR: The company was very responsive and provided detailed information beyond that requested on the surveys.

WOMEN'S ISSUES: This was the company's lowest score. Although 46% of Unilever's workforce is female, only 20% of management and senior management positions are occupied by women and there are no women on Unilever's 10-man board of directors. In response to our question on formal employment equity programs, the company said that it hires and promotes on the basis of responsibility and merit.

CHARITABLE GIVING AND COMMUNITY INVOLVEMENT: Unilever is not on Imagine's list and provided very little information about its corporate donations, saying only that the company "follows good Canadian practice based upon surveys of similar size companies." The company is involved in several community projects, including sports team, health and arts support and education funding. In the March, 1990 edition of the *Corporate Ethics Monitor* Unilever said its 1989 donations amounted to $463,252 (not including goods and free time).

PROGRESSIVE STAFF POLICIES: Unilever is on the Honour Roll in this category. Its employee assistance program provides substance abuse counselling and referrals for other services, such as financial and marriage counselling. Its health promotion program includes intramural sports activities, health and fitness club subsidies and corporate marathons. Company newsletters, rewards for cost-saving ideas and a policy of open-door management are some of the ways in which Unilever and its subsidiaries encourage communication between plant employees and management. As well, it conducts annual written performance reviews and runs a scholarship fund for employees' children. The company has extensive in-house training programs and offers up to full reimbursement for outside training.

LABOUR RELATIONS: The company has a formal job security program and uses retraining, relocation and financial compensation to reduce the impact of layoffs or plant closures. However, the company has no gain sharing programs in any of its operations.

ENVIRONMENTAL MANAGEMENT: Unilever has no full-time environmental affairs official and did not specify the number of employees with environmental responsibilities. However, it does have a written environmental policy, which requires the use of raw materials, processes and packaging that not only meet government standards but "are judged by Unilever and society to be safe for our workforce, the consumers and the environment." As well, Unilever has an environmental committee of the board and makes reports to the board of directors three times annually.

ENVIRONMENTAL PERFORMANCE: The company is also on this Honour Roll. It carries out a comprehensive annual environmental audit of all of its operations, and applies environmental criteria to everything from manufacturing and office procedures to purchasing decisions. The company and its operating divisions employ extensive recycling programs, make use of recycled materials in much of their packaging, use environmentally friendly suppliers as far as possible and attempt to recycle all chemicals and packaging. As well, the company has invested significant resources in developing more environmentally friendly products, reducing product packaging and implementing a pollution control program. Lever Brothers was fined $12,000 for exceeding pollution limits in 1987, but Unilever has no other violations on record.

Management Practices and Consumer Issues: Unilever is again on the Honour Roll. The parent company's written code of ethics is complemented by a Canadianized code, prepared in 1992, which employees read and sign annually. The company has no record of consumer or Competition Act court cases and provides a consumer toll-free phone number on the packaging of many of its products.

Notable Facts

Unilever Canada does no animal testing, either in-house or through contractors. The parent company does conduct animal testing elsewhere, but is actively seeking other methods of testing — in fact, it has spent $1 million (US) a year for the last 10 years on research in this field.

The company closed three plants, two in Toronto and one in Montreal, over 1990-91. Two of the closings were directly related to the acquisition of new companies, which were merged with existing operations. One merger occurred in January, 1990, when Unilever bought Salada Inc. and integrated it with its Liptons operations. Two hundred and four employees lost their jobs as a result of the three plant closings.

The parent company has subsidiary operations in South Africa.

Options For Action

We didn't write this book to promote any particular political agenda or course of action – but we do hope to promote action. What it is depends on you: use the information in this *Guide* to help you decide which companies you'll support and which you won't. Look at the issues that matter most to you and take the next step: don't just choose and reject products, contact the company. Make your opinions known.

Companies take note of opinion polls and what consumers tell them in focus group interviews, but the real test (and the real impact on their bottom line) is what people do at the cash register. So the apparently simple step of buying or rejecting a company's products is in fact very powerful. On the positive side, it's a way to support a progressive company as a whole or to encourage particular policies – less packaging for a product line, for example, or more use of recycled materials. Negatively, it withdraws your support from a company whose policies or practices you reject.

If enough people join in, the negative message can be extremely powerful. One famous example is the international boycott of certain companies that make infant formula because of the way they market their product to developing countries: the campaign, backed by UNICEF and the World Health Organization among others, charges these firms encourage the poorest women to abandon breastfeeding for a product they could not afford or use consistently and safely. Some firms, American Home Products (see p. 123) for one, have responded with marketing codes of conduct and are no longer on some boycott lists.

Even as a single individual, however, you can multiply the impact of your actions. Don't just stop (or start) buying a company's products: *tell the company what you're doing, and why*. This is especially important when the reason for your action is the company's own behaviour rather than some characteristic of the product. They'll never know how you feel about their lack of female senior managers (or community involvement or job security programs) unless you tell them.

So pick up the phone or, better yet, write a letter. The sheer physical presence of a letter gives it continuing life within a corporation and commands a response – especially when you make sure the company knows you have sent copies to appropriate government departments, advocacy groups and media.

Be persistent. Keep track of your calls and letters, make sure you get a reply and then follow up. Let the company know what you think of its reply to you and of its subsequent action (or lack of it) on the situation in question. And remember: praise is a powerful tool. Take time to let people know when you like what they're doing.

If the company that interests you is publicly-traded, you can also expresss your approval and disapproval as an investor. Purchase shares in companies whose practices concern you and use the annual meeting to raise those concerns. On the positive side, look into ethical investing. Some progressive firms also meet rigorous investment standards and give you a way to support the company while earning a return on your money. Seek professional advice, however. Unless you're an experienced investor, this is not the place to go it alone.

On the other hand, you may wish to be less dependent on commercial products, companies and systems of distribution. If so, think about how and where you shop. You can buy more fresh foods and bulk products, for example, join a food co-operative or grow at least some of your own produce. Options like these are growing in number and feasibility all the time.

The real key to effective action is to get involved in things in which you have a true personal interest or stake. Look in the next section of this book, Sources for Action (see p. 266), for groups that share your particular concerns. They can provide you with information, like-minded colleagues and perhaps projects that you'd like to join.

Finally, please make EthicScan one of the organizations you contact. Using the form on p. 283-84, mail or fax us an account of your experiences with a company mentioned in this *Guide*. What happened when you called or wrote to ask for information, express an opinion or explain a decision to use or avoid its products? Did you receive an answer? Was it relevant? Will it influence your future consumer purchase decisions? At what level in the company was your question or opinion handled? Which strategy did you find worked best in dealing with the company? Your experiences, combined with those of other Canadian consumers, will help us get a good sense of companies' responsiveness to consumer suggestions and complaints. Future editions of the *Guide* will reflect this information.

Sources For Action

The following is a list of some of the advocacy groups, government offices, publications and other sources you can consult for more information on the kinds of issues covered in the *Guide*.

Sources for Action is divided into four sections:

- Environment
- Women
- Management/Consumer Issues
- Labour

The organizations listed here have no affiliation with EthicScan Canada or *The Ethical Shopper's Guide to Canadian Supermarket Products* and do not necessarily endorse any or all aspects of the *Guide*. Similarly, EthicScan does not necessarily endorse these organizations. The definitions of their activities have been supplied by the groups themselves.

Environment

Non-Governmental Organizations

Canadian Environmental Law Association
517 College St., Suite 401, Toronto, ON M6G 4A2
(416) 960-2284

The Canadian Environmental Law Association (CELA), founded in 1970, is a public interest legal clinic. CELA represents clients with environmental problems and advocates for law reform and improved public participation in environmental decision-making.

Canadian Environmental Network,
PO Box 1289, Station B, Ottawa, ON K1P 5R3
(613) 563-2078

The Canadian Environmental Network is a national network of environmental organizations comprising 11 regional or provincial networks. Purpose: to facilitate information exchange among such organizations and other sectors nationally and internationally.

Environmentally Sound Packaging (ESP) Coalition
2150 Maple St., Vancouver, BC   V6J 3T3
(604) 736–3644

The ESP Coalition advocates the development and use of packaging that has minimal impact on the environment and, in cooperation with industry, government and the public, will promote the reduction, reuse and recycling of all packaging materials.

Friends of the Earth,
251 Laurier Ave. W., #701, Ottawa, ON   K1P 5J6
(613) 230–3352

Friends of the Earth is a national voice for the environment, working with others to inspire the renewal of our communities and the Earth, through research, education and advocacy.

Greenpeace Canada,
185 Spadina Ave., 6th floor, Toronto, ON   M5T 2C6
(416) 345–8408

Harmony Foundation of Canada,
19 Oakvale Ave., Ottawa, ON   K1Y 3S3
(613) 230–7353

Harmony is dedicated to achieving environmental progress through cooperation and education. Harmony's programs and publications for individuals, workplaces, educators and communities, encompass environmental values and practical skills for positive action.

Pollution Probe,
12 Madison Ave., Toronto, ON   M5R 2S1
(416) 926–1907

For over 23 years Pollution Probe has been dedicated to achieving positive and tangible environmental results through advocacy, research and education.

Recycling Council of Ontario,
489 College St., Suite 504, Toronto, ON   M6G 1A5
(416) 960–1025
or 800–263–2849 (outside Toronto)

The Recycling Council of Ontario is a non-profit corporation founded in 1978. Broadly representing individuals, government, industry, environmental and community organizations, the Council has been instrumental in advancing reduction, reuse and recycling initiatives in Ontario.

West Coast Environmental Law Association
1001–207 W. Hastings St., Vancouver, BC   V6B 1H7
(604) 684–7378

The mission of West Coast Environmental Law Association and Research Foundation is to provide legal services, research and education to promote protection of the environment and public participation in environmental decision-making.

World Wildlife Fund,
90 Eglinton Ave. E., Suite 504, Toronto, ON   M4P 2Z7
(416) 489–8800

The World Wildlife Fund's mission is to conserve wild animals, plants and habitats for their own sake and for the long-term benefit of people.

Government Agencies

Environment Canada
Ottawa, ON   K1A 0H3
(819) 997–6820

B.C. Ministry of Environment, Lands and Parks
810 Blanshard St., Victoria, BC   V8V 1X5
(604) 387–9419

Alberta Environment
Oxbridge Place, 9820 – 106 St.
Edmonton, AB   T5K 2J6
(403) 427–6267

Saskatchewan Department of Environment and Public Safety
3085 Albert St., Regina, SK   S4S 0B1
(306) 787–6113

Manitoba Environment,
Adminstration Building 2, 139 Tuxedo Ave.,
Winnipeg, MB   R3N 0H6
(204) 945–7100

Ontario Ministry of the Environment
135 St. Clair Ave. W., Toronto, ON   M4V 1P5
(416) 323–4321

Ministere de l'Environnement du Québec
3900, rue de Marly, Sainte-Foy, PQ   G1X 4E4
(418) 643–6071

New Brunswick Department of the Environment
PO Box 6000, Fredericton, NB   E3B 5H1
(506) 453–2558

Nova Scotia Department of the Environment
PO Box 2107, Halifax, NS   B3J 3B7
(902) 424–5300

Prince Edward Island Department of the Environment
PO Box 2000, Charlottetown, PE   C1A 7N8
(902) 368–5000

Newfoundland Department of Environment and Lands
PO Box 8700, St. John's, NF   A1B 4J6
(709) 729–3394

Northwest Territories Round Table on Environment & Economy
c/o Government Leader, PO Box 1320, Yellowknife, NT   X1A 2L9

Yukon Council on the Economy & Environment
PO Box 2703, Whitehorse, YK   Y1A 2C6
(403) 667–5939

Women

Non-Governmental Organizations

Canadian Daycare Advocacy Association
323 Chapel St., Ottawa, ON   K1N 7Z2
(613) 594–3196

The primary role of the association is to promote expansion and improvement in the quality of the Canadian childcare system. The Association advocates the development of high quality, affordable, not-for-profit, accessible childcare for all Canadians who require it.

Canadian Women's Foundation
214 Merton St., Suite 208, Toronto, ON   M4S 1A6
(416) 484–8268

The Canadian Women's Foundation is dedicated to long-term systemic change that will bring about the equality of women and girls in Canada. The Foundation grants funds for innovative and diverse programs and projects designed to help women and girls achieve greater self-reliance and economic independence.

National Action Committee on the Status of Women
57 Mobile Dr., Toronto, ON   M4A 1H5
(416) 759–5252

The National Action Committee is the largest feminist organization in Canada, a coalition of over 500 member groups that represent three million Canadians.

Ontario Coalition for Better Child Care
500A Bloor St. W., 2nd floor, Toronto, ON   M5S 1Y8
(416) 538–0628

The Coalition is an umbrella group of provincial organizations, provincial sections of national organizations, local child care advocacy groups, parents, child care programs, trade union locals and women's organizations.

The Women and Environments Education and Development (WEED) Foundation
736 Bathurst St., Toronto, ON   M5S 2R4
(416) 516–2600

WEED's objective is to provide a forum for communication and conduct research on issues relating to women in the fields of planning, health, ecology & environment, workplace design, community development and urban and rural sociology.

YWCA of/du Canada
80 Gerrard St. E., Toronto, ON   M5B 1G6
(416) 593–9886

The YWCA works actively for the development and improved status of women and for responsible social and economic changes that will achieve peace, justice, freedom and equality in Canada and around the world. (YWCA of Metropolitan Toronto publishes a *Guide to Women's Groups & Resources*. Call (416) 961–8100.)

Government Agencies

Status of Women Canada
360 Albert St., Suite 700, Ottawa, ON K1A 1C3
(613) 995–7835

BC Government – Ministry of Government Management
Responsible for Women's Progress
Parliament Buildings, Victoria, BC V8V 1X4
(604) 387–0413

Alberta Women's Secretariat,
Kensington Place, 8th Floor,
10011 – 109th Street, Edmonton, AB T5J 3S8
(403) 422–4927

Saskatchewan Government – Women's Secretariat
1914 Hamilton St., Regina, SK S4P 4V4
(306) 787–2329

Manitoba Women's Directorate
450–500 Portage Avenue, Winnipeg, MB R3C 3X1
(204) 945–5022

Ontario Women's Directorate
480 University Ave., 2nd Floor, Toronto, ON M5G 1V2
(416) 597–4500

Secretaire Generale Assoc. à la Condition Feminine
Gouvernment Du Québec – Ministere Du Conseil Executif
Edifice H, Bureau 2700, 875 Grande Allee Est
Québec, PQ G1R 4Y8
(418) 643–9052

New Brunswick Government – Women's Directorate
Centennial Building, King St., Room 413
Fredericton, NB E3B 5H1
(506) 453–2143

Nova Scotia Women's Directorate
PO Box 486, Halifax, NS B3J 2R7
(902) 424–5820

Newfoundland Government – Women's Policy Office
PO Box 8700, St. John's, NF A1B 4J6
(709) 729–5009

Northwest Territories Government – Women's Directorate
PO Box 1320, Yellowknife, NT X1A 2L9
(403) 920–8928

Yukon Territory Government – Women's Directorate
PO Box 2703, Second Ave., A-13, Whitehorse, YK Y1A 2C6
(403) 667–3030

Management/Consumer Issues

Non-Governmental Organizations

Allergy/Asthma Information Association
65 Tromley, Suite 10, Etobicoke, ON M9B 5Y7
(416) 244–8585

The Association's mission is to develop societal awareness of the seriousness of allergic disease, including asthma, and to enable allergic individuals, their families and care givers, to increase control over allergy symptoms by providing leadership in information, education, and advocacy, in partnership with health care professionals, business, industry and government.

Animal Alliance of Canada,
221 Broadview Ave., Suite 101, Toronto, ON M4M 2G3
(416) 462–9541

This organization is committed to the preservation and protection of all animals and to the promotion of a harmonious relationship between people, animals and the environment.

Canadian Advertising Foundation – Standards Council
350 Bloor St. E., Suite 402, Toronto, ON M4W 1H5
(416) 961–6311

CAF's mission is to champion the Canadian advertising process as an economically important professional enterprise, which operates with high ethical standards of practice within a framework of responsible self-regulation, and to provide dialogue between the practitioners of the advertising process and those who have an interest in it or who seek to influence it.

Canadian Centre for Ethics and Corporate Policy
George Brown House, 2nd floor, 50 Baldwin St.
Toronto, ON M5T 1L4
(416) 348–8691

The Centre is a non-profit organization founded in 1988, devoted to exploring and promoting the role of ethics in the conduct of organizations. It provides resources for business, government, labour and other groups in society that are concerned with ethical issues in management.

Canadian Centre for Philanthropy
1329 Bay St., 2nd floor
Toronto, ON M5R 2C4
(416) 515–0764

The Centre's mission is to promote the generous application of charitable time and funds, and strengthen the philanthropic community through education, research, training and the exchange of information. The Centre's Imagine initiative encourages, among other things, an increase in the standard of corporate giving to a minimum of 1% of average, domestic pre-tax profits.

Consumers' Association of Canada
307 Gilmour St., Ottawa, ON K2P 0P7
(613) 238–2533

The Consumers' Association of Canada, founded in 1947, is a voluntary, non-profit and non-governmental organization representing consumers across Canada.

EarthShoppers
329 Eglinton Ave. E., Toronto, ON M4P 1L7
(416) 487–8141

EarthShopper's mandate is to create a consumer voice for environmental and social accountability which will encourage business to develop and implement more responsible policies.

EthicScan Canada Ltd.
Lawrence Plaza Postal Outlet
P.O. Box 54034, Toronto, ON M6A 3B7
(416) 783–6776

EthicScan Canada is a research house and think-tank in the field of consumer and corporate ethics.

Project Ploughshares
Conrad Grebel College
University of Waterloo, Waterloo, ON N2L 3G6
(519) 888–6541

Project Ploughshares advocates reduced military spending globally and maintains a database on military contracts for Canadian companies.

The Social Investment Organization
366 Adelaide St. E., Suite 447, Toronto, ON M5A 3X9
(416) 360–6047

The Social Investment Organization (SIO) is a membership-based, non-profit organization dedicated to the promotion of socially and environmentally responsible investment and financial decision making.

Task Force on Churches and Corporate Responsibility
129 St. Clair Ave. W., Toronto, ON M4V 1N5
(416) 923–1758

The Task Force is a national ecumenical coalition of the major Christian churches in Canada. Its role is to assist its members in implementing policies adopted by them in the area of corporate social responsibility. Areas of special concern include human rights and aboriginal rights, environment, military exports, and corporate governance.

Government Agencies

Consumer & Corporate Affairs Canada
(819) 997–2938

BC Ministry of Labour and Consumer Services
1019 Wharf St., Victoria, BC V8V 1X4
(604) 387–3194

Alberta Consumer & Corporate Affairs
10025 Jasper Ave., 22nd floor, Edmonton, AB T5J 3Z5
(403) 422–3935

Saskatchewan Justice, Consumer Protection Branch
1871 Smith St., 1st floor, Regina, SK S4P 3B7
(306) 787–5550

Manitoba Consumer & Corporate Affairs, Consumers Bureau
114 Garry St., Winnipeg, MB   R3C 1G1
(204) 956–2040 or 800–782–0067

Ontario Ministry of Consumer and Commercial Relations
Consumer Services Bureau, 555 Yonge St., main floor
Toronto, ON   M7A 2H6
(416) 326–8555

Direction des Entreprises
800, Place d'Youville, 6e etage, Québec, PQ G1A 4Y5
(418) 643–3625

New Brunswick Department of Justice, Consumer Affairs Branch
PO Box 6000, Fredericton, NB   E3B 5H1
(506) 453–2659

Nova Scotia Department of Consumer Affairs,
PO Box 998, Halifax, NS   B3J 2X3
(902) 424–8946

PEI Department of Justice, Consumer Services Division
PO Box 2000, Sullivan Building, 1st floor
Charlottetown, PE   C1A 7N8
(902) 368–4580

Newfoundland Department of Justice, Consumer Affairs Division
PO Box 8700, St. John's, NF   A1B 4J6
(709) 729–2591

Labour Relations

Non-Governmental Organizations

Canadian Labour Congress,
2841 Riverside Dr., Ottawa, ON   K1V 8X7
(613) 521–3400

Bakery, Confectionery and Tobacco Workers International Union
(AFL-CIO/CLC)
Canadian Office
3329, rue Ontario est, Montreal, PQ   H1W 1P8
(514) 527–9371

Bureau of Labour Information Directory of Labour Organizations in Canada, published by the authority of the Minister of Labour, Government of Canada.

The *Directory* is a compendium of data on union membership and unions, congresses and other labour organizations in Canada. The 1992/93 edition is available from: Canadian Government Publishing Centre, Supply and Services Canada, Ottawa, ON K1A 0S9. Or call (819) 997-3117 or 800-567-6866.

Retail, Wholesale and Department Store Union
(AFL–CIO/CLC)
Canadian Office
15 Gervais Dr., Suite 310, Don Mills, ON M3C 1Y8
(416) 441-1414

United Food and Commercial Workers International Union
(AFL-CIO/CLC)
Canadian Region
61 International Blvd., Suite 300, Rexdale, ON M9W 6K4
(416) 675-6916

Government Agencies

BC Ministry of Labour and Consumer Services
1019 Wharf St., Victoria, BC V8V 1X4
(604) 387-3194

Alberta Labour
10808 – 99 Ave., Room 506, Edmonton, AB
T5K 0G8
(403) 427-5585

Saskatchewan Department of Human Resources, Labour & Employment
1870 Albert St., Regina, SK S4P 3V7
(306) 787-2413

Manitoba Labour
Norquay Building, Room 611
401 York Ave., Winnipeg, MB R3C 0P8
(204) 945-2295

Ontario Ministry of Labour
400 University Ave., Toronto, ON M7A 1T7
(416) 326-7565

Ministere du Travail du Quebec
425, rue St-Amable, 2e etage, Quebec, PQ   G1R 5M3
(418) 643–4817

New Brunswick Department of Labour
PO Box 6000, Fredericton, NB   E3B 5H1
(506) 453–3298

Nova Scotia Department of Labour
PO Box 697, Halifax, NS   B3J 2T8
(902) 424–4680

Newfoundland Department of Employment & Labour Relations
Confederation Building West Block, PO Box 8700
St. John's, NF   A1B 4J6
(709) 729–2716

Prince Edward Island Department of Labour
PO Box 2000, Charlottetown, PE   C1A 7N8
(902) 368–5550

Index of Company Abbreviations

Product Index

Air Fresheners see Household Cleaners

Aluminum Foil see Food Wraps

Anti-Perspirant see Deodorants

Artificial Sweeteners see Sugars, Sweeteners & Syrups

Apple Sauce see Fresh & Frozen Fruits & Vegetables

Baby Powder see Other Baby Needs

Baby Food see Baby Food

Bagels see Breads & Rolls

Baked Beans see Rice & Beans

Baking Soda see Baking Needs

Baking Chocolate see Baking Needs

Baking Cups see Baking Needs (see also Food Wraps)

Bathroom Cleansers see Household Cleaners

Biscuit Mix see Baking Mixes

Bleach see Laundry Supplies

Bottled Water see Bottled Water

Bouillon see Soups

Bread see Breads & Rolls

Bread/Roll Mix see Baking Mixes

Butter see Butter

Cake Mix see Baking Mixes

Cake Decorations see Baking Needs

Candy see Confectionery

Cat Food see Pet Foods & Supplies

Cereal, Hot see Cereals

Cereal, Cold see Cereals

Cheese Slices see Cheese

Cheese Spread see Peanut Butter & Other Spreads

Chocolate Bars see Confectionery

Chocolate Chips see Baking Needs

Chocolate Syrup see Sugars, Sweeteners & Syrups (see Cocoa & Other Drink Mixes)

Chocolates, Boxed see Confectionery

Chopped Nuts, Baking see Baking Needs

Chutney see Condiments & Sauces

Cocoa see Cocoa & Other Drink Mixes (see also Baking Needs)

Coffee Filters see Paper Products

Coffee see Coffee

Coffee Whitener see Milk & Cream

Conditioner, Hair see Hair Care

Cooking Spray see Baking Needs

Cooking Oil see Margarine, Shortening & Oils

Corn Syrup see Sugars, Sweeteners & Syrups

Corn Starch see Baking Needs

Cottage Cheese see Cheese

Cotton Swabs see Miscellaneous Personal Care

Cream Cheese see Cheese

Dental Floss see Oral Hygiene

Denture Cleaner see Oral Hygiene

Denture Fixative see Oral Hygiene

Deodorant see Deodorants

Diapers see Diapers

Dish Detergent see Dish Detergents

Dog Food see Pet Foods & Supplies

Dough, Refrigerated see Frozen & Refrigerated Doughs & Pastry

Drain Cleaner see Household Cleaners

Dried Fruit see Baking Needs

Dusting Sprays see Household Cleaners

Entrées, Frozen see Frozen Prepared Foods

Evaporated Milk see Milk & Cream

Extracts see Baking Needs

Fabric Softener see Laundry Supplies

Feminine Protection see Feminine Hygiene

Floor Cleaners see Household Cleaners

Flour see Flour

Food Colouring see Baking Needs

Freezer Bags see Food Wraps

French Fries see Frozen Prepared Foods

Frosting see Baking Needs

Frozen Desserts see Desserts

Frozen Dinners see Frozen Prepared Foods

Fruit, Canned see Canned & Frozen Fruits & Vegetables

Fruit, Frozen see Canned & Frozen Fruits & Vegetables

Fruit Drinks, Powdered see Cocoa & Other Drink Mixes

Fruit Snacks see Snacks

Furniture Polish see Household Cleaners

Gel, Hair see Hair Care

Gelatin, Flavoured see Desserts

Gelatin, Unflavoured see Baking Needs

Graham Crackers see Crackers

Granola Bars see Cookies

Gravy Browning see Condiments & Sauces

Gravy, Canned see Condiments & Sauces

Hair Spray see Hair Care

Hamburger Buns see Breads & Rolls

Hot Chocolate Mix see Cocoa & Other Drink Mixes

Hot Dogs see Prepared Meat/Poultry

Hot Dog Buns see Breads & Rolls

Ice Cream see Desserts

Iced Tea see Tea

Icing Mix see Baking Mixes

Incontinence Products see Incontinence Products

Infant Nursing Supplies see Other Baby Needs

Infant Formula see Baby Food

Insect Repellant see Miscellaneous Personal Care

Insecticides see Miscellaneous Household Supplies

Juices, Frozen see Juices & Fruit Drinks

Juices, Prepared see Juices & Fruit Drinks

Ketchup see Condiments & Sauces

Kidney Beans see Rice & Beans

Lard see Margarine, Shortening & Oils

Laundry Detergent see Laundry Supplies

Lemon Juice see Baking Needs (see also Juices & Fruit Drinks)

Luncheon Meats see Prepared Meat/Poultry

Maple Syrup see Sugars, Sweeteners & Syrups

Margarine see Margarine, Shortening & Oils

Marmalade see Jams & Jellies

Marshmallows see Confectionery

Mayonnaise see Condiments & Sauces

Meal Replacements see Cocoa & Other Drink Mixes

Meat, Fresh see Fresh & Frozen Meat/Poultry

Meat Pies see Frozen Prepared Foods

Meat, Canned see Prepared Meat/Poultry

Meat, Prepared see Prepared Meat/Poultry

Melba Toast see Crackers (see also Breads & Rolls)

Milk, Fresh see Milk & Cream

Milk, Condensed see Milk & Cream

Milk, Powdered see Milk & Cream

Mincemeat see Baking Needs (see also Desserts)

Mint Sauce see Condiments & Sauces

Mousse, Hair see Hair Care

Mouthwash see Oral Hygiene

Muffin Mix see Baking Mixes

Mustard see Condiments & Sauces

Nacho Chips see Snacks

Nail Polish Remover see Miscellaneous Personal Care

Napkins see Paper Products

Noodle Dishes see Prepared Foods

Oatmeal see Cereals

Olives see Condiments & Sauces

Pacifiers see Other Baby Needs

Pancake Mix see Prepared Foods

Pancakes, Frozen see Frozen Prepared Foods

Paper Towel see Paper Products

Pasta Sauce see Condiments & Sauces

Pasta, Canned see Prepared Foods

Pasta Dinners see Prepared Foods

Pasta, Fresh see Pasta

Pasta, Dried see Pasta

Pastry, Refrigerated see Frozen & Refrigerated Doughs & Pastry

Peanut Butter see Peanut Butter & Other Spreads

Peanuts see Snacks

Pepper see Salt, Seasonings & Spices

Pet Treats see Pet Foods & Supplies

Petroleum Jelly see Skin Care

Pickles see Condiments & Sauces

Pie Shells see Frozen & Refrigerated Doughs & Pastry

Pie Filling see Baking Needs

Pizza, Frozen see Frozen Prepared Foods

Plastic Wrap see Food Wraps

Polish, Furniture see Household Cleaners

Polish, Metal see Household Cleaners

Popcorn see Snacks

Potato Products, Frozen see Frozen Prepared Foods

Potato Chips see Snacks

Poultry, Fresh see Fresh & Frozen Meat/Poultry

Powdered Chocolate see Cocoa & Other Drink Mixes

Powdered Drink Mixes see Cocoa & Other Drink Mixes

Pretzels see Snacks

Pudding see Desserts

Razors see Shaving Needs

Relish see Condiments & Sauces

Rice Dishes see Rice & Beans

Rice see Rice & Beans

Rubber Gloves see Miscellaneous Household Supplies

Salad Oil see Margarine, Shortening & Oils

Salad Dressing see Salad Dressings

Salmon, Canned see Canned & Processed Seafood

Salsa see Condiments & Sauces

Salt, Road see Miscellaneous Household Supplies

Salt, Table see Salt, Seasonings & Spices

Salt, Water Softener see Miscellaneous Household Supplies

Sandwich Bags see Food Wraps

Sardines see Canned & Processed Seafood

Sausages see Prepared Meat/Poultry

Seafood, Fresh see Fresh & Frozen Seafood

Seafood, Frozen Prepared see Canned & Processed Seafood

Seafood, Canned see Canned & Processed Seafood

Seasonings see Salt, Seasonings & Spices

Shaving Cream see Shaving Needs

Shortening see margarine, Shortening & Oils

Skin Lotion see Skin Care

Snack Cakes see Snacks

Soap, Face and Body see Skin Care

Soft Drinks see Soft Drinks

Soup, Canned see Soups

Soup, Dried see Soups

Sour Cream see Milk & Cream

Spaghetti Sauce see Condiments & Sauces

Spices see Salt, Seasonings & Spices

Stain Remover see Laundry Supplies

Steak Sauce see Condiments & Sauces

Stewed Tomatoes see Canned & Frozen Fruits & Vegetables

Stuffing Mix see Prepared Foods

Sugar Substitutes see Sugars, Sweeteners & Syrups

Sugar see Sugars, Sweeteners & Syrups

Suntan Lotion see Miscellaneous Personal Care

Table Syrup see Sugars, Sweeteners & Syrups

Tampons see Feminine Hygiene

Tea see Tea

Tissues, Facial see Paper Products

Toilet Paper see Paper Products

Toilet Bowl Cleaners see Household Cleaners

Tomato Sauce see Condiments & Sauces

Tomato Paste see Condiments & Sauces

Toothbrushes see Oral Hygiene

Toothpaste see Oral Hygiene

Tuna, Canned see Canned & Processed Seafood

Upholstery Cleaners see Household Cleaners

Vegetable Juice see Juices & Fruit Drinks

Vegetables, Frozen see Canned & Frozen Fruits & Vegetables

Vegetables, Canned see Canned & Frozen Fruits & Vegetables

Vinegar see Condiments & Sauces

Waffles, Frozen see Frozen Prepared Foods

Waxed Paper see Food Wraps

Whipped Topping see Desserts

Whipping Cream see Milk & Cream

Window Cleaner see Household Cleaners

Worcester Sauce see Condiments & Sauces

Yeast see Baking Needs

Yogurt, Fresh see Yogurt

Yogurt, Frozen see Desserts

The Ethical Shopper's Action Report

Your Name (optional) and province of residence:

Company(ies) contacted, and when:

1 I communicated with the company by:
letter __ telephone call __ consumer hot line __

other, please specify:

2 I communicated on behalf of:
myself __ my family __
a social or advocacy group __

other, please specify:

3 The issue(s) I raised:

4 I complimented the company for some aspect of its
social behaviour __
I told the company why I was going to avoid its product __
I asked for certain details about its operations __
I told the company what changes I wanted it to make before I would
buy or continue to buy its product __
other, please specify:

5 A copy of my letter is attached
Yes __ No __ No letter involved __

6 Did the company respond?
Yes __ No __

7 What did you think of the response? Circle one number for each comment (1 is least satisfactory; 5 is most):

overall satisfaction	1	2	3	4	5
timeliness	1	2	3	4	5
quality of information	1	2	3	4	5
quantity of information	1	2	3	4	5
met my concerns	1	2	3	4	5
candour	1	2	3	4	5
caused me to change my behaviour	1	2	3	4	5

8 Overall, what strategies do you recommend for contacting a company?

9 Other Comments:

Send your comments to:

Joan Helson, EthicScan Canada
PO Box 54034, Toronto, ON   M6A 3B7.

Comment And Order Form

1 Overall this *Shopper's Guide* was:
excellent __ very good __ good __ fair __ poor __

2 Its biggest strength is:

3 Its major limitation is:

4 I would like these additional companies to be profiled in a future edition:

5 I would like these additional groups or resources to be mentioned in a future edition:

6 I would like these ideas to be included in the Options for Action section of a future edition:

7 I would like you to publish an *Ethical Shopper's Guide* to these other industries (e.g. pharmaceutical companies, retail outlets, supermarkets):

8 Please send me information about the discount price for bulk orders of this *Guide* as a fundraiser for my organization:

9 Please send me detailed research profiles on the following companies profiled in this *Guide* $11.60($10 + .80 pst + .76 pst), typically 6-12 pages:

10 Please send me the following from the EthicScan bookshelf:
Profitable Ethical Investing, by Eugene Ellmen @ $6.42 ($6.00 + .42 gst)
EthicScan research reports from *The Corporate Ethics Monitor*
@ $11.60 ($10 + .80 pst + .76 gst) each, typically 3-6 pages:

Credit Unions __
Trust Companies __
Chartered Banks __
General Insurance Companies __
Select Chemical Companies __
Please make cheque or money order payable to:
EthicScan Canada, PO Box 54034, Toronto, Ontario. M6A 3B7

Name

Address